Teresa Moorey has written over 30 books on witchcraft, astrology and related subjects, including the best-selling *Witchcraft: A Beginner's Guide*. She is a practicing counselor, hypnotherapist and astrologer, and is also a tutor for the Faculty of Astrological Studies, having gained a Diploma and Gold Medal in 1989. During her adult life she has explored the mysterious and the mystical, following the ancient paths of Goddess worship and witchcraft.

She lives in the Cotswolds, England, drawing inspiration from the beauty of the landscape, with her husband and four children.

To the Goddess

May Her wisdom live on
in our sons and daughters

ACKNOWLEDGEMENTS

Special thanks to Samantha Hudson, 16, who has given me her advice and comments and significantly contributed to this book. Thank you, Sam; have a wonderful life!

Thank you to my editor, Sue Lascelles, for all her helpful suggestions—especially her brilliant choice of title.

As always, thanks to my friend and confidante Jane Brideson.

Spellbound

The Teenage Witch's Wiccan Handbook

Teresa Moorey

Ulysses Press

Published by:
Ulysses Press
P.O. Box 3440
Berkeley, CA 94703
www.ulyssespress.com

Library of Congress Catalog Card Number: 2002101119
ISBN 1-56975-312-1

First published in 2002 by Rider,
an imprint of Ebury Press, Random House

Printed and bound in Canada by Transcontinental Printing

1 3 5 7 9 10 8 6 4 2

Interior illustrations: Rob Loxton

Cover illustration: "Figure with Chalices" by Emma Harding,
New Division, UK/Stock Illustration Source

CONTENTS

**The Wheel of the Year and the Phases of the Moon
(See Chapters 6, 7 and 8)**

Introduction

Witchcraft is fascinating! The word "witch" is one of the most loaded words in our language. For some people, it conveys images of evil, terrifying creatures in children's stories, from *Snow White* to Roald Dahl's books. For others, it is even more dark and powerful, suggesting devil worship, people who can harm by thought, and the ghastly cruelty of medieval times and before. However, the witch may also be seen as gorgeous and beautiful, drop-dead sexy, and an example of feminine power at its greatest. Through her clever spells she can have the money and the men she wants, *and* turn bad guys into frogs.

If you have picked up this book, chances are you have an inkling there's more to witchcraft than this—and you are right. Witchcraft is an ancient path, and one that requires discipline. By definition a witch cannot worship the devil—she doesn't believe in him; and what's more, witches are committed to helping people and the world in general. So why have witches had such bad press? The answers to this question are complex and historical, and we'll be looking at them in the first chapter. Can witches be gorgeous? The answer is definitely "yes" because the witch has "girl power" in abundance. As for turning people into frogs, even if she could she wouldn't, because her greatest rule is "Harm none." In fact, she probably likes frogs, along with all other forms of life, and she wouldn't insult the species by turning her ex-boyfriend into one!

So is there anything in the witch thing for guys? Definitely, yes! I know many male witches. They work on building sites, with computers and even lecture at the universities. Witchcraft offers modern young men a chance to develop talents that are traditionally seen as feminine, such as intuition, gentleness and receptivity. Far from making these men wimps, witchcraft enhances their masculinity, allowing them to draw on wells of power unavailable to most men, and often makes them extra-attractive to girls, too!

Witches worship a Goddess as well as a God. They are nature-worshippers because they see the natural world as a manifestation of the Divine. But witchcraft is mainly about developing your own inner awareness and your ability to determine your own life, "spelling out" what you want to do and be in harmony with the rest of Creation. It is a spiritual path, but also a practical path. A witch may be a mystic, but a witch is also an achiever.

The greatest gift I believe witchcraft can give to the world is a true appreciation of all things feminine—from the Goddess Herself downward. We are so used to accepting that maleness comes first that we tend not to notice that God is always "He," that children take their father's surname and that males often still have priority over females in matters of inheritance. Nowadays girls laugh at the idea that they might be inferior because they frequently are at the top of their class and beat guys to the best jobs. However, many areas that are specifically "feminine"—like having babies, child-rearing and caring for the family—are still not given their due respect. "Feminine" talents like intuition are still ignored in favor of logic. Witchcraft, at a deep, spiritual level, pays much attention to these factors.

Socially, witchcraft offers new perspectives, but it also has a specific personal relevance for teenagers. Because witchcraft encourages personal revelation, it offers a spiritual path free of dogma. No one tells you what to do. No one disempowers you, imposes sets of rules on you, or puts you at the bottom of a hierarchy that makes you feel defeated before you begin.

Witchcraft has one clear rule—that you must never harm any person or thing. It gives you a beacon to follow—to be the best that you can be—and it gives you inspiration, that of a love for all beings. But it doesn't teach that to be spiritual you have to be self-denying. In contrast with many other paths, witches do not see the material world as base, but rather as a manifestation of Spirit. Enjoying yourself, having what you like—these are gifts of the Goddess and experiencing delight is one of Her rituals.

Witchcraft can certainly make you a stronger person, and a successful one, but never by interfering with others, only by developing yourself. This book describes how a true witch lives, how the circle is cast, how spells are made and which festivals witches celebrate. It is a practical book, with lots of easy exercises so you will be able to see your abilities develop. If you decide this is the path for you, and if you follow through the ideas sensibly and thoroughly, there is every chance that you will feel stronger and your awareness will be expanded. And you'll have fun, too!

Chapter 1

The Craft of the Wise

Are you a natural witch?

Before you picked up this book you probably already had ideas about witchcraft. Perhaps you are attracted to it because it somehow feels familiar. Perhaps some things you have heard just seem very natural—maybe you feel you just "know." Many witches believe in reincarnation, that we are reborn again and again into different times and places. This may be with the same people, perhaps because we are trying to work through issues in our relationships. If there is a period in history that really evokes strong feelings for you, perhaps you were alive then—and perhaps you were a witch! It is said, "Once a witch, always a witch." Perhaps you don't feel particularly attracted to any historical time, but witchcraft seems to be in your blood anyway. Or perhaps it's all new to you but really fascinating, and you just want to find out as much as you can as quickly as you can.

Work through this flowchart to see what kind of a witch you might be. If it seems that you were a witch in a past life, perhaps this chapter will ring some bells for you. If you are a natural witch, you will start to feel at home. And if you're just very interested or a potential new spell-weaver—just enjoy!

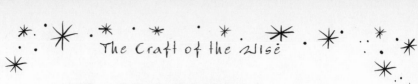

What kind of a witch are you?

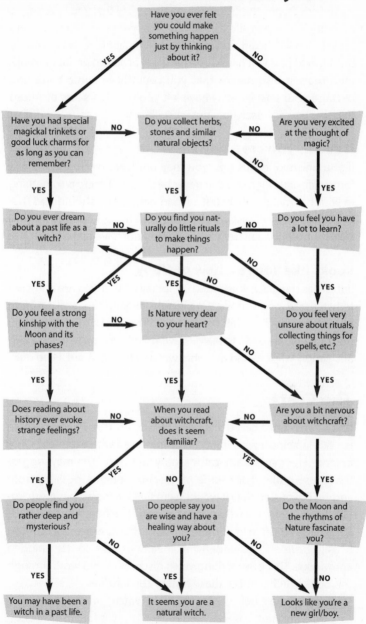

Have you ever felt you could make something happen just by thinking about it?

YES → Have you had special magickal trinkets or good luck charms for as long as you can remember?

NO → Do you collect herbs, stones and similar natural objects?

NO → Are you very excited at the thought of magic?

Have you had special magickal trinkets or good luck charms for as long as you can remember?

NO → Do you collect herbs, stones and similar natural objects?

NO → Are you very excited at the thought of magic?

YES ↓ Do you ever dream about a past life as a witch?

YES ↓ Do you find you naturally do little rituals to make things happen?

YES ↓ Do you feel you have a lot to learn?

Do you ever dream about a past life as a witch?

NO → Do you find you naturally do little rituals to make things happen?

NO → Do you feel you have a lot to learn?

YES ↓ Do you feel a strong kinship with the Moon and its phases?

YES ↓ Is Nature very dear to your heart?

NO → Do you feel very unsure about rituals, collecting things for spells, etc.?

Do you feel a strong kinship with the Moon and its phases?

NO → Is Nature very dear to your heart?

YES ↓ Does reading about history ever evoke strange feelings?

YES ↓ When you read about witchcraft, does it seem familiar?

YES ↓ Are you a bit nervous about witchcraft?

Does reading about history ever evoke strange feelings?

NO → When you read about witchcraft, does it seem familiar?

NO → Are you a bit nervous about witchcraft?

YES ↓ Do people find you rather deep and mysterious?

NO ↓ Do people say you are wise and have a healing way about you?

YES ↓ Do the Moon and the rhythms of Nature fascinate you?

Do people find you rather deep and mysterious?

YES ↓ You may have been a witch in a past life.

NO → It seems you are a natural witch.

Do people say you are wise and have a healing way about you?

YES → It seems you are a natural witch.

Do the Moon and the rhythms of Nature fascinate you?

NO → Looks like you're a new girl/boy.

You may have been a witch in a past life.

It seems you are a natural witch.

Looks like you're a new girl/boy.

5

You may have been a witch in a past life

If you ended up in this box, there is a possibility that you have vague memories of a past life as a witch. This means you may be very attracted to witchcraft, and can very easily adapt to it. You learn very quickly and find you naturally have ideas of your own for developing rituals. It also means that you could have some hang-ups, because your past life may have left you with fears and attitudes that you haven't resolved—but you will!

It seems you are a natural witch

If you finished in this box, you may not have been a witch in a former life (although one can never be sure!) but there is something in you that makes witchcraft second nature. You should find that you learn quickly. Trust your instincts, but always keep your mind open to new possibilities that you might not have considered.

Looks like you're a new girl/boy

If this was the place you ended up, it may be that you are attracted to witchcraft because the time is right for you. You may not have thought about witchcraft before, or even realized it existed. But you don't have to be a fish to learn to swim. Perhaps you're just curious and simply want to find out what witchcraft is all about. Read on!

The Craft

Witchcraft is often called "the Craft" by witches. This is because there is a skill in being a witch that can be improved with experience and practice. Freemasons also call Masonry "the Craft." This may suggest that these paths share some of the same origins, possibly from ancient Egypt. Certainly it would seem that witchcraft has more significance in our past than most history teachers would let on. History itself is often important to witches because ancient customs usually have special underlying meanings and contain hidden knowledge. This is something you'll discover as you work through this book. Witchcraft can make history come to life.

Some people believe that the word "witch" has the same roots as "wise." Witchcraft has always been about the wisdom of instincts—things you just *know*. It's likely that people had more of this wisdom

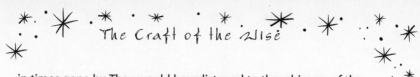

in times gone by. They would have listened to the whispers of the wind in the leaves, watched the flight of birds and smelled the sweetness of the earth when the rain fell. Nowadays we have television, phones and computers, and we don't think about the natural world, except when we get cold, wet or sunburned. We're much more comfortable physically, of course, but at the same time we've lost something important. Nature puts us in touch with something deep inside of us and makes us listen to our instincts. Think about how you feel when you get up on a spring day and the sun is shining. Doesn't your mood change? You feel great. Even if you have an exam or you've had a fight with your best friend, everything looks better when the sun shines. This is just a very simple example of how Nature can change your mood.

Try switching off your cell phone so no one can get hold of you, and lean with your back against the bark of a tree for a while; you may find that your mood changes. This is because you are tuning in to the natural world. This is a great stress-buster, but it also awakens you to Nature. You should feel more a part of life, but also more in contact with the real *you*.

People thought and acted very differently when they were close to Nature all the time. Of course, during those days life was such a struggle for survival that there wasn't much opportunity for people to think about bettering themselves. Today we are lucky and can have the best of both worlds.

Witch kings and queens

It is believed that girls and boys have different talents and our brains are wired differently. Men have better spatial skills, probably because of their need to be good hunters in times gone by. Because of this your dad can probably park the car better than your mom can. This doesn't mean he's a better driver, however, because women have other talents. For instance, your mom might be better at considering other drivers. Women are better at perceiving patterns and they are ace communicators. These different characteristics are the building blocks of our society.

Some people believe that in the Stone Age everyone worshiped the Mother Goddess, and that women were regarded as especially powerful. Giving birth was something that was thought of as very valuable—magickal even. Women would have helped each other, and probably had power. There was always someone to help look after the kids so the mother could go and do her work—and that "work" could have been as a tribal elder or leader. It isn't hard to see that in such a society more instinctual things would have been respected.

It can be difficult to appreciate what societies of long ago were like. Dotted throughout this section are exercises to bring history to life. They involve using your imagination as well as some more practical activities.

Imagine ...

… people dressed in skins and furs. They live near the forest in round huts, and pick berries and hunt animals. When the people are hungry and the hunters need to track the wild boar, the priestess drinks the juice they have fermented from the berries. She goes into a trance and dances around the fire. Her crazy shadow is as tall as the trees. Then she sits and the rest of the tribe is still. The leader of the hunt goes up to her and she gives him a special pouch…

Things to do

Go somewhere where you can be alone with Nature—where there is no traffic or phones. Close your eyes and imagine that you have been transported to some prehistoric forest. Smell the scents and listen to the sounds. How does it feel? Are you changing inside? What might you do, feel, believe?

As time went by attitudes changed. Conquest and power became more important than caring for the land and the tribe. This was probably a good thing in some ways because it meant everyone's brain got sharper. (It helps you concentrate if you're running through the woods trying to dodge a spear in the back!) Humans started to plan, to build, to fight and to gain power. Some of these activities were more natural to men than to women because of the hormone testosterone, which gives men their aggressive charac-teristics. Sadly, though, women began to be dreadfully oppressed, and this meant that not only did they suffer but the whole of society suffered as well. The world became a crueler place. There was a particular harshness about a society that didn't care for Nature. Western society developed, using logical ways while ignoring feelings and instincts, ignoring Nature and the power She gives us—thinking only of bigger and better without considering where that would lead us. Today girls do what boys do and no one thinks about it. However, in many ways women have had to beat men at their own game and the intuitive ways have been lost.

Imagine ...

... a woman wearing a coronet with the crescent moon carved upon it. In her hands she cradles another crown. She is standing in the center of a stone circle, and the rays of the morning sun streak beneath the lintel-stone and fall upon the crown she holds. Towards her comes a man, a great warrior, clad in armor, scarred from battle. His long shadow falls upon her, but as he kneels before her, the sun again kisses the crown with fire. She holds it high, and then lowers it upon his head. The people outside the circle cheer. She takes his hand, motions him to rise, and they walk hand in hand towards the rising sun...

Things to do

Imagine going to a stone circle when it is misty or rainy. What were the people who built this place like? How does it make you feel? What was it for? What would you like to do here now?

Even once society had begun to change, the "witchy" ways contin-ued—and not always underground. The Celts, for instance, had a strong sense of the "Otherworld," and understood that there is more to life than meets the eye. Women were powerful in their society. You may have heard of Boudicca, who led her tribe against the

Romans, all painted blue and howling savagely as they cut their invaders to pieces! She was proof that a woman can be warlike! There were cults in Ancient Greece and Egypt that held instinct to be important. In Egypt, the great goddess Isis was worshiped. In the early centuries C.E. (Common Era, same as A.D., or *Anno Domini*) these cults influenced "Gnosticism." Gnosticism taught that what your heart said was the way you should follow—that the way to the God or Goddess was through your own inner experience. We shall be developing the way to "inner experience" in the next chapter when we talk about visualization.

Imagine ...

... the Great Pyramid, white in the moonlight, and the sky behind it powdered with stars. A warm breeze blows from the desert and the night air swells with chanting. You hear the words "Isis, Osiris" over and over again, in a strange dialect. Towards you comes a procession, headed by a tall priestess. Her hair, blacker than the sky, falls straight about her shoulders and on her head is a head-dress shaped like a throne. She walks towards the opening in the pyramid and the procession follows her. You can hear the chanting continue now, higher, but muffled. ...

Things to do

Close your eyes and imagine the desert sands, a cool temple with many imposing effigies of the Gods, the scent of incense, the sound of chanting. What might it mean to be a priestess or priest in these ancient times? What do you think you could learn?

When Christianity came along, laws became harsher. This faith taught that everyone had to do what the priest said. The message of love brought by Jesus was overlooked by those who used Christianity for political reasons and personal power. To such a government, anything "witchy" was regarded as very subversive and witches were horribly persecuted in the Middle Ages. The things done to witches were worse than anything you see in horror films. In fact, the great majority of those persecuted weren't witches at all—they were just people who got on the wrong side of someone powerful, or had something someone else wanted—witches' goods were often given to the "witchfinder." A kind of hysteria engulfed communities and sometimes entire villages were wiped out by witch persecution.

Some Christians have a very deep-rooted fear of Hell and the Devil (neither of which witches believe in) so they thought that if they stamped out "evil" in the guise of witches they would be guaranteed a place in heaven. The witches were used as scapegoats, rather like people who are picked on nowadays by a gang and bullied. (Bullying makes everyone in the gang feel more like they belong, that they are normal because they have someone to look down on. But secretly everyone is worried that one day they will be the ones that are turned on, and so they bully all the more.) This kind of feeling was behind much of the persecution.

Imagine . . .

… a small medieval village. It is winter, the sky is grey and the bitter wind whistles in the nooks and crannies of a tiny cottage. A young couple sits huddled by the little fire, while in the corner an older woman works. In front of her on the table is a disk on which is engraved a five-pointed star. Fiery serpents seem to writhe on its bronze surface, which the fire-glow catches. The woman is mixing herbs, crushing them with a pestle and mortar, placing them in a small, chipped bottle. She stops the neck with a piece of rag and hands it to the young woman. "There, my dear," she says. "That should help you to conceive by Yuletide. But tell no one. Tell no one." She peers fearfully through the window as hoof-beats approach…

Things to do

Imagine going to a small village as unspoiled by time as possible. What might it have been like to live here four or five hundred years ago? How would it have been different from

today? What would you hope for? What would you fear? How could you deal with these things?

Because of this fear and cruelty, witches became pictured as ugly, fearsome hags, with hooked noses and black teeth, waiting to catch children and boil them up in a cauldron. Roald Dahl's book *The Witches* is about that sort of witch. But real witches were wise women and cunning men, who knew all about herbs and who could cure poor people who couldn't afford a doctor. The witches were the people who had "the sight," and knew what was going to happen in the community—who was in love with whom, who was going to die, or who was going to have a baby. They knew these things because they were in tune with Nature and their own intuition. They probably crept off to the woods when the Moon was full to worship Nature and the Great Mother in the old ways.

No one is sure how much of this actually survived, but it seems that some of the kings of England came from a witchcraft tradition. The English royal surname Plantagenet comes from the Latin *planta genista*, which is the name for the plant broom, from which the besom was made. (The besom is the broom on which witches were traditionally believed to fly.) There is a romantic story about King Edward III, who lived from 1312–1377. He was dancing with a countess known as the Fair Maid of Kent when her garter fell to the floor. The king knelt to give it back to her, saying, "*Honi soit qui mal y pense*," meaning "Evil be to him who evil thinks." (In those days royalty spoke French.) He said this to all the nobles and churchmen who were standing around stroking their beards and fingering their swords. What the king probably meant was, "If any of you lot want to make something of this, you'll have me to reckon with." The garter was a sign of witchcraft and the Fair Maid was probably a High Priestess to whom the king was giving protection.

Imagine . . .

... a gaunt castle. Braziers spit in its dark corners and a spiral staircase leads upward into the shadows. A door creaks open on a candlelit room where the king and his lady stand before an altar. Marble statues of the Goddess and the Horned God, naked as the king and the lady, stand on a velvet cloth. As the moonlight streaks in through the glassless window, the lady holds high a crystal and the lord kneels before her. "Open for me the secret way," he begins. But a shout goes up, "My Lord, my Lord, the enemy is at the gates…"

Things to do

Imagine going to a medieval castle and being alone for a while on a spiral staircase in a chamber. What would it have been like to have lived there? What would the people have felt, thought, done? How does the place inspire you?

There are many other possible historical connections between the monarchy and witchcraft. For example, William Rufus was an English king who lived from 1056–1100 CE. He died in the New Forest at the festival of Lughnasadh at the end of July. (When you read Chapter 7 you will find out the importance of this festival.) Rufus died at this time because of the tradition that the old king be sacrificed at harvest time to keep the land fertile. Four hundred years later Edward IV met Elizabeth Woodville and married her on May Day—there are many pagan elements in their love story. Edward's brother, Richard, who became Richard III, was the last of the Plantagenets. His symbol was a white boar, which is a very pagan symbol.

In England witches were not usually burned at the stake, but were more likely drowned. They were not supposed to be tortured. On the European Continent and in Scotland, however, this wasn't the case. Thankfully, in the eighteenth century people became more reasonable and logical and the persecution of witches died off. So although everything was becoming more scientific, the occult and witchcraft were revived and interest in them grew. In 1951, the Witchcraft Act was repealed at the express wish of Winston Churchill, who objected to the way it had been used against the medium Helen Duncan. Around this time witchcraft was publicized by Gerald Gardner, and although some witches were appalled by this, we could see that going public was a good thing.

Where are the witches?

Today there are witches in many walks of life—teachers, counselors, nurses, bricklayers, civil servants. There are young witches and old witches, men and women. Some of them like to dress in Gothic style and wear pentagrams while others are very ordinary to look at. There are many different witchcraft traditions as well. The best known is Wicca. This was really started, in its modern form, by Gerald Gardner. Gardner was initiated into a coven in the New Forest. No one is quite sure how much of Wicca he made up and how much is truly "traditional," but this doesn't really matter. Often when we make things up, we are, in fact, plugging in to something very meaningful without knowing it—instinct again.

Gardner's form of Wicca is known as "Gardnerian," but another is "Alexandrian," after Alex Sanders, who came later. We don't have to bother about the differences between these forms because they are similar. Wiccans gather in covens led by a High Priestess and a High Priest. They celebrate the seasonal festivals and do magick.

There are also other traditional paths with their own ways. It isn't possible to know how many of these there may be because some are no doubt still secret, and they aren't talked about as much as Wicca. However, more and more information is becoming available, for instance, through the Internet.

Another form of witchcraft is called "Dianic." This has a feminist bent, and not all Dianic covens admit men. While there is a very definite lesbian influence in this sort of witchcraft, it is also inspiring to heterosexual girls who wish to concentrate on the Goddess and the feminine mysteries. You don't have to be lesbian to feel that the Goddess is of prime importance and to feel that you are closer to Her in an all-female situation.

There are also "open" groupings, involving community events and such things as counseling, performing rituals to cleanse new houses and similar such occasions.

Another type of witch is the "hedgewitch." This is someone working (witchcraft is called "working") on her own. The term "hedgewitch" may come from the fact that the Celts respected boundaries as mystical places, like the "cross-over" from one world

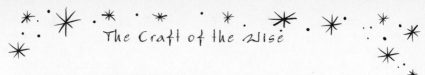
to another. It could also refer to the fact that in olden times witches grew high hedges near their houses for protection. (Hawthorn was a favorite.) Witches who work on their own and are especially interested in using herbs and potions may be called "kitchen witches," and often use basic kitchen utensils to work their spells. This may have been common in the old days when people didn't have enough money to buy special equipment—and what could be suspicious about a bowl, a knife and a broom?

A witch can actually fall into several different categories. For instance, a hedgewitch could work sometimes with a partner, or with others in a coven, while a kitchen witch might also be a Wiccan, and so on. As you progress as a witch, you may move from one path to another until you find the one that is right for you.

Explaining witchcraft

It is quite hard to explain the craft because it often involves things that we don't have words for. However, here are some facts about witchcraft.

* Witchcraft is Nature worship. Witches celebrate the seasons because the seasons are the gift of the Goddess and the God. Witches need no more proof that the Goddess exists than to look at the world around them—Nature is Her.

* It is a spiritual path rather than a religion because it has no dogma. The only rule is "Harm none." It is a way of developing your spiritual side—to witches this is fun and enlivening. To witches, the body isn't "unspiritual." It is a gift that can offer ways to spiritual experience. No one who denies her body n the name of religion can call herself a witch because that is an insult to the Goddess and the God who gave us our bodies.

* It is a magickal system. This means that witches know or make up spells in the spirit of their tradition. Within limits, witchcraft can get you things you want. It develops your power, but this must always be power *to*, certainly never power *over*.

＊ It is a way of developing yourself. Studying witchcraft will help you to get to know yourself better and to become a more whole person. It helps you to respect yourself and thus gain the respect of other people.

What witchcraft isn't

We have already talked about how witchcraft isn't "devil worship." Witches don't believe in him (or her!). In fact, we see no reason for such a being to exist because it implies that there is continual strife in the Cosmos. Of course, there are evil people and they need nothing more than their own selfishness and hatred to "tempt" them into doing awful things. Witches don't worship anything evil or nasty, but it is partly because we refuse to see the body as unholy that we have been regarded as worshipping the devil. If you have a religion of fear and damnation then you're going to see many things in life that appear evil. Witches have been a victim of this kind of thinking. But witchcraft is truly about love, with no concept of some kinds of love being pure and some impure.

Neither are witches "black magicians." There *are* some sick people who get pleasure from vile rituals, but these are not witches. Witches have, above all, a respect for life. It may help other people's understanding to say you're a "white witch." Although we do our best, we all have mixed motives. But destruction and ill-wishing have no part in true witchcraft. Neither do exploitation and abuse, sexual or otherwise, of anybody—and certainly not of children.

Ethics

This brings us to the important question of the ethics of witchcraft. We have already mentioned the rule "Harm none." This is very important to remember. Every witch knows that what you do comes back to you in some way, and some say it comes back with three times the force. So if you want to turn that mean guy into a toad or your math teacher into a pig, that's fine. That is, it's fine to *want to*. You can dislike someone all you want—that's human. The dislike is yours, so talk about it, deal with it, but don't ever use it in magick. Spells rarely work in any way that might be called obvious.

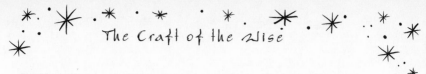

But if you set out to harm someone you'll harm yourself. *You have been warned.*

Visualization plays a large part in practicing magick, and if you try to do something nasty you saturate yourself with horrible energies, like a sponge soaking up foul water. After your ritual you'll feel wretched. Yes, there can be a satisfaction in revenge, but it's usually short-lived.

Let's not be mealy-mouthed about this. You can find curses in other books if you want to—there's nothing to stop you. And yes, covens of experienced witches do occasionally do spells to bind a rapist or catch a murderer, but this isn't anything a person should decide to do on his own. It isn't fair to try to harm another because there may be circumstances that you don't understand. Besides, "getting" at someone isn't all that easy; we each have our own psychic protection, even if we are unaware of it, and some people have a strong armor. If someone has hurt you or been deliberately nasty, you can do spells to protect yourself and better your life. This is much nicer, and you'll feel good after the spell, too. "To live well is the best revenge!" Never forget it.

What do witches believe?

Witches don't have any gospel or dogma. "Believe" isn't really a word witches use often. Their spiritual path is more about what they do and how they feel rather than about putting their faith *in* something. Witches don't rely on anyone's words to tell them about the Goddess or God. They aren't told what they have to believe about life after death, or made to accept any one story about what happened in the past. There is no overall leader, saints or prophets. A witch may choose to "follow" someone for a while in order to learn, but most are very independent people. Each person makes up her mind about what is important and there can be lively debates between witches! The point about witchcraft is that it encourages you to think for yourself in a responsible way and to get in touch with your own feelings about the Goddess and the God. But we can say some things about witches' beliefs.

✳ They worship Nature in some form or fashion.

✳ They believe that life is sacred and that all living things are part of the Goddess. The Goddess is very important, indeed, to witches because the Craft is a spiritual path that holds this world to be very sacred, and the Feminine has long been linked to physical things. The Goddess is in the fertile earth, the blossoms, the Moon among the stars, the deep waters and all the gentleness, caring and nurture that is around us. She is also, in her "dark" aspect, in the fearsome side of Nature—the biting winds, the dying leaves, the barrenness of winter. We all know that nothing creative can be completed without some destruction, weeding out and casting away. A lovely garden demands the death of weeds, for instance. This side of the Goddess has often been feared and turned into a demon, but it is simply part of the cycles of life, and cosmic and natural law. The Goddess also has three aspects: Maiden, Mother and Crone, which we shall look at more closely in Chapter 8.

✳ Most witches believe in a Goddess *and* a God. However, their God is very different from the Father-God idea, the old-man-in-the-clouds who gives laws and threatens. The witches' God is full of life, mischief and laughter. He is very sexy and very protective. He is the life force that rises in the spring, the strength of the stag, and the robust golden corn. His force is often seen as coming and going, while the Goddess is ever-present. The God is often represented with horns and called the Horned God. The Christian church turned him into the Devil, but, in fact, His horns show His connection with the instincts of the animal kingdom. The Horned God is an exciting figure—very strong and wise—and He leads the way in the mysteries of Nature. One way of understanding this is by seeing the God as traveling the cycle of the seasons, and the Goddess as the cycle itself. In addition, witches like to think in terms of many different Goddesses and Gods, which are all aspects of the one. However, they don't believe in them in quite the same way as someone has to who is told, "This is real and true. This happened." Witches know that the spiritual

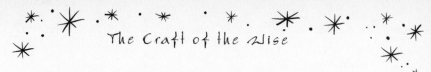
world has many levels and there are many ways of getting close to it.

✳ Witches believe that it is up to each witch to develop her or his own awareness of spirituality and to follow the path that is right for the individual. Some people say this means nothing but disagreement and strife. To this witches may reply that "disagreement and strife" of the most violent kind have surrounded the dogmatic religions throughout history. Perhaps anyone who claims "I am right and this is the only way" is asking for trouble!

✳ Witches believe that sex is sacred and a person's body is a gift of the Goddess, to be enjoyed in a way that harms none, especially one's own self.

✳ Most witches believe that we go on in some form after we die, and probably the majority believe we are born again in new bodies.

✳ Most, but not all, witches do magick. This means, basically, they believe that the material world can be influenced by thought.

How does that sound to you as a set of ways to run your life?

What makes you a witch?

The short answer is that *you* do. A witch is a witch is a witch. Witches are initiated, either by their own selves, or by another person or group. This is how they dedicate themselves to the Goddess. It's a commitment. Witchcraft is something you get a feeling about—you *know* you're a witch because of something inside of you. But to be a true witch you have to realize that you're on a learning curve—that is, if you want to be the best witch you can be!

Coming out of the broom closet

Today witches are very open about their way of life, but there is still persecution and prejudice. Many people do not understand or want to understand witchcraft. This is partly because the word makes people think of evil things. So why not call it something else? Witches are often a bit mischievous, not to mention stubborn! To them, the word means simply "a wise person" and if other people choose to twist the meaning that's their problem. Witchcraft links us with a very old tradition, and with many people who have suffered. However, even in the year 2000 a teacher in England was suspended from his job for being a "witch" or "pagan," although he was given back his job after the Pagan Federation fought for him. So, who you choose to tell and who not to tell about your beliefs is still an important decision.

If you go around school saying you're a witch some people are sure to laugh at you. It will sound as if you are claiming to have special powers or are trying to draw attention to yourself. Some people are going to challenge you to see if you can put a spell on them because they don't know what being a witch is all about. Until things change a lot more, there is sure to be someone, somewhere, at some point in your life who is going to laugh at you, think you're crazy or evil, or feel scared of you—so be prepared. If your teachers know you're a witch, they might have a different attitude toward you. Being open about being a witch could affect whether or not you get a job or get accepted into a course. Think carefully about whom you tell, and why you are telling them. Never do it to make an impression or to scare someone.

If you feel you need company in what you do, why not show this book to your best friend or other good friends? Don't say you are a witch, just that you're interested in witchcraft. Perhaps they would like to look into it, too. You could explore it in a group. But please remember that real witchcraft isn't like the films *The Craft* or *Practical Magic*. It isn't that easy or that dramatic. It requires work and lots of common sense and grounding. Real witches do not take the occult lightly. They do their rituals properly and they follow certain rules, which you will learn about. Like driving a car, learning to be a witch should be taken slowly. But once you can do it, you never lose it. And like driving a car, it can be dangerous unless it's done properly. Take things step by step and you will find out what it means to be strong and wise.

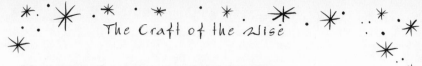

Your truth, your responsibility

If you are drawn to witchcraft chances are you're an exceptional person, and you will become even more so. You have a responsibility here. Remember this is an ancient tradition and you are (or will be) a representative of it. It is also something that has had very bad press. Of course, this isn't your fault, but it does mean that every witch needs to be careful of the impression she gives so that everyone will eventually see that this is a path of dignity and self-respect.

Taking on the mantle of the witch means you are spiritually aware, that you love Nature and that you value and look after the unique creature that is *you*. You care for others, you think deeply, your body is your shrine and the world is your temple. Hold your head high and draw closer to the sacred flame. Welcome home, young sisters and brothers!

Vegetarian or not?

Here is a question to ponder. What would a witch think about vegetarianism? This is a really good question and needs to be thought through very carefully. The most important thing to realize is that there is more than one answer. Witches have one law and that is "Harm none." They revere all life and Nature. However, death is a part of Nature and animals that eat meat are also a part of Nature.... The difficult thing about this sort of question is that there isn't one right answer. Witches try to accept this—to realize that things aren't necessarily black or white and what may be right for one person at one time may be wrong for another.

In the end, the characteristic response of the witch isn't to decide what is right and what is wrong in a rigid way. Remember, witchcraft is about what you do. But it is in keeping with the way of the witch to attempt to see another's point of view and to be open-minded—to sympathize where possible with both sides of an issue and to accept that there may be more than one solution.

What sort of a witch are you?

This questionnaire is really for the girls, but the guys can adapt it. For example, you could substitute male mystery groups for Dianic

covens. Go through the following questions, answering a, b, c, or d, as appropriate.

1) Your favorite night out is: a) with the girls, you like that feeling of intimacy and confidence; b) with the gang, guys and girls together; c) with your own special guy, or possibly in a foursome; d) you often prefer to be on your own.

2) At school you prefer: a) doing projects in a supportive group; b) lectures that involve the whole class; c) a structured course where you know what you're supposed to learn; d) private study.

3) When you dream of achievement is it usually: a) something that gets you acceptance and belonging; b) something that gets you public applause; c) something that gets you sound achievement; d) Something that gets you love.

4) If someone disagrees with you, you usually: a) concentrate on reaching agreement and mutual ground; b) try to win the argument; c) find someone who can tell you both what is right; d) prefer not to argue because what you feel *inside* is what counts.

5) When shopping for clothes you: a) go for something your friends will like; b) choose something that's going to turn all the guys' heads; c) pick an outfit that's going to make people think you're cool, stylish and loaded; d) choose something that is really "you."

6) When going out, you prefer: a) a girls-only party with some riotous friends; b) clubbing; c) a party with friends; d) an intimate meal or moonlit walk.

7) Your dream guy is: a) very thoughtful and sensitive; b) a lively extrovert; c) a high-flying achiever; d) passionate and devoted.

Your score

Mostly a's. You could favor the Dianic type of witchcraft, where the mysteries of the Feminine are explored in an all-girls group. You feel

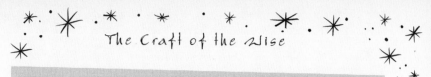

safest when it's all girls because you know you'll be understood and accepted. You feel that women together are stronger. Go for an all-girls group where you feel secure enough to blossom.

Mostly b's. Probably you favor the more open style of the Craft, where practices are fairly loose and there are lots of events going on in the community, such as planting trees, celebrating festivals, and so on. This is more "pagan" than specifically witchy. Look for like-minded people with which to develop this—and have fun!

Mostly c's. Wicca, with its structured approach and hierarchy of initiations, is probably for you. In time you might look to be initiated into a friendly coven. (Most covens won't take you before the age of 18, and some not until you are 21.) Meanwhile you can still read books and study if you like.

Mostly d's. You sound like a hedgewitch, liking the quiet life, able to draw close to Nature on your own or with one special partner. It might be hard for you to express just how you feel—go with your instincts and take things step by step.

Remember that what you have chosen today might not be your preference in a few months' time. You can change—it's your privilege! Also, you might like more than one path. This may be reflected in a close or equal score between two paths. For instance you might like the closeness of a Dianic group as well as the privacy of lone working. Or the extrovert activities may appeal and also the feeling of learning and getting there that you could have with Wicca. Don't be afraid to approach things in different ways. Remember, "change is the only constant"!

For you to do

You may need to read much more before you have any clear idea of whether the Craft is for you, or you may already feel sure one way or the other. If you have made up your mind that this is your path, take the time to jot down the reasons you are attracted to it. Take as long as you like, and be as honest as you can. Keep the list to look back on as you develop as a witch and see how you feel over the coming months. Comments on some possible answers are given at the back of the book on pages 247–48.

Chapter 2

First Steps in Magick

What is magick?

In this book I refer to "magick" with a "k" to distinguish it from "magic" in the sense of conjuring tricks. Chances are that it's the magickal aspect of witchcraft that fascinates you most. So what is magick? Magick takes place when something happens that is outside the laws of science. Notice that word "outside." Magick isn't contrary to science. You won't see money appearing in your hand or find that the person of your dreams materializes from the vapor in your cauldron. When your spells work it will just be in a fairly ordinary way, but you will know, and it will feel good.

Magick and science

In our culture science has taken the place of religion. We almost believe that science can, or will, do anything, and that it has all the answers. To admit to believing anything else is to risk being labeled a bit weird. The major religions such as Christianity and Islam are tolerated, because they don't interfere with science and are part of the Establishment. To believe in God, the miracles of Jesus and an afterlife in Heaven will get you called religious, but unless you try to walk on water yourself, you probably won't get laughed at. Even if you do, there are plenty of people to keep you company! Science and religion have settled in two separate camps—science is based in the here-and-now, while religion builds on parts of the past. Religion also has the possibility of a future after death and a God who is outside Creation because He doesn't interfere on a day-to-day basis. How long this convenient truce can continue depends on how long it takes scientists to label the precise part of the brain that contains the soul. They are trying!

However, on the fringes of science things are happening that are weirder than witches! Most of us still think of the Universe as a kind of clockwork model, as described by Isaac Newton. However, modern physicists have a different view. The behavior of sub-atomic particles seems to be influenced by somebody watching! Physicists such as Niels Bohr and James Wheeler have advanced the Copenhagen Interpretation, which states that no elementary phenomenon is a phenomenon until it is observed. This amounts to saying that the mind influences reality—witches have been saying this for a long, long time!

There are other theories that support magick in a roundabout way. For instance, the idea of "synchronicity" was put forward by the psychologist Carl Jung, who observed that events were often meaningfully connected, but not connected by cause and effect. In other words, one thing did not have to cause another, or two things did not have to be caused by the same thing in order for them to belong together. We tend to call this "coincidence," but sometimes it seems that there is more than just chance at work. This matches up with the concept of doing spells; a little ritual you do won't *cause* you to pass your exams, yet there is a connection.

Another example of fringe science is Chaos Theory. Chaos Theory tells us that science has, as yet, no way of mapping the forces at work in certain complicated systems. There are things about the Universe that we do not understand. When there are lots of forces playing together a very, very slight variation in one place can cause an enormous change in another. So the Chaos Theorists believe that a butterfly's wings flapping in one part of the world can cause a storm in another. There was a "Chaotist" played by Jeff Goldblum in the film *Jurassic Park*. In fact, in a rather clichéd way, the film showed that science does not always control nature, however clever it may be.

So if anyone laughs at you for being stupid to believe in witch-craft, you can quote some of the above examples. Of course, scientists are very careful to use scientific language and they would never use words like "magick" because their colleagues would ridicule them. However, some of the most notable (and brave) scientists are coming close to it, it seems!

Your psychic senses

The "logical mind" lives in the left side of the brain (if you are right-handed) and controls the right side of the body. It is the right-hand side of the brain that directs our more intuitive part. The right brain houses pattern-perception and creativity. The connections between the two sides of the brain (called "hemispheres") are better in women than they are in men. There are many theories about which part of the brain holds the "psychic" parts and they may all be right—or it may be that being psychic has nothing to do with the physical brain at all. Be that as it may, things that help us relax and chill out (that help the right brain as opposed to the left brain) are good for letting the psychic senses open. You do not need to be a full-blown psychic to be a witch, but you need some awareness of the world of the Unseen. Words like the "ether" or the "astral" are often used to describe this world. Again, this isn't "scientific." It means that there are unseen energies behind the material world; and it is here that magick and the supernatural operate.

"Supernatural" is a rather misleading word; nothing is really "supernatural"—it's just that we don't necessarily have an explanation for it. So a good way to get your psychic awareness into gear is to be close to Nature. Get out and about in parks and woodlands. Go for walks. Stop thinking and start looking, listening, smelling, touching and sensing. This will relax you (another requirement for being psychic) and put you in touch with the world around you, which is the first step to that mysterious "world beyond." Look also at the night sky, watch the phases of the Moon—these all form part of the rhythms that we live by, the things that have formed our blood and bones. They are all interconnected, and when we can tune out the "white noise" inside our heads and tune in to Nature and the Cosmos, we begin to waken up.

Extroverted people are also said to be more psychic. In our culture introvert is a bit of an insult, which is a shame. It's natural for some people to be quiet and thoughtful, and to like their own company. It certainly doesn't mean there is anything wrong with them! But it is the relaxed, open, fun-loving quality of the extrovert that keeps the lines buzzing. If you prefer to be alone, don't forget to play and laugh.

Your body, your temple

Witchcraft is unusual in that it holds the body very sacred and regards physical pleasure as a type of celebration because it is a gift of the Goddess. Your body is a gift, and like all gifts it needs to be treasured. So make sure that caring for your body is one of your top priorities. If you start to take a serious interest in developing your magickal awareness, please don't lose sight of the importance of good health. It isn't "witchy" to be tired and haggard, or to put yourself in physical or emotional danger. Personal safety is also important, so please don't go anywhere remote and dangerous on your own. Always take someone you trust with you, and always tell someone where you are going and when you'll be back. Take your cell phone, if you have one, and only switch it off for those periods when you are tuning into the natural world. Of course, each circumstance needs to be considered according to its own merits—just don't take chances.

Witchcraft teaches you how to alter your consciousness and we shall be looking at this in greater detail later on. Of course, a short-cut to altering consciousness is to take drugs. Please, don't do this. Drug-taking is far more likely to interfere with your development than to help it. It is true that in some cultures drugs are taken to open the perceptions, but (and this is a big but!) all of this is con-trolled by someone who knows exactly what they are doing and who cares for the person who is in the trance state. The drugs aren't taken for fun or to see what happens. In other words, they aren't recreational. Besides, these drugs, although tremendously strong, are made from plants and are rather different from the manufac-tured chemical things available when you go clubbing, and so on. Taking drugs is silly and dangerous. Taking drugs means that you put yourself in someone else's control—and witches like to keep

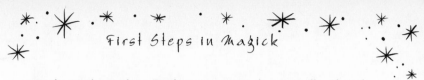
control over themselves. Furthermore, most drugs are illegal, and witches are usually aware that they don't need any more bad press! Get your kicks more safely.

Another safety angle to consider is the Internet. The Internet has brilliant resources for witchcraft and lots of chat rooms. Take advantage of this, but don't ever give out personal details such as your address, and never arrange to meet strangers alone.

Body-image and eating are often important issues for teenagers. (We talk about this more in the section on Beltane in Chapter 7 because Beltane is a festival of the senses.) In our culture eating has become a real problem for many people. This is because we have an unlimited supply of cheap food, specially designed by clever use of additives, to be as delicious as possible. Never in recorded history has there been so much available in the way of food as there is in the developed nations today. We have so many choices and we can afford to be fussy. It is easy to forget that this was not the case until quite recently. At the same time it seems to be the fashion to be thinner and thinner, possibly because we always want what we can't have! In a culture where we have to do very little physical work, where the food is so refined as to be fattening, and where all kinds of foods are easy to come by, it is not easy to be thin unless you have a super-charged metabolism. But super-charged metabolisms are not genetically favored because they cannot withstand famine. By natural selection they are weeded out. Survival of the fittest is survival of the fattest! Our culture also puts great pressure on women to conform to certain ideals—many women still have the idea that they aren't quite good enough. This harks back to centuries of women and their bodies being considered "vessels of the Devil." The ideal of being thin denies the body, and diseases like anorexia and bulimia are related, in some part, to these ideas. But it isn't just girls that suffer from these diseases; anorexia and bulimia are also becoming more frequent in teenage boys. In contrast, witches believe that anything you do that gives you pleasure without harming anyone else is an act of worship of the Goddess. It isn't magickal to deny your bodily needs—witchcraft is about getting in tune with them. So try to listen to your body; eat well and carefully and know that this will only make you more powerful in your spells and in your life.

Alcohol and cigarettes are also part of our culture but are illegal for younger people. For this reason they have become a symbol of independence and maturity—which is exactly what they aren't! As a witch you'll start to listen to that inner voice that tells you what is right for you and enables you to respect yourself—which will without fail lead to you being respected by other people.

As you develop your ability to perform rituals and to expand your awareness, you will need to be careful that you stay grounded. Keep regular eating and sleeping habits, go out with your friends, have a laugh, do your schoolwork—because these are all part of the picture. If you think about it, in magick your word really has to mean something, and if you say "As I will, so shall it be" while doing a spell, that resonates in your subconscious mind. Of course, if you regularly slough off school, don't keep your word to friends and family, and generally ingest things that you know aren't good for you, your sub-conscious also registers the fact that your word doesn't actually mean very much. This will have an effect on your spell. Magick works best for those who are effectual in other ways. Make your choices from a position of strength.

Sex and witchcraft

To witches the act of sex is very sacred. In having sex we are, in a sense, mirroring the patterns of creation. Good sex is a very magickal rite, where we come close to the Goddess and the God. This doesn't mean that adult covens have orgies because they don't—that isn't what witchcraft is about. Obviously some witches may have many partners, like many non-witches, but most are in committed part-nerships and they are as faithful as anyone else. The magickal use of sex in a coven is really symbolic "gender magick," where wine is passed from male to female, and where the *athame* (sacred knife) is plunged into the chalice to consecrate the wine. When a couple are both witches, they may use the sexual power raised in their love-making for magickal purposes, but this is very specialized magick and I'm not covering that in this book. In any case, as you develop as a witch you will know instinctively how to do these things.

Sex itself can, and should be, an act of worship—of the male by the female, and the female by the male. Homosexual love is just as

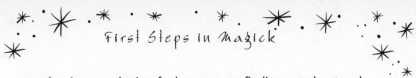

sacred, as is masturbation, for here you are finding out about and pleasuring your own body—all acts of love and pleasure are smiled on by the Goddess. Witches honor this in their rites, where there are many examples of sexual symbolism. The cauldron and the chalice both symbolize the womb, whereas the athame and wand symbolize the penis. The feminine principle is especially exalted in witchcraft because life comes from the womb and women protect and nurture it. Many covens work naked when they do their rituals. However, this doesn't mean that everything is raunchy—witches tend to say "Get 'em on" instead of "Get 'em off"! Nudity isn't very arousing—it's too unsubtle, but it is yet another salute to the natural world and the gifts of the Goddess, of which our bodies are one. Many people get giggly or give knowing looks when they hear about ritual nudity, but you have to be there to appreciate that it isn't particularly sexy!

Sex should be caring and respectful. Because witches believe you should harm no one, they are especially careful not to exploit young people. This is one of the reasons that people under 21 are rarely admitted to covens. It is very much against the principles of witches to do many of the things that they have been accused of, such as child abuse. This is particularly horrid to anyone who worships the powers of creation. Because witches are so open about sex and their own sexuality they avoid hypocrisy. Witchcraft isn't about mistreating or misusing anything; it's about respect and love for all of life.

Having said all of this, there are always those who do exploit the young and unwary under the guise of witchcraft. Initiations may be offered to young virgins, or an aura of occult power might be used to seduce. Keep well away from anyone who links sexual favors into training you as a witch or who tries to impress you with their knowledge in order to get inside your pants. Don't be dazzled! Also have nothing to do with anyone or anything that makes you feel uncomfortable—and never consent to be alone with any person you don't know well just because they claim to be a great witch. If they do so, they aren't!

Part of being a witch is to have the utmost respect for your own body. Choose partners with care—and don't allow yourself to be pressured into doing anything that you feel unhappy about. Of course, if you decide to take things further, do so in your own time, in a way that feels respectful and affectionate to you, and of course always practice safe sex. Your sexuality is part of your power—feel the glory of it, nurture it, value it and it will energize your rites and your life.

Nature worshipping

Witches are basically Nature worshippers. They celebrate eight festivals, based on the seasonal cycle, that help them to get attuned to the reality and the beauty of the world. I'll be covering this in Chapters 6 and 7. The seasonal cycle has links with mythology, and the "Story of the Goddess and God" brings it to life. It also has links with what happens in our minds and with our emotions. We can use the seasons to help us come to terms with things, to make use of opportunities, to get in touch with how we are really feeling and also simply to celebrate, for there is magick all around.

Your magickal training starts with becoming aware of Nature. Just open your eyes. Look upwards to see the stars at night. Watch the Moon and the changing shape of the crescent, appearing at different times of the day and night. Watch the birds and clouds. Feel the earth beneath your feet, comfortingly solid as you walk. Smell flowers—and other less pleasant scents! Spend a few minutes each day in a park, garden or field, just soaking it up and "being." Don't go there to think about a problem, to eat a snack or chat on your cell phone. Go just to be.

Practical exercises

Up to this point, we've done a lot of talking and finding out. If you want to be a witch this is where your training can really begin with the following exercises.

Exercise 1

Your Book of Shadows

A Book of Shadows is the record witches keep of their spells and rituals. Some prefer to call it a Book of Illumination, but "shadows" may be a better term, for what is written does not always come close to what is experienced. Your Book of Shadows can start with your first thoughts about what witchcraft is and what it means to you, together with your first experiences of inner journeys and communion with Nature.

Choose a nice, big book with room to paste in pictures and cuttings if you like. A wipe-clean hardback may be best because this will be durable.

As a simple dedication you may like to hold your book up towards the New or Full Moon, and ask the Goddess for inner wisdom.

Exercise 2

Relaxation technique

Tension is the greatest barrier between us and the vast sea of subconscious energy that surrounds us. It will help your magickal development if you learn to relax your body. Try to practice the following exercise regularly. Five or ten minutes a day is much better than once a week all Sunday morning!

Pick a time when you won't be disturbed. Lie on your bed, which gives an immediate message to your subconscious that you are going to relax. Close your eyes and imagine relaxation flowing down like water from the crown of your head over your body. Alternatively, tense and relax every muscle in your body in turn, starting with your toes and working upwards, until every muscle is relaxed. Once you feel completely relaxed, hold a pleasant picture in your mind or just allow yourself to drift. When you are ready to come back to everyday awareness, take a deep breath, stretch, pat yourself all over and have a drink of water.

Before doing any of the visualizations in this book, it is a good idea to do a relaxation exercise.

Exercise 3

Communing with trees

Earlier on we looked at how important it is just to *be* with Nature. Trees in particular often have a powerful, abiding presence that is very wise and peaceful. The Native Americans call them the "Standing People." Trees offer us so many things, and their wood has always been important to human life. They are also the "lungs" of our planet. The symbol of the tree can be very spiritual because old traditions use the shape of a tree as a map of the different spiritual realms—the roots being in the Lower World, the trunk in Middle World and the branches in Upper World. These different worlds are different sections of what we may call the "astral" define or spirit world (and Lower World has nothing to do with Hell!). People sense that there is something special about trees; it may be that they form an entrance to a magickal world.

Hugging a tree has become a subject for laughter to some people and so if you are at all shy you may like to commune with your tree in a way that won't be noticed. First choose a tree that you really like. Find a time when you won't be disturbed and sit with your back against the tree. Close your eyes. Feel the warmth of the tree flowing into you and relax.

Imagine you are the tree. Become conscious of your roots, penetrating deep into the soil, twisting, grasping, sucking, fingering. Now feel your trunk, strong and hardy, standing straight and tall. Now be conscious of your branches, spreading out into the air. Feel the wind in them, feel your leaves blow in the breeze and the birds' tiny feet as they curl around the small twigs. Feel all of this as best you can—don't worry if it is difficult.

Now come back to yourself. Be conscious of the aura of the tree. Imagine it as a peaceful green bubble extending several feet from the tree. How do you feel in this aura?

Try to listen to the tree. Is there a message from it? What is coming into your mind? This could be a picture, a sound, a smell, taste or sensation or just a feeling. Don't reason yourself out of anything, just experience it. Perhaps you have a problem or a question—do you feel you would like to share this with the tree? What answer comes back to you?

When you have finished you should feel a sense of peace. Thank the tree—you may like to bring an offering such as crumbs for the birds, in return. There is no need to tell anyone about your experience, but you may like to make a note of it in your Book of Shadows. It is part of your forming magickal identity.

Exercise 4

Forming a protective bubble

Later on we'll be looking at the magic circle and how to cast this. The bubble is really a mini-circle and it is very useful for protection of all kinds while working magick. It is also a good practice in visualization. While we are on the subject of visualization, you don't have to be able to do this to be a witch, and your skills will develop in time. Some people will always be more visual than others. To help, you can use props, such as a circular rug. You can also use other senses—you may "feel" that your bubble is there, or hear it humming like an electrical wire, or even smell it. Or you can simply tell yourself firmly and clearly that it is there.

Your bubble is useful when you are doing a quick spell, to contain your power until you have completed it. It is also a very helpful technique for any time when you feel a bit frightened or threatened, such as when going to a party where you know hardly anyone. Your "bubble" can make you feel safe and keep you calm. Be careful, however, that it doesn't keep others away from you! In a social situation it is best to visualize a golden or pink bubble to project warmth.

To make your bubble, just imagine an egg-shape of light around you. This "egg" should extend about a yard from your

body. It is a membrane that will allow anything through that you are happy with, in either direction, but nothing goes out or comes in that you don't want. Blue is often a favorite color. Imagine this egg several times a day, make it appear in your mind's eye, really feel it is there and then re-absorb it, for it is made from your life-energy. Always remember to dispel the egg afterwards. After a while this will become second nature and a help to you in many mental exercises and situations.

If you can't keep the skin of your bubble from turning hard and brittle, so that nothing can get through from either direction, then simply concentrate on making light flow out from you, forming a glow around you.

Exercise 5

Setting up an altar

It is very early for you to set up an altar, but it is worth setting aside a shelf or space in your room for objects that are magickal and devotional. You can use this for your attunement to the seasons (see in Chapters 6 and 7). If you do not want your altar to be on view, a shelf in your closet will do—although of course you won't be able to burn candles on it. The first articles for your altar could simply be candles, an oil-burner and perhaps a special stone, pebble, sea-shell or anything that you have collected that you feel connects you with Nature. Perhaps you have a picture that means something to you.

The idea of the altar is that it is a kind of anchor, a place of focus. As you progress, this altar may be useful in your rituals and a place for you to put your ritual items, such as your Goddess and God figures and your pentagram (see Chapter 4). Tend your altar, placing fresh flowers if you wish, rearranging it, keeping it dusted and free from clutter. It is your witchy working-space. Don't reason yourself out of anything you want on it; it is part of your witchy identity and your unconscious mind is teaching you about your own inner self.

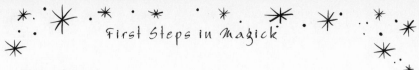

Exercise 6

Building your inner temple

This is your first major visualization exercise and you may need to do it several times before you feel comfortable with it. If you find it hard, practice just the first section until you feel comfortable. There are lots of things you will learn in the following pages, but really your most important training as a witch involves becoming aware of the inner planes, because it is there that you will find teachers of your own with a personal relevance for you. Again, if you cannot actually "see" with your inner eye, describe the scene to yourself, or imagine that you can feel, hear or smell things. You can record the instructions onto a tape if you like.

Begin by imagining that you are in a theater, and before you there is the stage. The curtains are drawn across it and as you look they slowly open, revealing not a stage prepared for a play, but a beautiful landscape. This is an entrance to the Otherworld. Look at the hills, trees, the sky and the fields. Do you want to go in? If so, go towards the stage, climb the steps and find yourself in another land. If not, let the curtains close for now and come back another day.

If you go in, take the time to notice all that is around you. Look at it and admire it. Look down upon the ground and find there a brown, hooded robe. Put this on. It is yours for protection.

Now you are going to build your astral temple. It is called an "astral" temple because the astral is the name for the world of spirit or the "Otherworld"—whatever you prefer. Is the astral real or imaginary, inside you or outside you? The answer is that it is all of these.

See a place you would really like to be—a place that is beautiful and safe. This can be anywhere. Many of us think that our ideal place is some sunny beach, but when you come to think about it, maybe that isn't where you feel your best. It really doesn't matter whether your special place is at the bottom of the sea or in an airplane in flight. It is up to you.

Although this is called a "temple," it doesn't have to be shaped like a temple if you prefer something else. The point is that it should be a haven for you. The word "build" here doesn't have to mean a building, but merely filling in the details of your special place to make it real. It may also help if you have an idea of where North, South, East and West are in your temple, for the purposes of inner rituals later on.

Take the time to imagine the details of your special place, making alterations here and there to make it more comfortable, safer and more *you*. You may find helpers appear—possibly animals or people. You should always challenge them with the words "Do you come in love?" and if they confirm this then let them proceed—and be prepared to learn from them.

When you have done as much as you can to build your temple, bid it farewell and come back to everyday awareness. Make notes in your Book of Shadows but tell no one about your temple, not even your best friend.

Ground yourself after this exercise by patting yourself all over, touching the floor and having a little to eat or drink. Remember this ritual of grounding for all future occasions.

Exercise 7

Meditating

Meditation is entering a slightly different type of consciousness where you're more in contact with your intuition and instincts. It is the way you feel when you find yourself staring into space. It is also similar to that feeling you get each day as you are waking up and going to sleep—lovely and drifty.

This type of consciousness is the same as the one you used when doing the visualization exercise described above. It can be like a waking dream, and it can be directed and described, partly described or open and exploratory. It is good to meditate in your magick circle every time you cast one. It is also good to meditate at each of the festivals (see Chapters 6 and 7) and at the full and new Moon. You can either meditate

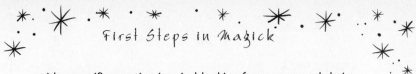

with a specific question in mind, looking for answers and clari-
fication, or your meditation can be simply adopting a relaxed
and reflective state of mind—not one where you are thinking
things through logically but just letting things drift through
your consciousness.

To meditate to find an answer to a problem or to enter into
the correct frame of mind for a ritual or seasonal celebration,
burn a white candle. In your oil burner, heat up a few drops
of oil of rose, ylang-ylang or bay. Make sure you won't be
disturbed and sit or lie comfortably, breathing steadily. Ask the
Goddess for protection. Imagine before you curtains opening
onto an inner stage, or simply keep your eyes open and stare
at the candle flame. If you have a specific question, formulate
it clearly when you begin, but don't keep asking it. If your
meditation relates to a specific season or God or Goddess,
have something before you that connects you with the
subject, like a flower, a leaf or an image. Ask to be connected
to the subject in question. All of this should be gentle, peaceful
and enjoyable. Don't try to do it for too long. Write down
anything that seems important in your Book of Shadows.

Chapter 3

The Four Elements

Magick is based on the belief that everything is energy, and to witches there are four main types of energy. Ancient people believed that there were four basic substances from which everything was made—Earth, Fire, Air and Water. Although we now know all about atoms, electrons, protons, quarks and all sorts of other particles, this still holds good. All substances are either solid, liquid, gaseous or in a state of combustion, and in these states they vibrate at different rates. These four different rates of vibration also work on the spiritual planes and in the human personality. They connect with colors, symbols, substances, plants, crystals and all forms of human thought, feeling and activity. In other words, to a witch, everything is connected with one or more of these elements. This will become clearer when we look at the elements in detail.

This is an important idea in magick because "like attracts like." When you have the knowledge of what things link up with your magickal goal you are halfway to making up a successful spell. This means that you would choose colors (for candles), herbs and such that go with the element you think is best. For instance, which element do you think might link up most successfully with a healing spell? For now, take a guess based on your first feelings and impressions of the elements. (The answer is at the end of the chapter.)

There is also a fifth element—ether. This is the unseen energy that lives within everything and witches set this in motion in magick. (The Chinese have a system of five elements.) However, it would not be very useful to try to compare the two. It is important to accept that there may be more than one system and that, mysteriously, they both work in their different ways.) As witches we use the time-honored Western tradition of the four elements.

As a witch, the four elements will come to be very much a part of you and your magickal consciousness. These four elements play a part in the formation of the witch's circle because they are called into being—or invoked—at the four quarters of the circle. "Invoked" means inwardly called up; that is, we imagine they are there. (But this doesn't mean they aren't really there, it's just that we can't see them with our ordinary eyes.) The elements are called up at each of the points of the compass: North is the place for Earth, East for Air, South for Fire and West for Water. When you make your circle you need to have a rough idea where North is and go from there. You will come to know and love the elemental powers. The circle is a perfect shape and it connects us to the spirit world. The four elements make a square that fits into the circle and this keeps us grounded—because square things are very stable. The elemental powers protect us and help us with their power.

The four points of the circle where we call the elements may be termed the Guardians, the Watchtowers, or the quarters. If you have seen the film *The Craft* you may have noticed the witches "called in the corners" when making their circle. I'm not aware of an actual witch calling them the "corners," but the idea is still correct. When you call up the quarters you can imagine them in the way that works best for you. Many witches actually think of a Lord and a Lady of the Watchtowers, and all their attendant spirits. There is a different name for each type of elemental spirit, as we shall see. Or some think about the legions of spirits themselves thronging in. Still others concentrate on the element itself—for instance, you could imagine water rushing over you as you invoke the Western quarter. Still others imagine all of these things in a complex and dramatic scene. See what evolves for you as you progress, but for now keep it simple. When you invoke the elements properly it can be a very strong feeling, especially when calling up the one that is most special to you.

As well as having their Lord and Lady and legions of spirits, different Goddesses and Gods naturally belong in certain quarters. For instance the goddess Bride that we talk about in the passage on Imbolc (see page 117) belongs more in the East/Air and South/Fire part of the circle, while a mysterious goddess like Hecate goes in the West/Water and possibly North/Earth section. There really is a wealth of links, but do not expect to understand or recall them now. Get to know the elements themselves first.

The Earth element

As you might expect, this element is solid, long-lasting, strong, real and physical. It connects with things we can touch and feel. It is about the practical, the grounded, the common sense and the wisdom that we carry in our blood and bones. Earth is situated in the North of the circle because that is the dark part of the sky where Sun and Moon do not travel.(Witches in the Southern Hemisphere usually change this around so that Earth is in the South.) In many ways Earth is the most important quarter to witches because we believe that the spiritual is found within the physical and we also work with hidden things. Because of this the altar in a witch's circle is usually placed in the North.

Earth/North is linked to the season of winter and the feast of Yule, to midnight, old age and to the phase of the Moon known as dark Moon, which we shall discover more about in Chapter 8 (even though the Moon, dark or otherwise, is always in the South for people in the Northern Hemisphere). Do you see how the associations are growing? These things feel connected, do they not? The North's colors are dark grey, brown, black and dark green. One symbol witches use to mean Earth is a stone. The signs of the zodiac that come under the Earth element are Taurus, Virgo and Capricorn.

The spirits of Earth are called the Gnomes. You can picture them looking after the soil, the trees and the flowers and being close at hand when you do the gardening. The Gnomes also tend the minerals within the earth, the crystals and precious stones. When you call on the Earth quarter you can think about all these industrious little beings marching up to your circle.

Earth
North
Gnomes

Water
West
Undines

Air
East
Sylphs

Fire
South
Salamanders

The Four Elements

The Air element

We always invoke the quarters in a clockwise direction, because that is the way the sun moves when looked at from the Northern Hemisphere, and witches try to follow the patterns of Nature wherever possible. However, in the Southern Hemisphere the Sun moves counterclockwise, so Southern witches should really invoke in a counterclockwise direction. A word for clockwise that witches use is "deosil." You may like to remember that—it's very witchy! But strictly speaking deosil means "in the direction of the sun," which is different in the Southern Hemisphere. The opposite of deosil is "widdershins," or counterclockwise, and is usually considered to be a bit on the nasty side. Some witches avoid moving widdershins at all while others say it is perfectly appropriate for some tasks that involve undoing, such as when saying goodbye to the Watchtowers. For the moment, stick with deosil and see how you feel.

So, moving deosil (clockwise in the Northern Hemisphere, counterclockwise in the Southern Hemisphere) we come to East and the element of Air. This element is mobile, light and free. Molecules as gas are in their most mobile state. We cannot see Air, but we can see its effects, such as when trees blow in the wind. In the same way we cannot see thought, although we can appreciate what it does. Air is linked to movement, to freshness, to thought and to communication. It connects with the rational and logical thought processes, studying, and the theories that are hatched in the mind. Today it also relates to things like telephones and computers.

Air/East is connected to spring (particularly the Equinox), youth, dawn and the waxing Moon. One of the things that witches associate with Air is incense. Air's colors are bright blue and yellow. The Air signs of the zodiac are Gemini, Libra and Aquarius. The Air spirits are called Sylphs. They swoop and dive on the wind, ride on the backs of birds and perch on treetops; they are graceful, beautiful, swift and elusive. They keep the atmosphere clean and keep lines of communication open and buzzing. They are with you in the fresh air, especially in high, windswept places. They are also hovering about when you are doing your best to pass on your ideas. When you call up the East and Air, imagine all these exquisite beings borne on the wind to your circle.

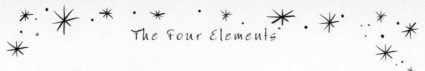

The Fire element

Fire is vibrant and volatile. Molecules in this state are excited and in the process of changing from one substance to another. Fire is bright, warm, energetic, consuming and invigorating. Flames leap and dance. Fire relates to inspiration and creativity, drive, passion, wide perspectives (although these are also Air), spirituality and imagination. Fire in its basic form has largely disappeared from our lives. We cook in microwaves and heat our homes with central heating, not with an open fire in which you can see "pictures." No wonder we love fireworks! Fire today is especially magical.

In the Southern Hemisphere Fire should really be related to the North, where you see the Sun burning brightly. In the Northern Hemisphere Fire's home is the South. It is connected to summer, the festival of Midsummer, to midday, full Moon and young adulthood. Its most obvious symbol is the candle, and its colors are red and orange. The Fire signs of the zodiac are Aries, Leo and Sagittarius. The Fire spirits are called Salamanders and they leap and twist and sparkle in the flames. Look for them in the heart of a bonfire. They are also useful for creativity and inspiration and we can imagine them energizing us. When you call up the South (or North, depending on your location) and Fire, imagine the Salamanders sparkling at the edge of the circle.

The Water element

Water is gentle yet tremendously powerful. Like Fire it transforms, more slowly yet just as completely. Molecules in the liquid state are free and fluid. Water is cleansing, nurturing, life-giving and healing. There is a rhythm and a beauty to the waters, and the human body is over 70 percent water. Water is linked to empathy, compassion, caring and developing. All of life comes from water and depends upon it. Water flows in and around things, taking the shape of the vessel that contains it, yet escaping through any cracks. It appears deceptively gentle, yet it can erode stone. Water is a mystical element relating to the emotions and feelings that may not be expressed.

Water/West is linked to waning Moon, evening, the beginning of old age, the Autumn Equinox and the season of autumn. Its symbol is the chalice, and its colors are green, deep blue and purples. Water signs are Cancer, Scorpio and Pisces. The Water spirits are called Undines and they are strange and beautiful creatures. They haunt all stretches of water, slipping smoothly in and out of the water with scarcely a ripple, ducking and diving, dancing in the waterfall, riding on the waves. When you call up the West imagine these lovely creatures borne up to your circle on the tide.

Your element

You may be realizing, if you haven't before, that magick and witch-craft are about a "Cosmic web" in which everything is connected. This means that a waning Moon may be connected to water, to old age, to a cup, to the season of autumn, to purple and green—and many more things. It also means that abstract things, such as your personality, are connected to one of the elements. You may have spotted a clue to this because I mentioned three of the signs of the zodiac under each of the elements. Your own sign of the zodiac is the sign where the Sun was when you were born and this has a strong effect upon your personality. Maybe you already feel a link with the element you were born under and when you read about it something clicked into place.

You don't have to know anything about astrology to be a witch, but many witches are very interested in it and use it to some extent. After all, the phase of the Moon is important to witches and that is a part of astrology. Astrologers believe that the positions of the Sun, the Moon and all the planets at the moment when you were born link up with the type of person you are. Scientists often scoff at this, yet astrology is used successfully by many people to understand personalities and predict the future. Newspaper columns are really just a bit of fun, but they are based on astrological principles. If you study astrology you will find that it works.

One of the most important points, if not the most important point, in your birth-chart is your Sun sign. This is the sign that you were born under and almost everyone knows theirs. If you don't, all you need to do is pick up a paper or magazine and look for the astrology column to find the dates. For instance, if you were born between August 24 and September 23 you are a Virgo. The dates

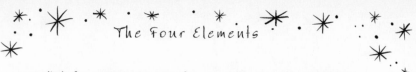

vary a little from year to year, so if you were born on September 22, 23 or 24, you really need to ask an astrologer what sign you are because you could be a Libra *or* a Virgo. It all depends what the date is exactly when the Sun moves from one sign to another.

So you already know your important element through your Sun sign. If you are Taurus, Virgo or Capricorn, you are an Earth person; if Gemini, Libra or Aquarius, you are Air; if Aries, Leo or Sagittarius, you are Fire; and if Cancer, Scorpio and Pisces, you are Water. Of course, it is possible that for some reason this doesn't feel right. This could be because you have a strong representation of another Element in your chart (for instance you may have the Sun in earthy Virgo, but the Moon, Venus, Mercury and Mars might be in airy Libra). Before we look more closely at the elements and what they mean to your personality, take this questionnaire to find out which one is strongest in you.

Which is your element?

1) What sort of pictures do you like to have in your room:
a) pictures of flowers, animals, wildlife and landscapes?
b) pictures that give a feeling of openness and freedom, or perhaps maps and diagrams? c) fantasy pictures or things you dream about? d) pictures of family and friends or things that were given to you by someone special?

2) What sort of films do you most enjoy: a) a good story, with a beginning, an end and a middle? b) a whodunnit, or possibly a documentary on your favorite subject? c) sci-fi or fantasy? d) a weepy romance?

3) There are many things that go toward making a person pleasant to be with, but you prefer to be with: a) a sensible, reliable, capable person, because you know where you are with them; b) a truthful person who says what they mean and is reasonable; c) an interesting, imaginative person who makes you feel inspired; d) an affectionate, understanding person.

4) You value your own room for many reasons but mostly because: a) it's your base, it's comfortable and you have all your things there; b) you feel free there, with your books,

computer and cell phone close to hand; c) it's your space to dream, make plans, sort out your life; d) you feel safe there, and it's a private place to bring your friends.

5) In life in general it's most important to you to feel: a) secure; b) free; c) inspired; d) protected.

6) Your main ambition, when you leave full-time education, is to: a) get a reliable job or profession; b) be independent; c) see the world; d) find someone special and settle down.

7) Which comes closest to your favorite night out? a) somewhere familiar, especially if the food is good and the surroundings pleasant; b) it doesn't matter really as long as you can get out and about, have a laugh, see your friends; c) you'll try anything—you'd rather not go to the same boring old place every time; d) it's the people that you're with that count the most, and often you're happy at home.

8) You are most interested in: a) doing things, getting results in the here-and-now; b) working out what things mean and discussing it; c) whatever may be possible in the future; d) how people feel, what they like, how they react.

9) Your ideal vacation would be: a) sea and sun on the Costa Mucho; b) doing this and that and whatever takes your fancy; c) something unusual and adventurous; d) it's who you go with that counts.

10) When someone comes to you for advice, do you: a) give practical advice about what they could do? b) analyze the situation with them and come up with loads of ideas? c) enjoy getting them all fired up with possibilities? d) try to make them feel as good as possible?

Your score

Mostly a's. It looks like Earth is your strongest element. You are down-to-earth and generally practical. It may appear that you are logical (and you may certainly think so!), but actually it isn't sweet reason that makes you tick so much as what is most workable. You probably handle money and sex fairly sensibly, but your imagina-

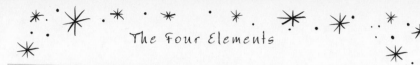

tion may need developing. Your strong point is your sound contact with things of this earth and you may have a talent with herbs, oils, incense and all the practical witchy things, which will make you feel "connected." It is probably easiest for you to invoke the North/Earth quarter. Fire may be your most difficult element because it may seem a bit iffy. Also you may distrust people who are very intuitive and spiritual, although they may also be very attractive to you. This is because you are trying to develop that part of yourself. When you invoke the Fire element you are helping yourself to balance out. It may help to meditate in the South of your circle, asking for the gifts of Fire.

Mostly b's. Air seems your strongest element. You are generally fairly emotionally detached although you probably have a lot of friends and like to talk a lot. You like to work things out in a logical way and like to think you are fair and reasonable—you are, but sometimes you don't understand emotions and may deny that you have some feelings that aren't "nice." Truth is important to you but you need also to be honest with yourself about how you feel. You are reasonable, friendly, pleasant, often light-hearted and possibly clever. You are good at working things out. Your strong point is your ability to see how rituals work and to make symbolic connections— you may also be good at writing rituals and understanding theory. It is probably easiest for you to invoke the East/Air. Water may be your most difficult element because it may seem overwhelming and confusing. Also you may distrust people who are very emotional and empathetic, thinking they are soppy, although you may also be drawn to them. This is because they represent something that you lack and instinctively feel you need. When you invoke the Water element, you are helping yourself to become more whole. It may help to meditate in the West of your circle, asking for the gifts of Water.

Mostly c's. Fire seems your strongest element. You are adventurous, either mentally or physically—or both. What is important to you is the possible, the exciting, the futuristic, the mythological and the fantastic. You may be very imaginative. Probably you have tremendous energy of a bodily or spiritual kind and you may be very creative. In rituals you are all too ready to enter the other realms and to expand into the magickal Otherworld—and to create in it. What you may not be so good at is remembering the matches, and you may get halfway through your rituals before you realize that you have forgotten something! People probably find you inspiring and energizing, although you do not always see what's under your nose and you may not care about it if you do! You aren't the most realistic of individuals but because you may be dynamic you may seem more practical than you really are. Many witches are like you, for you are generally intuitive and spiritual. It is probably easiest for you to invoke South/Fire; North/Earth may be hardest because it may seem suffocating and obscure. You may get irritated by people who are very practical and down-to-earth. You may feel that they are trying to clip your wings. At the same time you may also be drawn to them because deep inside you know you need those qualities. When you invoke the Earth element you are helping yourself to be more complete and it may help to meditate in the North of your circle, asking for the gifts of Earth.

Mostly d's. Water seems to be your strongest element. You are empathetic, intuitive and dreamy, but also very attuned to the needs and feelings of others. You may have a healing presence and enjoy looking after people and making them feel more secure. Kind and emotional, you may be over-sensitive at times and unable to stand back and detach yourself from people and situations. You may be an excellent judge of character but you are probably nice to everyone, regardless! It may not be easy for you to be rational, to work things out and to understand logical arguments. Your witchy gifts are that you can go with the flow, sense the undercurrents both magickally and emotionally and choose your companions wisely—that is if you can manage to say "No." Probably you find it easiest to invoke Water/West while East/Air may be your most challenging element. You may rather dislike people who are very detached and logical. You find them cold, but nonetheless you seem to end up with them! This may be because you are seeking something of that detachment to balance yourself. It may help to meditate in the East part of your circle, asking for the gifts of Air.

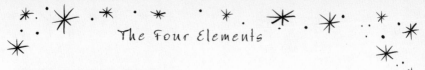

Practical exercises

Exercise 1

The elements in Nature

Go for a walk and find something that links with each of the elements to place on your altar. Examples could include a stone or soil for earth, a feather or wind-borne seed for air, a red flower or dried wood for fire and rainwater or a shell for water. Stones of different colors could actually symbolize the elements—brown for earth, blue for air, red for fire, green for water. See what else you can find. Remember—if it is important to you, then it is important!

Experience each of the elements. Earth can be connected with by gardening, planting seeds or by collecting stones to form your own mini stone circle. Air can be experienced by kite-flying or playing with balloons, Fire by watching bonfires and fireworks and Water by going swimming or paddling.

Exercise 2

Guided visualizations to meet the elements

The elements exist most powerfully in the subtle realms. The following four exercises will help you to become truly acquainted with them. If you wish, you can tape the instructions and play them back once you are in a state of relaxation. For each one, it is best to start in the "temple" that you constructed in Chapter 2, visualizing yourself wearing your robe, which you should leave behind in your temple when you finish. Whenever you finish a visualization, remember to ground yourself as described on page 38.

During the visualizations, you might decide that you don't feel up to carrying on; this is fine—just bring yourself back and ground yourself. You might also find that you encounter elemental beings; challenge them by asking them if they come in love. Treat them with respect and thank them for any advice they may give.

Earth

See yourself leaving your temple to walk down a forest path. It is getting darker and darker and greener and greener as you go deeper into the trees. There is a wonderful scent of pine and wet earth. Follow this path for a while noticing all the animals and plants—this is a lush place.

See before you a cave. Do you want to go in? If you do, walk on, feeling the hard floor of rock beneath your feet. Touch the solid walls of the cave, noting how cool they are. You are going deeper and deeper into the earth and the light is dim. Walk on.

Now you find yourself in a large cavern. Here it is very safe and secret. You can smell all the concealed scents of the inner earth. The walls and ceiling of the cave seem to have strange patterns etched into the rock—or is it merely the dim light playing on the uneven surface of stone? Are there any beings in the cave? If so, ask to see them, and make friends with them.

Stay as long as you like, exploring, perhaps talking and discussing. Are you given a gift? If so treasure it and give thanks. When you are ready, make your way back along the path to your temple and leave the gift there. Wait a while before coming back to everyday awareness. After your meditation do something for the earth, such as planting seeds or watering a plant, and make a note of your experiences.

Air

Start from your temple and make your way out into an open field. The wind is fresh and there stands a hot air balloon, ready to take off when you are ready. Do you want to get in? If so, step into the basket and feel it tremble slightly as it lifts gently off the ground. You feel light, light as a feather and the balloon wafts easily with your weight. You know that you are safe for you are part of the wind on which you are riding. There you go, up and up. Look at the clouds and the birds, feel the wind in your hair, see from horizon to horizon—be aware how free you are, and how open everything is.

Higher and higher you are wafting. The balloon is carried on the breeze. It is all so effortless. Feel how fresh the air smells, and look how far you can see. You are up with the clouds now—light, white fluffy clouds that seem to dance on the breeze. It is light and bright, airy and wonderful. You realize that you can leave everything behind on the ground and come up here to play with the breezes, where everything is different, clean and playful. You hear the breeze singing in the ropes—but is it the breeze? Or could those be voices that you hear, chattering, laughing? Are there beings there? Ask to see them and experience them. Stay there as long as you like, drifting and swaying, perhaps talking and asking questions. Perhaps you are given a gift; if so you should treasure it and give thanks.

When you are ready, ask to be returned to earth and feel yourself going slowly and gently downward until you land with a soft bump in the field where you started. Go to your temple and place your gift there, staying there until you are ready to come back to the everyday world. It is a good idea to do something to honor the element of Air—perhaps you could vacuum your room! Write down what you have experienced in your Book of Shadows.

Fire

Start again from your temple and find yourself on a wide plain where orange and red flowers grow thick and luxuriant. Do you want to go on? If so, walk through this place, enjoying its vibrancy, color and vivid life. Horses thunder past in the distance. Eagles wheel and dive, occasionally landing with fierce grace on the stumps of twisted trees. Walk along, feeling energetic and enthusiastic—where can it be that you are going?

It begins to get darker and before you now there is a brilliant glow. As you approach you see that this is an enormous bonfire. The flames are roaring and leaping skyward in brilliant shades of crimson and orange. Behind the bonfire fireworks soar into the night sky, bursting in showers of multi-colored sparks. Stand in front of the bonfire and feel the heat upon your face. How warm and lovely it is! How exciting all the fireworks—such as you have never seen in the real world—colors more scintillating, the display more luxurious. The flames are roaring and dancing—and deep within them, in the caverns of fire, you may see beings capering, bounding out like firecrackers, only to jump back in again with wild laughter. Is there anything you want to ask them, or to talk about? Are there any teachings that you need from the element of Fire? Talk for as long as you wish. If you are given a gift, treasure it.

When you are ready, make your way back across the plain through the brilliant flowers and into your temple. Keep your gift there as a treasure. When you come back to everyday awareness, celebrate fire by lighting a candle. Make a note about your experiences in your Book of Shadows.

Water

Emerge from your temple to find yourself in a cool grotto. Before you there is a lake, into which falls a waterfall in a neverending silver spray. Beads of moisture hang in the air. You can taste them on your tongue. How fresh and sweet they are!

Walk around the lake, touching the wet rocks, making your way through green fronds. Trees bend over the lake, making it dim and cool. Their reflections look back at them, broken by the occasional gentle ripple. Fish jump out of the water and gracefully dive back into the depths. You look into the water—it is green, purple and deep blue. Glistening and mysterious things seem to lie deep below the surface but you cannot quite see them.

Now you are close to the waterfall and it falls like a shimmering curtain. The stream plays on the surface of the lake in a neverending song. It really does sound musical. You are sure you can hear music—a strange, wild sound as of sweet voices singing to you. You climb upon a rock and see there is an outcropping. If you walk upon it you can go through the curtain of water and find what lies beyond. Do you wish to go?

If you do, take a deep breath and step through. Now you are in the kingdom of the waters. What do you see? Can you see the beings that are singing so beautifully? What would you like to ask them or talk to them about? Do they have a gift for you? If so, take it with reverence and stay awhile if you wish.

When you are ready, make your way back through the curtain of water and round the lake, back to your temple. Stay there for a while and place your gift there with care. When you come back to everyday awareness, make a note of what you have experienced in your Book of Shadows and celebrate the gift of Water by drinking a glassful.

Healing with the elements

Back on page 40, I asked you what element would be best for a healing spell. The answer is that Water is probably the principle element in healing. You may have realized this from practical matters—if someone is feeling ill we might offer them a glass of water, and if we have a cut we bathe it in water. More generally, there is a healing, soothing feel to water. We grow from a tiny fusion between a sperm and an egg in the waters of the womb, until we are born. However, Fire may also have a place in healing, burning off infection, and Earth helps strength and endurance. Air could possibly be involved for communication, if we were looking for a cure, and also for problems like asthma. Most spells can involve several approaches.

If you decided that Water was the main element then you could make up a healing spell using water in your cup or chalice, green candles and perhaps eucalyptus, which is an herb ruled by the Moon (and we all know how the Moon pulls the tides). You will be able to find out more in Chapter 9.

Chapter 4

Magickal Secrets

You may think there is some big secret that witches have, some hidden knowledge only given to a favored few. Well, in a way you are right. But this knowledge isn't something simple, like the exact way to say a magickal rhyme in order to make something happen. Nor is it knowing ingredients for some concoction in a cauldron, or having a magic wand with stars at the end. The secret is being aware that everything is connected in a Cosmic web. This isn't something anyone can point out to you—this awareness, if you do not have it already, comes with time. After a while you will see this, sense it, be truly conscious of it and know your way around it, and be aware of which strings to pull to get the desired effect. Spells and rituals are pulling the strings.

Your own mind is really important because it enables you to move around in magickal space, so to speak. Certain things have an effect on your mind, changing your consciousness, making it easier to visualize and think in a certain way; and because your consciousness has altered, so the universe around you alters—sometimes a great deal, but rarely in any obvious way. These days we are very aware of the mind, the unconscious and the way we can increase our personal power, but these ideas are comparatively new. A hundred or so years ago thinking for oneself was not regarded favorably (unless you happened to be a noble, and then you could get away with murder!) and to try to direct your life might, in some cases, have been considered arrogant. Go back further in time and the situation was worse. There was much less freedom and people who wanted to make their own choices were considered a threat to the authorities of the time. Besides, religion was very strong and people were taught that only the priests could connect them with God. Any thought that they might expand their own awareness and become directly conscious of deity (which is really what the Cosmic web is) would have seemed sacrilegious. Witches worked with subtle forces and sought to make changes of their own choice, and so were doubly threatening—hence their persecution.

But you are free! You can find out all you like, you can make a vision of your own future come true and you can make your own contact with the Goddess and the God in your rituals. But first you need to learn some basics.

Magickal symbols

Do you know what a symbol is? It is more than a sign. For instance, there are road signs, such as a bottleneck shape for "road narrows." These signs are for information. But consider a national flag—the British Union Jack or the American Stars-and-Stripes, for example. These are more than just signs. When someone looks at a flag it sets off a number of associations in the mind—patriotism, pride, belonging—and this changes the consciousness of the person, however slightly. They may puff out their chest and feel they are growing, or they may, of course, feel scornful and amused if nationalist fervor does not appeal to them. At all events a little old flag can have quite an effect.

With magickal symbols the effect is similar, only stronger and less easily described. For the most part these symbols have an effect on the unconscious mind. This is the part where your dreams and lots of memories that might give rise to automatic feelings are stored. For instance, you might feel really snug and safe whenever you smell lavender, but you don't know why. In fact, Granny loved that perfume and as a tiny baby you spent many happy hours with her. Perhaps she died when you were two and you can't remember her or the lavender, but deep in your unconscious the memory is lodged. So, for you, lavender has associations. But there are some things that have associations for the whole of a culture (sometimes even the human race as a whole) and these things are more a matter of race memory or possibly genetics. These symbols are very deeply implanted and they do something, to a greater or lesser extent, when you see them. This doesn't mean that you go into some strange trance when you see them or use them, for the effect is more subtle than that. But they do alter your mind and that is the first step in magic. The pentagram is one of those things.

The pentagram

Let us start with the pentagram. This is a five-pointed star and it is the essential symbol for witches. Most witches wear one as jewelry of some kind, regularly visualize the pentagram and can form one quickly and easily using "mind-power" and a finger or an athame. First, it is important that you understand the pentagram and get used to forming it.

The pentagram is a primary symbol of the Goddess for it looks like the female figure (the six-pointed star is linked to the male). Many flowers have five petals, the pentagram shape is linked to the orbital path of the planet Venus and if you study geometry you will find that certain shapes and proportions linked to harmony are connected with the pentagram. However, none of this matters that much—when you look at the pentagram you will know it is magickal and powerful. It's that simple.

The pentagram is also a symbol of the five elements: Earth, Fire, Air, Water and Ether, or the human mind working with the four elements. It is usually formed with one apex upward and two downward, like a figure standing with her legs apart and hands held out at her sides. It is also sometimes shown with two apexes upward and one downward. This is sometimes regarded as representing the horned head of the devil and is seen as evil, but there is no reason why this should be. It could mean the spark of consciousness hidden within the world of the material. However, it is only the upright pentagram that concerns us here.

So, you need to get used to forming a pentagram with your finger. Start at the top apex and go down to the left, up and across to the right, straight across to the left, down and across to the right, up to the top apex again and close the pentagram by repeating the starting-stroke. You can also draw pentagrams on a sheet of paper. Practice them over and over again until it flows with ease.

What is the pentagram used for? You can use it in any spell as a sign of power. Form it across a door for protection, or over food to bless it. Specifically, witches use it when calling up the four quarters or Watchtowers that we talked about in the last chapter. Some witches—Wiccans in particular—start with different points of the pentagram for the different elements. The one I have given is the Earth-invoking pentagram. But many witches use only this one at all times for each of the elements, and for the moment it will be fine for you to do this. Get to know and love your pentagram.

Spiral

The spiral has many meanings. It can symbolize an entrance to the Mysteries. These are the hidden things within ourselves and Nature that we explore as witches. It also means things coming into the concrete world and going out of it again, so it can mean death and rebirth. Water goes down the drain in a spiral, smoke may rise in a spiral, and the passage of the seasons in the wheel of the year is seen as a spiral because, although we go around and around, we never cover quite the same ground. Snakes, instinctual creatures that they are, move in spirals. (Snakes are important to witches because the fact they shed their skin regularly links them to womanly cycles like menstrual periods.) It is good, as a witch, to be aware of the meanings of the spiral because so much in myth, history and art is connected to it. For instance, the net, labyrinth and knot are all part of the same family. The knot was worn by the priestesses of ancient Crete in observance of this. Stories about labyrinths mean going into the Mysteries of life. The spiral is the witch's journey and the witch's dance.

The ankh

Some witches like to wear an ankh so it is a good idea to know what it means. It is a cross with a loop at the top, similar to the biological sign for female, a circle with a T-bar underneath, except that the circle is more like an oval. It is both a symbol of life and a key.

Triangles

There is a triangle to symbolize each of the elements. Fire is a triangle apex upward, and Water is apex downward. Air is like Fire only with another line inside drawn parallel to the base and Earth is like Water with a line within drawn parallel to the top line. The triangle also links with the Triple Goddess, Maiden, Mother and Crone (see pages 185–88) and ritual magicians use a triangle outside their magickal circle in which to conjure demons. (Needless to say, we won't be going there, because it is of doubtful value!

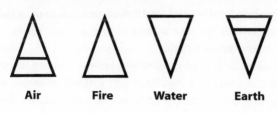

| Air | Fire | Water | Earth |

Ritual magicians use magick, but it is more complex and less a matter of instinct and nature. It's is not necessarily related to a spiritual path in the way that witchcraft is.)

The tools of the witch

There are several tools that witches traditionally use in rituals and spells. Of course each spell may have its own individual requirements, but certain tools are used to cast the circle, to bring specific energies into it and to honor aspects of life and nature. The tools also have something of the effect of symbols that we talked about above. They help you to change your consciousness and/or focus your mind. However, it may be a bit misleading to think that the witch's tools are only magickal because of their mental effect. They have their own power, being a highly charged part of the magickal universe. And they are also beautiful.

It is possible to do spells and even rituals with almost nothing in the way of props and tools if your powers of visualization are strong enough. But using tools helps you, strengthens your belief, surrounds you with reminders of who you are and what you are doing. And it's fun!

Candles

Candles are very well-known as tools for rituals of all kinds. They are associated with the element of Fire. They represent transformation, the lighting of the inner flame. A candle can be used on its own for a simple spell. You can have candles of different colors for different purposes; a list of the meanings is given in Chapter 9. However, white can be used for all purposes. It is usual to have a couple of candles on your altar and one at each of the other quarters when casting a circle.

This seems a good place to have a word about fire and safety. Using several candles is inadvisable in a small bedroom where curtains and linens can catch fire! Where possible, witches devote a room specifically to ritual and this then provides the necessary space for several candles. If this is not available then it's only common sense to be very careful. Never underestimate the power and resourcefulness of the Fire element. It is exuberant and rampant and we do not have enough of it in our lives to understand it for the most part. When uncontained, it can do ferocious damage quite quickly. Candles should not be left unattended. One witch friend was doing a spell to bring passion into his life. He lit many candles and then went to answer the phone. When he came back his bed was on fire! Quite apart from the safety aspect, if you set your room on fire it is going to put an end to much of your training as a witch, for a while at least, because everyone is going to nag you about candles. It's better to be safe than silly!

Athame

Pronounced "a-thay-mee," this ritual knife has been misrepresented in fiction as being used for sacrifices and all manner of dark deeds. In fact, the very term "ritual knife" gets people jumping up and down because some are rather anxious to believe that witchcraft is "evil." But witches don't believe in sacrifice—at least not in the sort that brings harm to anything, although they may decide that sacrifice is necessary in their own lives at some point. The athame is never used to cut anything material. It is used to cut "reality." When you draw a pentagram in the air at the quarters of your magic circle you are, in a sense, cutting through the visible world into the Otherworld, inviting the elemental powers in through the gap. The athame is used to focus your mental energy. You can visualize a blue light coming from the tip. The athame can be used to cast the circle or to direct power in any spell. Because it is linked to mental concentration it is associated with the element of Air and the Eastern quarter.

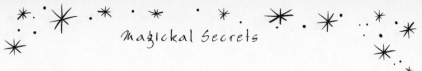

Wand

The wand is connected to the element of Fire, probably because ancient people believed that fire lay dormant within the wood, waiting to be awakened. Both the wand and the athame are rather phallic and so are linked to the positive, active male principle, while Earth and Water are receptive female elements. (This isn't to say that men can't be passive, or women positive, of course.) The wand aids visualization and inspiration, creating magickal energy. In some ways it is almost interchangeable with the athame, but the athame is more about directing, while the wand creates or works with subtle energy. For instance, you might stand before your altar and invoke the Goddess using your wand, held high.

Pentacle

A pentacle is the disk on which the pentagram is engraved (although pentagram/pentacle are often used interchangeably). The pentacle is an essential part of witchy equipment and it's placed on the altar as a symbol of Earth. The pentagram can be engraved on metal, wood or stone. In fact, if you can't get or make a pentacle to represent Earth on your altar, then a specially chosen stone can have pride of place on your altar instead, or possibly as well.

A stone is obviously a symbol of Earth. Choose one from a special place where you like to be, or pick one for its shape, for what it reminds you of, or any feelings you have about it. The pentacle and the stone aren't used actively in spells, though you may choose, for instance, to place objects on top of them when casting spells and performing rituals to benefit from their grounding energy.

Chalice

The chalice is a symbol of the element of Water. It is used for water, wine or fruit juice in rituals where you drink in honor of the Goddess. The chalice is womb-shaped, linking with the waters of life. It is a very important symbol because it represents the true, inner wisdom of the Goddess that we seek. This is probably what the knights who went in search of the Holy Grail were looking for. It is placed on the altar.

Cauldron

The traditional picture of witches is that they dance around a cauldron and stew up gross concoctions in it! Witches do have cauldrons, but like most things they are used symbolically. Like the chalice, the cauldron symbolizes the womb—but with attitude! The chalice holds the gentle blessing of the Goddess while the cauldron is Her transformative power. In most seasonal rituals the process of change is honored, and the cauldron may feature in these, wreathed with flowers or containing a candle. The Earth is both a womb and a tomb, if you think about it. The dead are laid to rest but life always comes back, growing from the earth. If you believe in reincarnation, the tomb and the womb are one, in a way. The cauldron is this sort of "womb," and it may be linked to darker aspects of the Goddess. Some witches who work in a community way may use a cauldron to brew up soup or stew, and so the cauldron feeds people in the way it was used in homes in the past. The cauldron is connected to the element of Water but because it is, as we have said, "transformative," it is also linked with Ether or Spirit. It may be placed in whatever portion of the circle is most suitable at the time, probably in the center or West.

Censer

A censer, for those unfamiliar with the term, is a vessel in which incense is burned. The censer isn't really a dynamic tool because it's used to set the scene rather than actively in spells, although there may be exceptions, such as when you pass an object through incense vapor in order to dedicate it to the powers of Air. Censers can be quite difficult to come by, and they need to be treated with caution because what they contain is very hot! They should be designed so that there is a chain which you pick up that stays cool, enabling you to lift it and waft the incense-smoke around your circle. Failing to get a censer, there are pots you can use to burn incense. Please be very, very careful. Don't use an ashtray; it isn't suitable for the prolonged burning of incense. Anything you use should be designed to cope with the job. The censer is connected to the element of Air.

White-handled knife

In contrast to the athame, this type of knife is used to cut things—not, of course, anything human or animal! It is used to chop herbs,

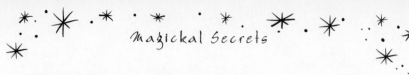

scrape ash from the censer and perform similar practical tasks. It doesn't have to have a white handle. You can use a pen-knife or even scissors, which are often better and quicker. You may feel it is nicer to keep something specifically for your magickal jobs. This knife isn't used symbolically in rituals.

Besom

This isn't your substitute for the bus or taxi but another ritual tool that witches do indeed use. The besom is for sweeping out your circle. Not literally, though: a vacuum cleaner does that much better! It is for getting rid of any negative forces that might undermine your magickal work. As you sweep with your broom you can visualize that you are sweeping out the grey clouds of ill-wishing, doubt, distraction, malevolent entities or anything at all that could contaminate the circle. The broom should be of the old type that you see in pictures, made from a large bundle of twigs with a wooden handle sticking out. This broom had several meanings. It meant fertility: the handle is like a penis and the brush is like a vagina, and the broom was "ridden" by the women over the fields to make them fruitful. The broom was probably also used for masturbation, where the tip of the handle was covered by a special ointment that was absorbed by the delicate tissues of the genitals to produce the sensation of flying. Powerful herbal concoctions may also have been taken by people close to Nature who knew what they were doing in ways now lost to us. Because of the sensations induced by all of this it is no wonder that the good old broom became linked to flying! Various trees were used in the making of the broom for they all had—and have—their magickal meanings. The birch was most commonly used because it is a tree linked to purification. Another old favorite was the broom plant, *Planta genista*. Like most of the tools used by witches, the besom was a normal household object and it only looks so lovely and witchy to us today because it is old-fashioned. It is a treat to sweep away the leaves at Halloween with a besom! The besom isn't linked to any element in particular.

Sword

If you go to fancy New Age stores you may see wonderful swords on sale behind glass cases—for wonderful prices! Wiccans usually use a sword to cast the circle but an athame serves just as well. The sword has a lovely presence to it, especially when wielded by the High Priestess. It is linked to the Air element. Many witches operate without a sword and some don't like the thought of using one. There's no need to try to get one—and your little brother's plastic one will not do as a substitute! However, if a family member is into medieval re-enactment or similar things, you may have access to a real, although hopefully blunt, sword. If so, use it if you like, with style!

Salt and water

These elements represent Earth and Water, and it is usual to use them to cleanse the circle, dissolving the salt in the water and sprinkling the space. Salt was sacred to Aphrodite and was a very valuable substance in times gone by. (Before the days of refrigerators and freezers it was widely used to preserve meats and other produce.) You can take a bath with a little salt dissolved in it to cleanse yourself before rituals.

Bell

There is a magickal quality to sound because it's a vibration and brings about change. The bell can be rung a symbolic number of times to mark points in rituals. Some simple meanings might be:

* one ring to signify a beginning or a single, concentrated goal
* two to signify a pairing
* three for a creative act
* four to ground and balance
* five to inspire
* six for harmony
* seven for profound wisdom
* eight for achievement
* nine for a move to a new cycle.

Or you can just ring the bell because you like it, or to snap you out of a meditative phase in your ritual when you want to go on to do

something else. The bell is an optional extra to rituals. The round shape of the bell links it with the Goddess.

Music

Doing a magickal working with someone who can play an instrument enhances the atmosphere beautifully. A penny whistle or pan-pipes make one think of the Horned God—and they can sound haunting. Drums, too, are excellent to dance to. Many witches play a suitable cassette or CD for their seasonal rituals.

Robe

It is a very good idea to get yourself a robe that you wear just for rituals. If this has a hood so much the better because it can envelop you more completely—if this is what you want. The robe you use will carry all of your personal "vibrations" and these will build up the more you use it for rituals. Many witches work naked (this is called "sky-clad"), and when you are alone you may prefer to do this. The subtle energies of the human body are said to flow better without clothing. In any case, wearing no clothes is a statement of pride in the body the Goddess gave you and symbolizes freedom from prejudice, prudery and constraint. Needless to say, however, you need to be very careful if you work naked because few things are more arousing to certain questionable types than the idea of an attractive female witch dancing nude by candlelight! It isn't "witchy" to take risks with this and adult witches who work in covens and alone are very careful not to compromise themselves. So if you choose to do this, lock your door, draw your curtains, plug your key-hole and, above all, don't tell anyone what you do because they may get unbearably curious! If you work with friends, make sure that they also are similarly careful, especially if you work in a mixed group. Make sure everyone has the right motives and attitudes.

Whether or not you work naked most of the time, it's still a good idea to have a robe for those times when you work outdoors or, for example, if you do blessing and space-clearing in houses of friends. You can very easily make a robe out of an old sheet if the material doesn't fray too much. Just cut a hole for your head and sew up the sides, shortening where necessary. Then the garment can be gathered together at the waist with a cord. Or you may find something in a second-hand store. If you are good at sewing, you can make a robe without a pattern as long as you have enough cloth and you cut it big enough—always err on the side of the enormous as you cut, and pare down later if necessary. What you need is a double length of cloth that you cut out with arms all from one piece. Just sew down the two sides and hey, presto! To form a simple hood, cut a big, deep collar or cowl neckline that you can pull up and over when you wish.

Your altar

Last but not least you will need some sort of altar to place your bits and pieces for rituals. This can be just a sturdy cardboard box covered with a suitable cloth. The altar is a working, devotional space, as opposed to a shrine, which is about honoring. Your magickal altar for your rituals is therefore different from the static altar you may have in your room to honor the Goddess. On your altar—which you should place in the North of your circle if you are in the Northern Hemisphere and the South if in the Southern—place your pentacle and/or stone, your athame (although if you can

get a sheath for your athame and attach it to a cord on your waist, so much the better) and anything you need for the spell or ritual. For instance, if this is a seasonal ritual, such as the ones given in Chapters 6 and 7, you will need space for flowers, fruit, nuts and so on. You will also need your salt and water, chalice, wand and possibly your censer—although you may prefer to put that in the East of your circle. Candles, of course, go here, as well as figures of the Goddess and the God. These you may buy in New Age stores, but you can use pictures or simple pieces of stone or wood that seem suitable to you. Have a space also for your Book of Shadows because you may want to refer to it.

Sacred space

All space is actually sacred because the Goddess is within everything. Witches don't split mind from matter, spiritual from worldly—they are all part of the same spectrum. It is especially important to witches to see life and the world as an expression of the Divine. We don't believe *in* the Goddess because She simply *is* all around us, and the God is the force within. At least that is one way of looking at it. Whatever view we take, all is sacred.

In the last few years the idea of space having more meanings than just convenience and a pleasant appearance has become popular with Feng Shui. This is a Chinese system, literally meaning Wind Water. It teaches that our living space is symbolic, that different parts of it have different meanings and how we use the space can affect our lives because it affects the flow of *chi,* or life force. By setting up a place as our living space we are causing a change in the ether. What we make of that space matters in ways that may be far-reaching. Our space is an energy-system.

When witches do their rituals they set up a place that is sacred, called the Magick Circle. You will learn exactly how to cast this in the next chapter. When you cast your circle you are saying, "This is my special place. This is where my consciousness meets the material world. This is where I make contact with the Otherworld." Space is "sacred" when it is blessed and where, in some fashion, the spirit world is expressly remembered and honored. Ancient places like Avebury, Stonehenge, Carnac and others were built for this reason.

Churches have that same function today. However, you do not have to have any sort of building or construction to make a space sacred. Some places are special and readily lend themselves to consecration (i.e., being made sacred) because of the significant nature of the unseen energies within and around them. It is worth thinking about this idea before we go into how to make your circle and what exactly, it means.

Ritual

Ritual is a term used a lot in this book. It isn't a word that is always attractive because it's also used to describe things that are meaningless and repetitive. Ritual is actually "mindless" because, although we may have worked out exactly what everything that we are doing means, what we do doesn't have a logical or visible result. A ritual can indeed be meaningless if the meaning has been lost or if we haven't clearly sorted out its purpose. There are plenty of things in daily life that can be meaningless rituals. For instance, a house-proud woman may vacuum every day because she feels she has to or she'll feel guilty, and she may go on doing this long after she has driven everyone away by her obsessive neatness. She is doing what she is doing out of some nameless fear, or to cope with something in her mind that she doesn't want to look at properly, such as an inner belief that she is "bad." On the other hand, another woman may vacuum every day as a "meaningful" ritual because once she has done that she has mentally cleared the way for something creative. Most of us do these little things and as long as we are aware of them and use them, as opposed to being taken over by an obsession, they can be productive and valuable.

The point of ritual is that it does, or should, change our consciousness, and this change is for a purpose. Magickal ritual changes our consciousness to a state where we are more in tune with the Otherworld. It also sends messages to our unconscious mind that certain things are taking place. Because the mind is also part of the material world, these changes do take place. Also, of course, rituals are simply magickal. There is something that we cannot define and it is wonderful. You will see!

The power

One of the things you will do in magick is raise power. This power can be sent out into the world as a healing force or you can direct it into a specific spell. What exactly is this power? It is the life force, called by various names, such as the Chinese *chi*. It is also called *prana*, *orgone* and many other names. It is the "force" that Luke Skywalker and Obi-Wan Kenobi use in *Star Wars*. This energy is within and around all of us and also within the Earth and Cosmos.

You can "raise power" by chanting, dancing or performing almost any rhythmic activity, or you can raise it internally by willing it. Clapping, humming and repeating can all do the same thing. Witches in a coven raise power by dancing in a circle holding hands. The power rises in a cone and can be sent off to do its work, or released by visualizing it as a fountain to bless the land. You can raise it in the same way dancing alone, if you wish. When you are working alone you may feel the power rise to a certain pitch and know it is ready for release. The spell you do may not have a specific point where you "raise power," but raising power is built into the process of the spell. For instance, you may do a simple healing spell by lighting a green candle for a friend and you may say over and over again, "Xxxxx, be healed." The internal repetition is a way of raising power.

This power exists in the subtle realms, or ether, and clairvoyants can see it in the same way as the aura can be seen. This power is usually seen as blue, violet or golden light. However, you do not have to be able to see it with your physical eyes in order to sense and direct it. As you progress as a witch you will do this instinctively. If you find it difficult, then go very slowly with your rituals, only doing small, simple things at first. Use the "as if" approach. Behave "as if" you could perceive and direct the power and this will become real after a while. Here you are using your imagination. Before anybody says, "Huh! Only imagination," it is important to remember that everything beautiful and enjoyable, in fact all of the man-made things you see around you existed in someone's imagination before they became real. What we imagine has a reality on the subtle planes and magick is a way of "fixing" that imagination so that its effects are long-lasting, and even physical. Let's recap.

* The power is the life force within you and the Earth.

* What you do and what you intend calls it up.

* Your will and your imagination direct it.

* It may be seen as a force-field or sensed, as an "atmosphere."

* This power is quite natural.

* Start slowly and carefully to enable yourself to get a sense of it.

Magick takes shape

Here is the pathway of magic, as defined by Jane Brideson, a witch friend of mine.

* It starts with your everyday self—the talking, thinking, awake, part of you that makes up its mind and gets going.

* The end product needs to be in harmony with your true self and purpose in life.

* Ritual and "power raising" get the message through to your subconscious. We could also call the subconscious your "Younger Self" because it is simple, instinctual and playful, although it is, in fact, a very ancient part of the mind.

* Because your "Younger Self" is so free and full of raw and exuberant life, the image and intent are magnified and channeled to the Higher Self.

* Higher Self is the part of us that contacts the Goddess and is part of the Cosmic web.

* Higher Self uses the power to make happen what we want, or alter it, from a position of simply knowing better.

* Change then happens in ordinary life, through ordinary ways.

(Acknowledgements are also due to the author Starhawk for expressing the concepts above in her work.)

Practical exercises

Exercise 1

Symbols

Make sure you learn your symbols well enough to describe their meaning simply to your friends. Make sure you can easily form your pentagram. Practice drawing it on paper a few times, then draw it in the air.

Exercise 2

Getting your tools

It is a good idea to start collecting some tools so you begin to feel you are moving magickally in the world, seeing the importance of certain things for your rituals and generally getting yourself prepared. This will be working on a mental as well as a practical level. You don't need to have all the following right away. In fact, some of them might not be particularly appealing, but it is best to have something to represent each of the elements.

Candles

Look out for reasonably priced candles and get yourself a stock of white ones. Almost any other color will come in handy at some point, too. Red, blue, yellow, green, pink, purple, orange, black, sky blue, rose, silver and gold all have their place in magick. Steer clear of multicolored ones since these may have mixed messages. Don't forget matches and some decent candlesticks.

Athame

You can work without an athame, for a fingertip will do. However, you will feel good if you can get one. You could carve one yourself out of wood if you have some skill. In flinty areas sometimes you may find a piece of stone of the correct shape. You could use a knife from the kitchen, cleansed and consecrated (which I'll cover later, see page 80), or buy a new one. Athames can be bought in New Age stores, but they may be expensive. Alternatively you may be able to buy an attractive paper knife, or find one in a junk shop. (Tradition states that you should never haggle over the price of anything you are going to use in magick.)

Chalice

You can use a wine glass for a chalice if you like. However, it is much better to have your own chalice rather than borrowing from the kitchen cupboard. A pewter or ceramic chalice won't cost very much. Look out for a chalice that is made out of something solid, such as pewter or stone.

Wand

Again, beautiful wands, sometimes with crystals at the tip, can be bought at considerable price. But you can make your own easily. Look for a friendly tree and ask it if you can cut a twig—make sure you listen in your imagination for the answer and leave an offering at the base of the tree to say "thanks," such as some herbs, seeds or water.

You can also use fallen wood to make your wand. You may like to explore the meanings of the tree to make your choice: ash for healing, willow for psychism, rowan for protection, birch for cleansing and new starts, oak for command, hazel for inspiration, hawthorn for fertility and yew for wisdom. (More details are given in *The Magic and Mystery of Trees: A Beginner's Guide*. (See "Further Reading and Resources," page 242)

Goddess and God figures

Lovely figures can be found in many stores. You may also find statues in Christian shops that you can use. It is really up to you to decide what works for you, but my advice is certainly to avoid crucifixes because their image of suffering is not in harmony with witchcraft.

Besom

A besom can probably be bought at low cost in a garden center—then your only problem is where to store it! Even if you have a large room, a besom in the corner may take some explaining! However, as your besom isn't used for the major part of rituals, but only for ritual cleansing by sweeping, maybe it could stay in the garden shed until you need it. Of course you can manage without this, too, for you can sweep your circle using motions of your arms and visualizing all negativity as greyness being swept out.

Pentacle

These are found in New Age stores. Wooden ones may be very reasonable. Or you can make your own from a flat piece of wood or stone.

Stones

Do take the time to collect a few of these. When you hold them you will find that some have strong feelings attached and that they truly connect you to Mother Earth. Go for a walk somewhere peaceful that you like and see what you can find. You may find something interesting waiting just for you.

Robe

Look for some material to make a robe or scour the thrift stores. Wash anything you buy, not merely to cleanse it physically but also spiritually.

Bell

These can often be found in junk shops. Try ringing your bell before you buy it to make sure you like the tone.

Cauldron

Again, look in junk stores. It is quite hard to find a real cauldron these days but you will find variations on the theme, such as old cast-iron pots. Great-granny's attic is another good place to look. But cauldrons are quite large things to keep in a small room so you could make do with a casserole dish or large bowl.

Censer, incense, oil-burner, joss-sticks

Please choose the container in which to burn your incense with care. If you are to be fully prepared to do a ritual, this needs to be sorted out. Incense is an important part of ritual because scent gets straight through to the most primitive parts of the brain.

You can use joss-sticks as a simple substitute; this is much better than using incense without proper thought or preparation. However, it is more difficult to choose an appropriate scent because they tend to have fancy names. Specific smells have specific purposes and they do not have to be "nice" and fragrant. But for now, something you find pleasant will certainly be best. Smudge sticks can also be bought; these are bunches of herbs (sage and sweet-grass) such as those used by the Native Americans. These really need to be held very carefully as they can easily drop little burning pieces.

An oil-burner is a good thing to have in your room because these are usually safe and solid. They will create a powerful scent and you can choose the right one for your ritual. However, they do not create smoke like incense, which has such a magical quality. An oil-burner is excellent for creating a generally good atmosphere in your room when preparing for a ritual or when thinking, writing or reading about magick.

A censer or suitable container can be bought for burning your incense. Use it with care, on a heat-proof surface. You will also need a packet of round charcoal bricks, some tongs and possibly a taper. Make sure you use proper incense charcoal, bought from a New Age or church shop, and not barbecue charcoal. Hold the charcoal in the tongs as if it were a wheel, keeping it well away from carpets and other soft furnishings in case it spits. Apply a flame from a match or taper to the bottom of the "wheel" and small sparks will start up. (Remember to keep your charcoal dry, or this stage could take several tries and make you frustrated!) Although you will not see the charcoal catch fire it will now slowly burn. Lay it down in the censer and sprinkle incense into the little dip in the middle. The vapor will start to rise. Aaaah!—the enchantment begins!

Incense can be bought in many New Age stores, shops attached to churches and abbeys, or you can make your own. The incense you buy could be quite expensive. You can blend your own with herbs from the supermarket, but these won't smell very nice unless you invest in some resins, which are more expensive, but less so than the blended incense. Frankincense smells gorgeous and deserves a place in your cupboard; copal is also lovely. Myrrh is useful to have, for although more gloomy, it has a place in rituals. Lists of meanings are given in Chapter 9, and different incense "recipes" are given in the following pages. Rosemary can be a poor witch's substitute for frankincense, although it doesn't smell as good. Sage, thyme, mace, cumin, coriander, mint, cinnamon, basil and bay are some of the cooking herbs and spices that you can use in incense. You should be able to get dried rose petals and lavender in craft stores. Essential oils, such as those you put in your oil burner, can also be used as part of the incense, sprinkled onto the dried ingredients in the mixture. Lavender is a favorite and ylang-ylang another— these are relatively cheap. You may get these in many outlets but always be sure they are proper essential oils, distilled from plants, not chemical substitutes. Natural therapy centers and health food stores are good places to try.

A simple incense to get you started, use rosemary, sage and thyme, blended and sprinkled on your charcoal. For a nicer effect use frankincense instead of the rosemary. Another suggestion is frankincense, cinnamon and grated lemon peel.

Take the time to experiment with your incense. Enjoy!

Exercise 3

Revision test!

Without looking at the book, write down what these mean and how you might use them: a) athame; b) candles; c) pentacle; d) chalice; e) cauldron; f) besom; g) wand. Now look

them up—how did you do? Well done if you were correct. And if you wrote a small paragraph, then you're a star (or even a pentagram!). Take the time to revise the meanings, maybe one each day. There's no rush; it'll all sink in in time. When you feel reasonably familiar with the tools and have collected the ones you want, you can proceed to the next chapter.

Exercise 4

Visualization

As you lie in bed at night preparing to sleep, visualize a pentagram at your door and another at your window to protect you. Visualize one at the foot, the head and each side of the bed, also. This is good practice for you and will be of real protective value.

Chapter 5

The Magick Circle

In the last chapter there was quite a lot of theory for you to absorb, so this short but important chapter is mostly practical. Spend lots of time on it. Here you will learn how to cast a circle—the basic skill of the witch. So what is the circle? Your magick circle has several functions.

* It is your working space for your rituals.

* It is a sacred space because it is dedicated to the Goddess and the God and your worship of them.

* It is a kind of halfway house between this world and the Otherworld.

* It is a place of containment. The force you raise will be kept inside until you decide to send it forth. Then the circle acts like a valve—it lets stuff out but not in. Many witches consider this to be the most important thing about the circle.

* It is a safe place. The force you put into the circle means it will keep out any stray entities, which often gather when magickal work takes place.

Entities

In the spirit realms there are many "energy centers." Some do not always have much of what we might call "consciousness"—they may be energies that have been generated by a person who is nervous or upset. Others are "elementals": these have some awareness but are essentially primitive and can occasionally be troublesome. Such entities are involved in poltergeist activity. There may also be spirits of varying descriptions such as faeries or spirit guides. These should not be a problem for a witch, who is, after all, not holding a seance! However, it is sensible to be aware of their possible presence. Part of the importance of proper ritual conducted within a properly cast circle is that it offers protection from such spirits.

To work, to work!

You have worked hard to get to this point: doing your visualizations, learning the meanings of symbols, and collecting your tools. Now is the time to start doing some real magick. Of course, this is work and can be quite draining at first. So choose an evening when you feel reasonably energetic and don't have to get up too early the next day. Make sure no one is going to disturb you when you are doing your ritual because they will disrupt the atmosphere you have created. So make sure your mom won't come in to collect your dirty clothes while you are in the middle of your working. It is best to explain what you are doing if you can. Even if people don't fully understand, they can at least give you privacy.

The ritual we are now going to do is to "consecrate," or dedicate, your working tools. The day before the ritual, the items that can be placed in saltwater should be. If you don't have an athame, don't worry. You can just dedicate your chalice/wine glass and stone. Of course, you do not always have to dedicate things like candles and incense before you use them, but if they can be it's never a bad idea. But regular working tools such as the athame and chalice should be properly dedicated. Only dedicate things you really intend to use magickally. You may also like to dedicate a crystal or necklace to wear for magick. Read through the chapter carefully before you start. However thorough I have been, nothing can take the place of your own experience, so take things slowly and follow your inner promptings.

Don't expect too much from your first ritual. There will be a lot for you to remember, which might worry you, or you might be thinking more about practicalities than anything magickal. You may also feel silly or self-conscious. That's natural at first. Ask yourself if you really want to go on with this and if the answer is "yes" then proceed.

Your first ritual

Magickal working is a bit like following a recipe with ingredients and a method! Before the circle is cast you need to make sure you have all your "ingredients" in hand. These might include a robe, altar (or put your things on a cloth on the floor), Book of Shadows, candles, candle-holders, matches, chalice, bowl of water, salt, athame, incense, censer/container, charcoal (or joss-sticks), stone, pentacle, Goddess and God figures, broom, cauldron, wand, white-handled knife/penknife, your favorite fruit juice, a nice cake or something similar—and this book! Of these, it is essential to have some sort of chalice, candles, joss-sticks and stone, water and salt. If you do not have a pentacle, draw a pentagram on a sheet of paper and place it on your altar. Fruit juice is also essential to celebrate. And for the moment, you will need this book to refer to unless you have memorized everything you need to say and do!

What you do

Before you start your ritual take a bath or shower. Use lavender oil or lavender shower essence if you can. Remember to go to the bathroom! Put on your robe if you have one. Slowly and peacefully get all your things together. Meditate for a few minutes, clearing your mind, thinking about the Goddess and offering all you do to Her. Ensure your privacy—lock your door if you wish. Light your candles and incense/joss-sticks. Put your altar or working space roughly in the North.

Begin by standing facing North and raise your arms. Say (aloud or in your mind): "Great Mother, be with me. Horned God, give me your protection. Bless me and guide me in all I do." You can add more words of your own if you like. For instance, you may have read about Goddesses and Gods that appeal to you and you might like to speak directly to them. (It is best to choose a God and Goddess from the same tradition, such as both Celtic or both Greek. You can find a list of them in Chapter 10.) Visualize light streaming in upon you.

You cast the circle by pointing your finger or athame and moving around deosil (clockwise) so that you draw a complete circle around yourself. Visualize blue light streaming from your finger or athame, creating a protective circle around you. In a way, the circle is also a sphere because it is three-dimensional. It can also be "cast" around the edge of the room, which may be more convenient. But it is good to use the circle idea because it is a perfect shape. If you have been regularly visualizing your protective bubble then the circle is just another step up, and you'll find it easy. Remember, you don't have to "see" the circle; just tell yourself it is there. Complete your circle and bow, saying, "So may it be."

Once you have made your circle try not to go outside of it. If you really have to go out, open a "doorway" with your finger or athame and close it behind you when you come back.

Now cleanse your circle, using the besom or your hands—or flap a duster if you like! Just see, in your mind's eye, anything negative or undesirable leaving your sacred space. Say, "I cleanse you," several times. Take up your salt and form a pentagram over it using your athame or finger. Do the same with your water. Now sprinkle a little of the salt into the water. Hold the saltwater up over the altar and say, "I dedicate this to the Great Mother of us all." Moving deosil, sprinkle the saltwater around the circle, saying, "Be blessed by salt from the earth and the waters of life."

Put the bowl down on the altar and take a few deep breaths. Now is the time to summon the four elements. Make yourself feel peaceful, if you can. When you feel ready, face North and form your pentagram, saying, "Great powers of Earth, powers of salt and soil, stone and bone, cave and root, valley and mountain, be with me, I pray you." Visualize the powers of elemental Earth in any way you wish. Bow and say, "Welcome to my circle, O powers of Earth."

Turn to the East, form your pentagram and say, "Great powers of Air, powers of wind and sky, gentle breeze, mighty gale, power that bends the trees and brings clarity and freshness of mind and body to our lives, be with me I pray you." Visualize the powers of elemental Air as you wish. Bow and say, "Welcome to my circle, O powers of Air."

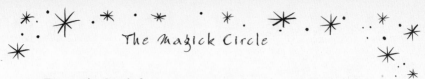

Turn to the South, form your pentagram and say, "Great powers of Fire, powers of heat and flame, giving your warmth and energy, consuming, transforming, inspiring, be with me I pray you." Visualize the powers of elemental Fire in whatever way seems right for you. Bow and say, "Welcome to my circle, O powers of Fire."

Now turn to the West, form your pentagram and say, "Great powers of Water, deep ocean, peaceful lake, tumbling stream, cleansing, healing, giving life, be with me I pray you." Visualize elemental Water in whatever way appeals to you. Bow and say, "Welcome to my circle, O powers of Water."

Now turn back to your altar. This may be a good point to light another joss-stick or add more incense. Sit in your circle for a minute, watch the smoke, and feel the atmosphere you have generated.

If you like, you can dance around your circle to raise some power (although power will be present already from your invocations). Or you could clap rhythmically or hum a suitable tune.

Now you are going to dedicate the working tools that you have. It doesn't matter how many or how few—you can always do this again to dedicate anything you acquire.

Take each article one at a time. Dab your fingers in the saltwater and rub them over the article. Be sensible here. If you are dedicating candles avoid dampening the wick, and if dedicating your chalice just do it around the outside or your juice will taste of salt! Most important of all, imagine the article being cleansed. Imagine holding it under a waterfall, a special magickal waterfall with sparkling energies that go right through into the article and deep-cleanse it. This is especially important if you are cleansing old objects from a junk shop or an attic. Say, "Be cleansed, in the name of the Great Mother."

Face North and hold the article up high over your altar. Say, "I dedicate this to the Great Mother and the Horned God. Please give it your blessing so it can be an instrument of your power and of my power as a witch."

Now go around to each of the quarters and ask for the blessings of the elements. When you get to the element that connects with the particular object, then say something special. For North say, "Great powers of the North, powers of Earth, fill this (stone/pentacle) with your force that it may be a source of strength, grounding and protection." For East say, "Great powers of the East, powers of Air, fill this (athame, censer) with your force that it may be a source of clarity, concentration and skill." For South say, "Great powers of the South, powers of Fire, fill this (wand, candle) with your force that it may be a source of inspiration, courage and energy." For West say, "Great powers of the West, powers of Water, fill this (chalice, cauldron) with your force that it may be a source of love, healing and compassion."

Place each article back on the altar. Now that your chalice is dedicated you can pour some fruit juice into it. Form a pentagram over the juice (possibly with your newly dedicated athame!) and drink it in celebration. Save some to sprinkle on the earth outside when you have finished.

Sit in your circle and reflect a while if you like. You may feel you want to "chat" with the Goddess, and if so, that's great.

Dismantling your circle

It is important that you do this properly. In effect, what you are doing is closing the openings you have made to the Otherworld and re-absorbing your own etheric energy. Please attend to this because if you don't, you could leave yourself vulnerable in some way and feel tired. When you aren't used to it witchcraft can sometimes be surprisingly tiring. Do things properly—start properly and keep it up and you'll be an efficient witch.

First you are saying goodbye to the elements or Watchtowers. Some witches call this "banishing." Start with the North and form your pentagram, but this time visualize the energy streaming back into your finger or athame, not out of it. Imagine the portals to the Otherworld shrinking and disappearing. Say, "Powers of Earth, thank you for being present at my rite. Hail to you, and farewell." Do likewise at the East, South and West.

Now stand facing your altar and thank the Great Mother and the Horned God for their presence. Imagine your circle fading and everything returning to normal. Put your palms to the ground, pat yourself all over and have some more fruit juice and your cake. Tidy all your stuff away, being especially careful to put out the candles.

Write down everything in your Book of Shadows that you have experienced or felt, even if it wasn't very much, together with anything you felt inspired about or would like to remember for next time.

Finally, go outside and pour the rest of your fruit juice and any cake crumbs onto the earth, thanking the Goddess as you do so.

And so now you have cast a circle and completed your first ritual. It's a good idea to practice this a few times before progressing to seasonal celebrations. Don't worry if the earth didn't move or if you feel nothing much happened. These things will grow in time. You have made a start! Well done!

Chapter 6

Darkness into Light: the Celtic Winter

One of the most important things you need to do as you become a witch is very simple. It doesn't happen in a darkened room, by candlelight. It needs no incense, symbols or rituals; it's watching the passage of the seasons. Sounds boring? Not at all. You can see the yearly story as a romance because it is a reflection of the Goddess and the God. You can see it as a mirror of your own life, where things come and go and then return. Feeling a part of Nature makes everything easier and more interesting because there is magic in the November mist, voices in the winter wind and a blessing in the sunshine. Witches worship Nature because She is beautiful. And witchcraft makes Nature exciting.

Long ago people respected the power of the seasons because there was little protection from the cold. People died in the depths of winter or, in some parts of the world, the height of summer. Although we know this still happens, primarily in the Third World, we're now insulated from extremes in our centrally heated houses. But Nature still rolls on and we are dependent on her—we just manage to ignore the fact. Apart from the damage this attitude is doing to the world by destroying our environment, it also damages

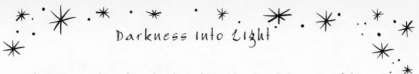

us because we have less depth and imagination. Being part of the seasonal round will give you soul.

Ancient people had many legends about the seasons and the yearly passage. Everything was believed to be the work of the Gods. Of course, this isn't scientific, as we well know. But science has made the world sterile. Witches know that there are things in life you can't measure. There is more to the seasons than the third rock from the Sun turning on its axis. It's all part of the great Cosmic pattern, and we humans fit into it in the same way as the Earth, Sun and stars—we're all part of the picture, part of the wholeness.

In Greek myth, the twelve labors of Heracles tells about the Sun's passage through the year during which Heracles met challenges in each of the months, or signs of the zodiac. Heracles was a Sun hero. For instance, the story about his struggle with the Nemean lion relates to the sign Leo. (Like all good stories this one lives on. Remember the Disney animated film *Hercules*, the Roman name for Heracles? Gilgamesh, in Babylonian myth, is a similar hero. There were twelve parts to his story as well. The cycle of the year and the Sun has been celebrated in tales throughout time.) Great men were compared with the Sun; in its fight with the demons of darkness, the Sun always wins. The Roman Emperors identified themselves with the Sun, and these comparisons have continued even into recent centuries—for instance, Louis XIV of France was called *le roi Soleil,* or "Sun King."

However, many ancient peoples, including Native Americans and the Celts, saw the Sun as a great Goddess. As the bearer of light and life, the Sun was seen as Mother. Most modern witches see the Sun as representative of the God, with the Earth as Goddess. All of these stories and ways of looking at the seasons have one thing in common—they bring the Universe to life. They are not true in the way that it is true you have two eyes, two legs and one mouth. But they hold a truth all the same, one that is important to witches.

Our story

Different witches tell the yearly story in different ways. Some aren't interested in any story and just enjoy the seasons as they are. For those of us who love the Goddess and God, here is a tale.

At the Midwinter Solstice, or Yule (three days before Christmas in the Northern Hemisphere), when the Sun stops retreating and begins to return, the young God is born. The Goddess is His mother, tender and caring, while the God is a small, vulnerable child. From the moonlight upon the sea a young Goddess is born, a bright Maiden. She grows in secret, sheltered by a seashore cave. Meanwhile the God grows in the Greenwood, nurtured by the wild creatures with whom he belongs.

At Imbolc, six weeks after Yule, the Mother Goddess slips away and the God gains in strength, but in the background. Yule was His time, but the festival of Imbolc celebrates the purity and energy of the young Maiden Goddess, who is still free, playful, making her choices and growing to maturity. As we shall see, this is a special time for teenage girls.

The next festival falls during the Spring Equinox, when day and night are equal over the entire globe but light is gaining in the Northern hemisphere. The young God and Goddess are not fully adult, but they delight in the blossoming of the flowers and the tender buds, as they do in their own independence. They celebrate springtime and we celebrate with them.

Beltane, which arrives at the end of April, is the next festival. At this time the God and Goddess fall deeply in love. This is a celebration of sexuality, as the God and Goddess make love. Of all the festivals, this is the time when witches consciously honor sex as something sacred.

Next comes Midsummer, when everything is in bloom and days stretch into nights as the light lingers. In a way the Goddess has given birth to all the brilliance of flowers and greenery. Nature is at its height, but again something is changing. Just as light seems supreme, it begins to die and the Sun starts to slip away. In the same way the young God changes. The responsibility of His partnership has altered Him and His youthful energy is to some extent waning, making way for something more mellow and serious.

At the end of July, at Lammas, also called Lughnasadh, the God knows He must die. Like a hero, He sacrifices his life for the Goddess so that the circle of life may go on. Death is a necessary part of life and He bravely shows that He can meet His, leading by example.

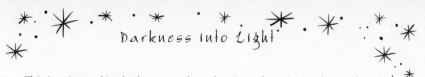
This is mirrored in the harvest when the ripe wheat is cut down. The God goes on His quest, which is an Underworld journey to confront the forces of darkness. But just as the harvest is "reborn" in loaves, preserves and all the food we eat, so the God mysteriously continues as King of the Underworld.

At the Autumn Equinox, when day and night are again equal over the earth but dark is gaining, we have another chance to celebrate harvest. Like Lammas this is a time that is melancholic as well as happy. The generous Goddess reigns alone, sad and soft—it is a poignant time.

Six weeks later comes Samhain/Halloween, when spirits stalk the land and the God beckons the Goddess from His Underworld throne. But She must remain awhile to give birth anew to the Sun God at Yule—and so the cycle begins again.

This story can be told in many ways and some books tell it in greater depth, and with twists of meaning. If you like, you can make up stories of your own to fit in with the way you see the seasons. Your story may be completely different. Also, there are many different Goddesses and Gods, as we will see in Chapter 10, who seem to fit in better at different times of the year. For instance, Maiden Goddesses like Diana seem best at Imbolc, while more motherly ones like Demeter feature at Midsummer or perhaps at Yule. Crone Goddesses and Goddesses of darkness, like Hecate, go with Halloween. It is the same with Gods. You can choose your favorites and honor them in their own seasons.

The eight festivals

No one is quite sure where the idea of eight festivals (or sabbats, as witches often call them) came from. Some traditions have only five festivals, and there are other variations. But most witches work with eight, and these are believed to be mainly Celtic. The Celts turned things around—for them day began at nightfall and the year began at the start of winter. They liked the darkness—they saw it as fertile. This is the order of the festivals, with their dates.

* *Samhain* (pronounced sa-win or sa-ween)—October 31. This is also called Halloween. It was the Celtic New Year.

* *Yule*—December 22. This is the Midwinter Solstice, also celebrated as Christmas.

* *Imbolc* (pronounced im-mo-lug)– February 2. Also called Candlemas.

* *Spring Equinox*—March 21.

* *Beltane* (pronounced bel-tayne)—April 30.

* *Midsummer*—June 22.

* *Lughnasadh* (pronounced loo-na-sa)—July 31. Also called Lammas

* *Autumn Equinox*—September 21.

Throughout the cycle there are different aspects of fertility, birth/death/rebirth, sexuality and creativity. In olden times the "sacred marriage" of the young God with the Goddess of the land was played out by the King making love with the High Priestess. It was believed that the King got his power from the land, and this celebration was a way of honoring the fact. It also honored femininity. As time went by this belief was forgotten. The King thought he could do what he liked with the land and men regarded women as their possessions rather than honoring them as representatives of the Goddess. Today things are changing and girls are stronger and more powerful again. Modern witchcraft is part of this change.

The festivals of Samhain, Imbolc, Beltane and Lughnasadh are believed to be the oldest and most powerful. They are connected to a time when herding was more important than cultivating. Although we give dates, in reality they would have been celebrated when it "felt right." The Equinoxes and Solstices are tied to the actual position of the Sun, and tying these festivals to their current dates may have developed at a later time. The Equinoxes were more important to farming communities. Naturally, in different parts of the world the height of spring comes at different times, and the celebrations of the Spring Equinox and Beltane may have themes in common for some witches.

An important point concerns witches in the Southern Hemisphere. There the seasons are the other way around. Some

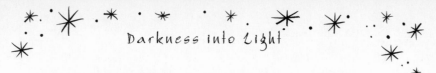

Australian witches still follow the European dates, celebrating Yule on December 22, even though it is Midsummer Down Under. However, it is probably much better to move the dates so that your celebrations fit in with the seasons in your part of the world.

Working through the festivals

In this chapter and the next, we'll be looking at rituals and magic for each of the festivals and at the old folk traditions that go along with them. This chapter focuses on the first half of the Celtic year, when the hours of darkness exceed the hours of light. Chapter 7 looks at the other half of the year, when day is longer than night.

You'll find it fun, as a witch, to know the old, true meanings for some of the traditional seasonal customs and to realize that the people doing them are actually behaving like witches without knowing it. This chapter and the next will also suggest fun things to do on your own or with your friends. These aren't magical things as such, but the idea behind them is to get into the spirit of the season. Also, if you don't have witchy friends, many of these things you can do with "ordinary" friends. The seasonal round should be fun, and hopefully make life fuller and interesting.

In addition to the activities given, you can make up lots of your own. Here are some suggestions.

* Keep a journal, diary or scrap book. In it you can record what you do, how you feel, how the season makes you feel. You can paste in clippings or postcards of things that remind you of the season.

* Write a poem or a few lines of prose about your feelings.

* Paint a picture or make a sketch.

* Listen to music—what music seems to go best with the season and how you feel? For instance, do you think techno is more summery or wintry? What about ska, or plain old rock, or classical music?

* What perfumes do you think fit with the season?

* Collect things for each festival, such as dried leaves, feathers, pebbles, pine cones, shells, pressed flowers, to remind you of

your walks. Some of these can be placed in a "medicine pouch" that you can make with a large piece of cloth, a hole-puncher and some cord (or you can buy a fabric drawstring bag). You can consecrate this in a ritual and use it to hold things you have collected for each of the festivals. "Medicine" to Native Americans means "power." This, then, will be your "power bag" for the year, filled with pebbles, feathers and such. You can use the contents of your "power bag" for rituals that are about completing things, making things whole.

✳ You can collect beads for each season, choosing an appropriate color and stringing them on a thread to make bracelets and necklaces.

✳ Choose nail polish and make-up to reflect your seasonal mood.

✳ Set aside a shelf in your room as a small altar and rearrange it for each festival, placing things there that seem appropriate. Candles are the easiest to change—here are the colors suitable to the festivals. (Remember, white candles will always do for a ritual if you can't get colored ones):

> *Samhain:* black or deep wine-red
>
> *Yule:* scarlet, rich green and/or gold
>
> *Imbolc:* white
>
> *Spring Equinox:* daffodil yellow or bright green
>
> *Beltane:* deep rose
>
> *Midsummer:* crimson or honey
>
> *Lughnasadh:* orange or pale gold
>
> *Autumn Equinox:* blue or blackberry purple.

At every festival it is a good idea to go for a walk. Once you are out and about, it can be exciting to find your way through the mist to a special natural place at Samhain. Wrap up well against the biting winter winds and watch the bare branches scratching the sky—then go back home and have a cup of hot chocolate. Nothing makes you appreciate comforts more than a taste of the elements.

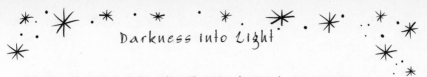

But there's more to it than that. There is a beauty in every season, a special scent, a unique experience. Becoming a witch is becoming part of that—it helps to develop your instincts.

Intuition isn't about candlelight and crystals; it grows from contact with Nature—feeling the earth beneath your feet, touching tree bark, watching the flight of birds. You don't have to think about anything, you just have to be there. Intuition and the psychic senses are only a matter of tuning in to what's around. You are teaching yourself to do this by soaking up the seasons. If you live in the country you have no problem; if you live in the city, visit parks, watch trees and the sky. (Always be safe—don't go anywhere dangerous and don't go alone to remote places. Being a witch is about respecting and caring for yourself as well as being "magickal.")

Start your journey on the merry-go-round as soon as you like, with whichever festival is closest. Here we begin with the Celtic New Year, at Samhain.

Samhain (October 31)

This is the most melancholy and the most eerie time of year, when brown leaves skitter in the wind and dusk creeps in earlier and earlier. It's getting colder, darker. It's good to get home by the fire and listen to the wind whimpering outside. But what might it be like with no warm house for shelter, no television, with fears of dwindling stores and harsh weather to haunt your mind? And other fears, too—of the evil things that creep closer in the lengthening shadows....

Goddess and God

We meet our hero and heroine at the saddest point in their yearly drama. The Goddess is alone. We picture Her now as a Crone, swathed in black, very wise, knowing lots of secrets, longing for what is gone, yet knowing that what must be must be. Yet She is magickal—we know that She transforms. At Yule She will be the shining Mother as She gives birth to the young God and the start of a new cycle.

The God is now deep within the Underworld. He is gone—and life and joy have gone with Him. But He is very powerful now because He has faced all His fears. He sits on His throne in his dark realm and calls for the Goddess to join Him. But She knows that She must stay because She is always needed. Even though light has gone, Nature continues, and while She continues there is always hope—hope of rebirth. It is good to respect the dark things, because dark things are in everybody. Our society prefers to see things differently, as if some things have to be forbidden, even from thought. But witches know you have to face the dark things, especially those inside you. This doesn't mean you do any awful thing you want—quite the opposite. But it means you never assume things can be all sweetness and light. The dividing line between good and evil isn't always clear, and there is no light without shadow.

In times of yore

This was the Celtic New Year. It is hard to imagine how anyone could think about something beginning just as everything seems to be ending. But if you think about it, there is a kind of sense in it. As soon as we see things are going, we're past the beginning. As we get close to the very depth of the year, at Yule, there is a kind of light at the end of the tunnel. At Samhain there is no light. We are in a sort of "cradle of darkness" and the only way is up! "Samhain" means "Summer's End." There is a type of good cheer in telling ourselves that something new is starting now.

In ancient times this was actually a very scary season. The truth was that no one could be sure of making it through the winter because stores might run out. People could die of starvation, wells could be frozen over and ravenous wild beasts would be hunting. The sick and the old might well not see another spring. Tough decisions had to be made, too. For instance, if there wasn't going to be enough fodder, certain livestock had to be slaughtered. People's lives might depend on a good decision being reached about this. It has to be said that human sacrifice also took place because some people thought the Gods needed to be pleased in order for there to be a mild winter.

The ancestors were honored at Samhain, and this was the start of the story-telling season. Bards would weave many a tale, their words entwining with the curling smoke as everyone sat close

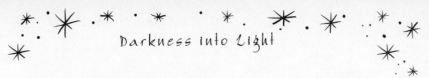

about the fire, drinking and listening to all that the Gods and the heroes had done when the world was young. People's lives were short, but there was a feeling that the thread went on. That thread also went back to the ancestors of the tribe, who were honored because they were the roots from which everyone came. This gave a sense of belonging. (We have lost this sense today with families scattered all over the place, divorce being commonplace and people thinking that freedom is the most important thing. Of course it is important, but knowing where you have come from and what you are part of is also important.) The ancestors were Gods, too, in a sense, and their stories were told and retold. In the days before people could write, their memory was much better. Incredibly long epics were memorized and passed by word of mouth from bard to bard down through the generations. In gatherings there was usually a "talking stick" that was passed around. When anyone held the talking stick, they could speak and everyone else was expected to listen.

The Christian church took over the old festivals, substituting dates in the church calendar. Samhain became All Hallow's Eve, followed by All Saints Day and then All Souls Day. In this way the tradition of honoring the dead was carried on. For us today this is still an eerie, ghostly time.

The custom of hollowing out a pumpkin and putting a lighted candle inside means several things (as most customs do!). It's saying, "Life goes on, deep inside the earth, and in vegetables that are full of seeds, like this pumpkin." The candle inside is like the light of life. But at the same time, the leering face reminds everyone that this is a scary time of year. Some say it's the face of the Crone, the Goddess in Her darker aspect. The pumpkin face is also there to frighten away evil spirits. Take your pick!

Like all the major festivals, Samhain is a Fire festival. Fire was, and is, very cheering in the darkness. But there is also a more sinister side to it. Some human sacrifice was by burning, and this has been passed down in Britain as Guy Fawkes Night, November 5. Originally the human sacrifice at this time was often the old king, who gave way to someone who was younger and stronger—rather like the God going down into the Underworld. With poor old Guy Fawkes we commemorate the death of someone who wanted to kill a king instead of the death of the king. It's an interesting twist. Fireworks are also part of the Samhain picture. There is a destructive side to Samhain, and there is also the reminder that life goes on.

Trick or treat is a "tricky" season. People used to play jokes on neighbors, leaving barn doors open, making animal noises in the night and generally acting crazy and unpredictable. This is part of honoring the darker side of life. We all have problems living with other people and have such feelings as hatred and jealousy that we don't indulge. Customs like this are a kind of safety-valve. They can also be good fun.

In the last century two of the most awful wars the world has ever seen took place. The fact that death was possible on such a large scale made something happen to people's awareness. Also, the media was able to broadcast what was happening, especially during World War II. Humans have always been warlike and destructive, but since the two world wars, we have become more aware of what we are capable of. Global destruction is now a possibility. It is very fitting that Veterans Day occurs at the beginning of November to commemorate all those who died in wars. Here we are reminding ourselves not only of the dead (our ancestors) but also asking ourselves about the meaning of violence and death. It's worth thinking about. In twenty years' time those of you who are teenagers now will be running the country. What sort of world do you want? And what sort of people do you think will create that world? Who do you want in power? The future is in your hands.

Things to do

Dressing up

Everybody knows this is a time for ghosties and ghoulies. People have Halloween parties without having a clue that this is the main festival for real, live witches! It's part of the tradition to wear a mask and dress up at this time of year. Some ideas for mask-making are given in the section on Yule on page 111. Samhain is an "Underworld" time, which means we look at our own private Underworld. So what are your "masks," the acts that you put on to get you through life? At school, do you like to "play it cool" so no one will know they can get at you? When you go to parties or out with friends, do you put on a different, flirty "you" to enjoy the evening? What about the face you put on when you want money out of mom or dad? These masks are all pretty obvious, but there are other parts you may play, even to yourself. You might hate selfishness. Perhaps lots of your friends seem selfish, but you think you aren't. Could it be that you're pretending to yourself? Sounds horrible? Well, it might feel horrible but actually we all do it, and Samhain is a time to try to be honest with ourselves *because it makes us stronger*. Knowledge is power. And knowing about yourself can be the greatest power of all because it makes it easier to make choices. It's a good thought for Samhain.

So the masks and the dressing up can be just for fun. But there are meanings behind the traditions. You could consciously dress up like something you don't want to be but think you might be on the sly. "Okay, so I am a jealous bitch, but no one's going to know this but me. But I'll paint my face green and put in some fangs to celebrate how honest I am with myself." You can dress up like a vampire, or turn yourself into a Buffy look-alike. You could be really, really sexy, because Samhain is about death, and sex is the other side of the coin. This is different from the Beltane sexy, which is more about warmth and laughter, whereas Samhain is slinky—long red or green nails, lots of mascara, black clothes. Another idea is to dress up as your favorite Goddess or God, but be careful here. Many of the old Gods had a very dramatic time of it in the stories told about them and funny things can happen if you take this too seriously. As a sensible witch, you will know that this is just a bit of fun, and to put the character away when you take off the gear.

Apple bobbing

If you're having a Halloween party, it's traditional to put apples in a big bowl of water and try to get them out using only your mouth. This custom arose because apples were traditionally fruits of the Underworld and belong to the people of Faerie. Apples were also believed to be the food of the dead. If you cut an apple in half cross-wise, you'll see a five-pointed star, which is special to the Goddess and to witches.

The Ancient Greeks also told a story about a golden apple that was given to the Goddess Aphrodite by a mortal man, Paris, who had the job of judging which Goddess was the most beautiful. Paris chose Aphrodite because she was the most seductive and because she promised him the most beautiful woman in the world as his wife. The only problem was that this woman was already married to someone else! Aphrodite helped Paris steal her away, starting the Trojan wars to get her back.

So, as you can see, the apple is connected to Halloween in many ways. Getting all wet is also part of it, but make sure your mascara is waterproof!

Out and about

Go out and watch the brown leaves chasing each other like demons in the wind, or wander around a graveyard, an ancient earthworks or a barrow-mound in the autumn mist. Then you can really feel the strangeness of the season and how it connects you to times gone by and to other worlds. You could go to a place that you have heard is haunted—local guidebooks often give details. Old places such as castles and old homes are a likely bet. Take a friend with you and return home and "ground" yourselves with hot tea and cookies so you don't get too spaced out. You may want to experience the Otherworld, but your place is in this one. Witches are practical people who know that life is for living. And if you see anyone who is wearing a pentagram, wish them "Happy New Year" and see what they say!

Ghost stories

You could have a quiet night in with your friends telling ghost stories, talking about relatives who have died and, perhaps,

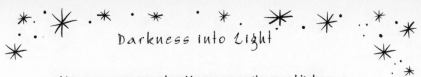

making up a story together. Have an egg-timer or kitchen timer handy, giving each person a set time to speak. When that time is over someone else should take up the narrative. If you're all in the mood for a giggle it can be hilarious. You could round off the evening with a scary movie or, perhaps, an episode or two of "Buffy."

Be careful if you are talking about people that have passed over. While it might be a bit sad to talk about your great-granny who died when you were four, it can really open wounds if someone has lost a close family member recently. No one should be pushed to talk, or even pushed to take part if they are reluctant. If anyone does get upset, it's up to the others to be supportive and helpful. In this way, as witches, we revive some of the old customs that brought people close. And please don't ever break a trust. Friendships may come and go, but the trust should still be there to be relied upon.

Trick-or-treat

Trick-or-treat is a favorite with younger people. It's good fun, but be sensible. Don't go alone, don't go into iffy neighbor-hoods, and don't go into the houses of strangers. Preferably trick-or-treat people you already know. And needless to say, never frighten old folks or little ones. A true witch likes to have a laugh but is mature enough to know who needs protecting.

Becoming psychic

Samhain is a time for turning inward and is traditionally linked to the psychic arts. Try this questionnaire to see if you are psychic.

Are you psychic?

1) When someone starts to speak, do you sometimes know exactly what they're about to say? Yes/No

2) Have you ever just *known* what's going to happen—and then it does? Yes/No

3) Have you ever seen anything inanimate move of its own accord, or willed it to move? Yes/No

4) Did you ever have a dream that came true in some way? Yes/No

5) Are your first impressions of people usually right? Yes/No

6) Have you ever felt sure a place was haunted because of what you felt, saw or heard, and later found out that it had a reputation for being ghostly? Yes/No

7) Have you ever felt that a dead relative or friend was trying to communicate with you? Yes/No

8) Do you have a strong sense that if you will something hard enough you can make it happen? Yes/No

Your score

0 Yes answers: chances are you are blocking your psychic gifts through self-doubt or skepticism.
1–3 Yes answers: your skills are developing.
4–6 Yes answers: you are definitely psychic.
7–8 Yes answers: Obi-Wan taught you well!

A traditional Samhain activity is to try to sharpen the psychic senses. But you must bear in mind that this is a scary time of year. Even if you usually laugh at danger, things can get under your skin at this time of year. Remember that anything you "see" or sense can have several different interpretations. For instance, the Death card in a tarot pack rarely means the actual death of a person. It's usually about changes. As the teenage years are full of these, the chances of this card being drawn are quite high!

Earlier chapters suggested ideas for protecting yourself. Use these if you feel the need at any time. Most importantly, please don't ever do the "talking glass," or ouija board. It is too open, and invites all manner of entities over that you may have no control over. Teenagers often have lots of natural energy that can be attractive to such stray spirits. It is not going to be an impressive start to your life as a witch to have some poltergeist hanging around you can't control. Also, it is a very bad advertisement for witchcraft to buy into

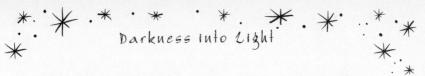

all the old stories about devil-worship and such. At the very least, it'll cause you grief. Don't do it.

Here are some things you can do to help you develop your psychism.

Tarot

Samhain is the traditional time of year to do a tarot spread (setting out the cards). There are many books available about tarot, and even if you aren't an expert with the cards you can still look up the meanings. The process will still work, though maybe not as well. A simple approach is to ask a question, then spread the pack out face down. Run your fingers lightly over the tops of the cards, using your left hand if you are right-handed and vice versa, then pick three cards. Often you will get a "feeling" for the cards you should pick, or your fingers may get hot and tingly when they pass over an appropriate card. Spread the three cards out—often they will describe the dilemma and give you extra clues about it. Then pick a fourth as an "answer." Don't take things literally and don't make dire predictions. The cards are there to help you make choices, not to scare the living daylights out of you!

Alternatively, there are plenty of other packs of cards available in New Age stores and bookstores. With these packs you can pick a card to give you a clue as to where you're at and ways you can develop. Think positively.

Scrying

This is a method of "seeing pictures." Traditionally it involves crystal gazing but you don't have to use a crystal ball. You can look for images in a bowl of water or any reflective surface. To scry you need to feel "dreamy" in the way you feel when you're about to drop off to sleep, but without feeling tired. It's best to do this in a darkened room by candlelight or moonlight. If you use a bowl of water, you might want to place a coin in it. Whatever you do, the aim is to look deeply into the "speculum" (the thing you are using to scry) as if looking into another world. Some people experience scrying as if literally seeing with their eyes, while others see with "the mind's eye." Whatever you see (or smell, hear, taste, feel) should be noted, even if it seems meaningless. If you see something scary like a skull, please do not terrify yourself or others. These things are always symbolic—a skull can represent your ancestors or signify deep changes for you. If you discover you have a real talent for scrying, it is up to you whether you choose to develop it or not. You can help yourself to shut down by regularly visualizing a protective egg around yourself and affirming that it is shutting out all unwanted influences. And if you find you aren't any good at scrying don't despair. If you feel bad about it you'll be shutting yourself off even more. You do not need the sight to be a powerful witch because there are many other ways of developing awareness and effectiveness on the subtle planes.

Telepathy

A pleasant exercise to do is to pair up with a friend and try to transmit something very simple telepathically. A color is possibly best. Sit facing each other with your eyes closed. You can hold hands if you like. Being a bit giggly can be good because a playful attitude helps more than being overly serious, but always remember "mirth with reverence." Both of you should be as relaxed as possible. One person gets ready to "receive" by having an open mind, perhaps by visualizing a blank TV screen. The other intensely imagines a color, while the "receiver" tries to pick up on what it is. See how many times you can get it right. Remember, if you're getting tired or fed up, your psychic abilities will probably fade considerably.

You could also use a set of cards with simple symbols on them—such as a square, circle, star, moon and triangle—and "send" one of them. Keep a record of your results and see if you can improve as the autumn progresses.

If you can't be with your friends at Samhain you could try some telephone telepathy. Both of the above exercises can be tried over the phone, or you could have pre-arranged times to send and receive. You could communicate impressions of the place you're in, how you're feeling—all sorts of things. You don't know until you try!

On your own

If you do some of the facing-up-to-yourself things that I mentioned in the dressing-up section, you'll be doing this on your own. If there are things about yourself that you would like to change, a simple

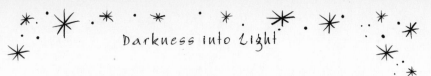

"spell" is to write them on a piece of paper, tear it up and flush it down the toilet. Make sure the paper is soluble, or all your rejects will stay, floating and looking up at you! Also, do be sure that the things you want to get rid of aren't going to cripple you as a person. It's fine to want to be without loneliness, poverty, worry, and so on, but do you really want to be without envy, for instance? You want to be without the pain of envy, and you don't want to be controlled by envy, but isn't it natural to feel a little envy? Doesn't it spur you on to improve, to achieve? There's no need to try to be an angel, just a well-balanced, sensible and effectual person.

Where appropriate geographically, the warm weather is now gone so you can get ready for winter by sorting through your summer stuff and putting it away. You are coming into a time of year when energy is likely to be less plentiful, so think about your priorities. Are there things you don't want to be bothering with? At school this is often a busy time as the new academic year really gets under way, so perhaps those nights out with the girls or the guys are best turned to nights in, studying together. Sit down quietly and think about how you want to reorganize your life for the winter. Make some notes to remind yourself.

Of course, this time of year isn't all serious. Even if there aren't any parties for Halloween, there probably will be over Christmas, which is only six or seven weeks away. So stock up on the party make-up while there's plenty to choose from in the stores. Get yourself some glitter, hair mascara or shiny body-powder to cheer up the miserable days—or treat yourself to a bright scarf and gloves.

You can practice your psychic skills on your own, perhaps by placing six tarot cards face down and seeing if you can guess which one your hand is hovering over. Or choose just one card for a personal message to yourself. Scrying can be practiced alone, too. Black candles in your room and a black cloth over your personal altar will set the scene. Cypress and patchouli are good oils to use in your oil-burner at this time.

Because Samhain is about remembering, you may like to start a photograph album or arrange photographs that you already have. Perhaps you have a special photo of one of your ancestors that you'd like to frame.

Do you like mysteries and puzzles? Now is a good time for delving and puzzling things out. If you like, find yourself some books and magazines with puzzles in them, or read stories about mysteries and ghostly happenings. Better still, write your own. If you like history, now is a good time to delve into it. Start with your own home town. Most bookstores have a local section and you may discover something that really interests you.

Memorabilia chest

Samhain is about remembering. You may be interested in finding a special chest or box to keep special things in. New Age stores sometimes have lovely boxes painted with moons and stars, but if you're short of cash you could use a shoebox. Cover it with crepe paper and decorate it yourself.

Because the herb rosemary is for remembrance, sprinkle some dried rosemary in the box before you place special photos and keepsakes and anything you find that's magical (special stones and shells) in it. You could also use your chest to store your ritual tools.

Recipe:

red hot fruit punch

Ingredients

3 oranges; 3 lemons; 4 oz sugar; 10 fl oz water; 2¼ pints of red grape juice; 2½ fl oz cranberry juice; some canned cherries.

Method

Cut the lemons and oranges in half, squeeze them and put the empty skins into a large saucepan with the water. Simmer for five minutes (not more), re-squeezing them every so often to get all the juice out. Strain the liquid and put it back into the pan with the sugar and fruit juice and three-fourths of the grape juice. Heat this through thoroughly but don't let it boil. Put it into a warm bowl with the rest of the grape juice and the cranberry juice. Float cherries on top. Serve warm.

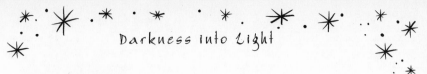

Samhain ritual

If you are feeling depressed think carefully about doing this ritual because it may be a bit heavy—change any bits if you are doubtful.

For this you will need some black candles, a piece of white bone (a chicken bone will do, or, if your family is vegetarian, substitute a piece of dried wood) wrapped in a black cloth, three dried leaves, a small white candle, some nuts and seasonal fruits for the altar, and a small hollowed out pumpkin with a candle inside. Apples cut crosswise are also a good idea. If you wish, you could place on your altar a photograph of a loved relative who has died. Make sure you have a delicious treat to consecrate at the end of this rather somber ritual, in order to cheer you up. Use an incense of cypress, allspice, patchouli and myrrh. Cast your circle as described on page 82.

Sit in your circle with two black candles lit on the altar, thinking quietly about the dark of the year, how you feel about it. Confide your feelings to the Goddess and ask for Her comfort if you feel you need it. When you are ready, light a black candle that you have placed in your cauldron. This should be in the West of your circle in honor of the Horned God who has made His Underworld descent. You may dance or sway to raise power, chanting:

Great Lord, in Mystery
Protect me and show to me
The wonders of land and sea
All of history, all of history, all of history.

Name each of the dried leaves for something that has to go from life. For example, you could say, "Summer must die in the land; let unkindness in humans also die, and let my shyness go, too." As you name each of these things, place a dried leaf in the cauldron.

Turn toward your altar and say, "Great Mother, it is dark, it is dark. What remains of life?" Now unwrap the bone, place it on your pentacle and say, "The bones remain, the bones stay."

Light the small white candle. Say, "Bone and stone so cold may be, but bright flowers in the spring we'll see." Repeat "Bright flowers, bright flowers" a few times.

You may feel like talking to your relative who has died. Send love and blessings. Now consecrate your treat and enjoy it. Think how much better you'll feel when, along with the old year, the thing that you want to lose from your life has gone.

After you've closed down your circle, dispose of the leaves outside. Also leave out some of your treat for the Faerie folk. Eat the apples and nuts.

Yule

We all know about Yule as Christmas, but we may not be aware of the pagan and witchy themes that underlie the celebrations. Many people complain that Christmas is too commercialized, and no doubt they are right. However, while the spirit of Christmas is certainly about giving to others, it is also about delicious indulgence in life's good things. There is a reason for this. Yule is the darkest time of the year and it is a good instinct to make it as merry as possible to keep our spirits up. Actually Christmas takes place about three days after the exact Solstice point, when daylight is shortest. At Christmas the fact that the days are now starting to get longer becomes astronomically obvious.

Goddess and God

Everyone knows the story of Baby Jesus and how He was born in a manger. Although this is a Christian tale, it is similar to many older stories in which a young God, who represents the Sun, is born again. It is the Great Mother Herself who gives birth to Him.

The God is a tiny baby at the start of life, and at the start of the year. However, He is also there, in a sense, as His adult self. (It is very convenient that Gods can be two people like this! But it is a way for us to understand the cycles of life and how they fit in with our human experiences.) St. Joseph, who was husband to the Virgin Mary, plays the role of the God in that he is a protective presence in the background.

The Goddess is very much Mother during Yuletide and we honor this. We can see the Goddess and God very much in a family setting, with peace and joy all around. No wonder Christmas is thought of as a "family time." However, the whole human race is one

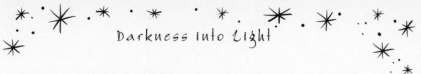

family and at this time of year the Goddess gives us a special blessing, as light and life return.

In times of yore

Yule was a time of festivity, but the purpose of this festival wasn't just to have a good time. People believed that they had to make everything bright and wonderful to tempt the Sun to come back. That sounds silly to us now—we know that the seasons are caused by the turning of the Earth and summer will return whatever we do or don't do. But there is more to celebrating than meets the eye. Many centuries ago people felt deeply connected to the earth and the seasons. They felt they needed to take part otherwise something would be lost. They were right. Nowadays we are so logical we *have* lost a connection with the earth and this is indeed doing damage to our habitat. We know this from deforestation, the holes in the ozone layer, pollution and all the other alarming things you have heard about in the news.

The Druids used to decorate pine-groves with bright objects at Yule. Pines and other fir trees are linked to birth. Evergreens keep their greenery all year round and are a promise of the new shoots that will come in the spring. Evergreens are especially sacred to the Goddess, for She stays with us in Her many different forms all year. There was also a tradition of decorating a "Moon tree" with lights and offerings to the sky Goddess. All these old customs lie behind the present-day Christmas tree. The Christmas tree has many meanings—about life continuing, brightness and delight coming to us—it's no wonder we love it.

The dear old fairy at the top of the tree is an image of the Goddess. She is also a reminder of the Otherworld. We know that trees can be an opening to the Otherworld, and as for decorations, the colors also have special meanings. Red and green are the traditional colors of life, of blood and vegetation; gold is the color of the Sun; silver and purple are the sky on a winter's night, with the full Moon gleaming. Of course, this all looks pretty, but the reason why it is so very magickal is because of the deeper meanings.

Do you secretly feel a bit sorry that you don't believe in Santa Claus anymore? Well, he's still with us because he's like the jolly horned God of Nature, except his reindeer have the antlers instead of him! The horns advertise joy in life and animal energy. Sadly, the Devil is shown with horns. That was probably thought up to put people off their horned God when Christianity became popular because it has often happened in history that the gods of the old religion become the devils of the new. Of course, there isn't anything evil about the horned God. It is interesting that Santa Claus is also called "Saint Nicholas" and the Devil is called "Old Nick."

Father Christmas is also a masculine form of the German Goddess Holda, who came down chimneys with presents. Lots of our modern Christmas customs come from such diverse roots as these.

The Yule log was a very important custom because it meant that new life could be rekindled from the old. A piece of the special log was kept to start the fire again next year. The custom of the Yule log may also have come from the Druids, who lit great bonfires at the Winter Solstice to entice the Sun to come back. Some people say the log should be ash, some oak, some birch. These days it is usually chocolate!

Holly and mistletoe have inner meanings, too. The holly was sacred to the God, especially during the times of growing darkness, from Midsummer through to Midwinter. As for mistletoe, the Druids liked it best when it grew on the oak tree, because the oak is a majestic tree. (One meaning of "Druid" is "wise man of oak.") The mistletoe was cut with a golden sickle, thus combining Sun and Moon importance. Because the mistletoe grew on another tree, not on the earth itself, it was taken to represent life at its very beginnings, when the soul enters the body. It also represents fertility and sprigs were given for good luck. And that is why we still kiss underneath the mistletoe.

Ivy is another important Christmas plant, used as a decoration and sung about in carols. Ivy was considered a feminine plant, the "mate" of holly. It is also sacred to Dionysus, the Greek God of wine!

Wassailing is an old custom that is still with us in the form of Christmas caroling. It originated in apple-growing parts of Britain. The apple trees were woken up with loud singing, music and dancing, while cider was poured on the roots as an offering and the trunks were hit with staves.

Things to do

Gifts

We all know Christmas is about gifts. This comes from the tradition of buying gifts for a baby. When we give presents to each other we are, in a sense, giving them to the God, or Baby Jesus, because we realize that there is something divine in everyone! Of course, we all like to get things given to us as well, and that is also what Yule is about—enjoyment—lots of it—in honor of the Goddess. So when you choose your presents for friends and family, remember you are honoring the God and the Goddess, too, which does actually have a bearing on your development as a witch. Being a witch is also about realizing the importance of the links we have with other people—and that love is what life is all about.

Decorations

Buy some decorations that seem to you to have special witchy meanings and hang them on your tree with wisdom and pride. For instance, it is easy to get five-pointed gold stars. Gold suns are a reminder that Yule is a solar feast, celebrating the Sun's return. Moons are special to the Goddess—as we shall see in Chapter 8. Many other figures have magical associations. Bows and knots are linked to the spiral, horses were animals believed to take people on journeys to the Otherworld, and pine cones are sacred (as is any seed) because they show that life carries on. Bells, as you also know, play a part in some rituals. Try to find a pagan, magickal or Goddess link to any decoration that takes your fancy.

Cribs

You can have a small crib in your room and place Baby Jesus in His bed on Christmas night. In this way you are linking the old pagan ways with newer Christian ones. This is actually a little ritual to bring light and life back to the world and to also bring new and promising things into your life. If you can, pin a golden Sun over your crib on Christmas Eve to show you understand the old meanings and the original Nature-worship.

Gift-gathering

Get together with your best friends to swap presents, but add a special something to the event. Each of you should have a piece of paper—choose a pretty color like pink or pale green. Put your name at the top of the paper. Then the paper is passed around and everyone writes on it some nice things about the person whose paper it is, saying why they think they are a good friend, what they admire about them and anything else nice, happy, encouraging and complimentary. Keep your paper with you to look at from time to time to keep you cheerful through the winter.

Out and about

Many ancient monuments were built to honor the return of the Sun, such as Newgrange in Ireland. Also certain barrow-mounds are constructed so the rays of the Sun at the Winter Solstice (but at no other time) can penetrate deep inside, into the darkness, making it light. If there is any such place near you, or a standing stone or mound, go and visit it at Yule, remembering that the earth, in her secret places, knows that the Sun is on his journey back. If it snows, get out and make a snowman or snowballs. Childish? Not really. It is important to get out and experience the season so that you're part of what is happening around you. Of course there's nothing magickal about a snowball down your back, but being in touch with Nature really does make you more alive.

If you live in a city, take a look at what is happening in your local park. Does everything seem dead? Look closely at some of the trees and shrubs and you'll see buds forming, ready to

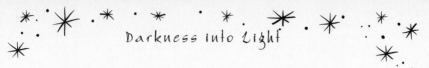

open out into new leaves and flowers in the spring. You could also study the sky and make a note of the different colors and appearances of clouds. After a while you might find that you can begin to predict weather patterns.

Making bracelets

This is simple and fun. You can do it with your friends or on your own to make inexpensive gifts. You will need some elastic thread, beads of your own choice, and some clear nail polish.

* First take an elastic thread and cut it to a length that fits comfortably around your wrist.

* Next tie a knot at one end of the thread, leaving some thread free.

* Dab some nail polish at the other end of the thread to stop it from fraying.

* Now choose the beads you want to make your bracelet. For example, you might choose a bead for each of the festivals, using the colors suggested for candles on page 92 and repeating this until the thread is full. Or you could use the colors of the rainbow.

* When you have finished, tie the ends of the thread together and dab on just a little more nail polish to secure it.

* Grin with pride at your cool new bracelet!

Mask-making

All you will need is some clay that hardens without firing. This is easy to get in craft stores or even large stationers and toy stores. Because you are going to apply it to your skin, check for allergies 24 hours in advance by pressing a small piece on your inner arm. If a rash develops, do not do this activity.

Flatten out a large section, like a thick pancake, and mold it to your face. Cut holes for the eyes, nose and mouth in whatever

shape most suits your purpose. Either leave holes to thread
ribbon through or insert a thin stick into the soft clay so that
you can hold the mask in place just as they used to do during
old-fashioned masked balls. You can make a mask that just
covers your eyes if you wish. Before the clay sets you can
make designs in it. To resemble the Green Man, draw leaves
and acorns; stick on feathers or fur to be a wild shaman; or use
glittery stones, flowers—whatever takes your fancy.

Recipe:

Yule log

Ingredients

About 25 cookies; 1 small pot whipping cream; 1
teaspoon cocoa powder; I teaspoon powdered sugar, and
some left over for decoration; 1 lb milk or plain chocolate.

Method

Whip the cream until it stands in peaks and then add the
cocoa powder and powdered sugar. Sandwich the cookies
together with the cream to make a roll and wrap this in foil.
Place it in the refrigerator for an hour to chill thoroughly.
Break the chocolate into pieces in a bowl and melt them in
the microwave. Do this in stages, testing every few seconds so
the chocolate doesn't get too runny. Pour the melted
chocolate over the chilled roll—it should start to set as it
makes contact. Now you can decorate it with powdered sugar
("snow") and any other Christmas decorations you like. Keep it
in the refrigerator, if possible, until you are ready to eat it.

Giving and taking

Yule is all about giving and receiving gifts, but we can have lots of
different approaches to this. What is yours? Take this questionnaire
to find out.

1) A friend gives you an unexpected gift, and you haven't
bought one for her. How do you react? a) really
embarrassed—why didn't you think…? b) awkward but

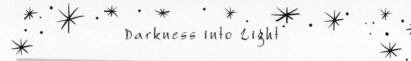

pleased—you'll go out and get something in return; c) delighted—how generous and thoughtful!

2) Christmas shopping is: a) really great, you save up for it for ages and get really nice presents; b) fun, but you worry about how much you're spending; c) something that has to be done—but you like it best when your own stocking is full.

3) You receive a gift that you really hate. What do you do? a) smile and say a big "thank you"—it's the thought that counts; b) try to hide your disappointment; c) say, "Oh, what a shame—it's not to my taste. Could we please change it?"

4) You are making your Christmas list—how much are you enjoying it? a) you never make a list—you are grateful for what you get; b) you don't like to ask for too much—but you put it all down anyway; c) great—half the pleasure is in the anticipation.

5) A friend has just won the lottery and tells you she will buy you anything you want for Christmas: a) you say, "Just give what you can afford to charity"; b) you try to find out what she is really prepared to spend; c) you gleefully present her with a list, starting with a new sports car, an entire new wardrobe and ending with an operation for Granny's hip.

6) The best thing about Christmas is: a) seeing the looks of pleasure on other people's faces; b) everything, really—the presents, the lights and parties and all that Christmas excitement; c) getting lots of lovely presents.

7) Your family and friends are all hard up and it's going to be a lean old Yule: a) you don't mind—you'll be working down at a shelter for the homeless anyway; b) you try to enjoy it but everything seems flat; c) you're sure something will turn up to make it a wonderful time.

8) What is your attitude to the modern Christmas? a) too commercialized—really it should be about what you can do for others; b) a bit over-the-top because we all eat, drink and spend too much; c) what the heck—you have a ball!

9) What do you think of the traditional Christmas story? a) there's a moral in it—it means there is a spiritual side to life; b) you feel a bit skeptical about it all; c) it's a lovely story as a background to the celebration.

10) It is often said "Christmas is a time for children." Do you think this is true? a) undoubtedly, they are what counts; b) perhaps you should think that, but you like it, too! c) yes, and you're still a kid, and always will be.

Your score

Mostly a's. You really enjoy giving more than receiving. This is great if you are genuinely identifying with the pleasure of others because it shows you are in tune with wider things in life. However, if you simply feel guilty about wanting things for yourself, ask yourself why. You, too, are a child of the Goddess and you should never be afraid to ask for things for yourself. You, too, are worth it, and you can give all the better to others if you have received things yourself.

Mostly b's. You aren't quite sure, are you? You just love getting things, but you feel a bit guilty, a bit worried that you're being selfish. You love giving things, too, but you are afraid to give too much and leave yourself short. Don't concern yourself—the Goddess will provide; when you are part of the flow you benefit from the flow. Give in order to make room in your life for the goodies to come that are rightfully yours—take what is given to you with joy.

Mostly c's. You're just a great big kid and a tad greedy, but we forgive you! You have a flagrant joy of life that is a celebration in itself and your exuberance rubs off on other people. Your gratitude and pleasure is enough reward, but remember, also, you have a great deal to give in other ways. Have you really thought what joy you can get from seeing a look of pleasure on the face of someone you love? When Yule comes why not buy a special present for a child in an orphanage or institution abroad? Spread your sunshine—we all need it!

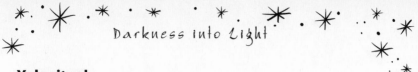

Yule ritual

For this rite you will need three candles—one green, one red and one gold. You can light more if you wish (if you have the room to do so in safety). Put holly, ivy and mistletoe on your altar and around your cauldron. Have some mince pie, or something similar, and some tasty fruit punch (or whatever you like) to celebrate. You will also need a large bay leaf, a pen, a pot with ash or soft compost in it and a small gold Sun, such as what you might hang on the Christmas tree. Incense could be made from frankincense, orange peel and cinnamon.

Put your golden Sun deep into the pot of dry compost or ashes before you start and place it on or before your altar. Light your green and red candles, placing them on your altar. Place the gold one, unlit, in the cauldron. Cast your circle, then kneel before your altar and say, "Great Mother, the Sun has gone and all is dark. The emptiness of eternal night surrounds us. Give birth, Great Mother, to the Divine Child, that all may live again."

Reach into your pot and draw forth the golden Sun. Hold it up over your altar and say, "The Son is born again, the sun is risen. By the grace of the Mother, Light and Life are born again. Blessed be."

Place the Sun on top of your pentacle. Light the candle in your cauldron and say, "Welcome young Sun, bright Sun, growing Sun. Lie warm upon the land. Joy and blessing to all."

Burn some more incense and celebrate with consecrated drink and mince pies. Think of all the good things to come—parties, gifts, the New Year, new plans, growing light as the spring comes. Feel as joyful as you can. Dance and sing if you wish.

When you are ready, sit quietly before your altar and think of a wish. Write this on the bay leaf. Kiss the leaf three times and ask the Mother for her special blessing. Hold the leaf in the flame of the gold candle with your incense tongs and let it burn away.

Celebrate again with the goodies and close your circle when you are ready. Hang the gold Sun on your Christmas tree as a blessing to your home and the land.

Imbolc

For a young witch, Imbolc (usually pronounced im-mo-lug) can be the most exciting of festivals. It is the time when priestesses and priests were often initiated. Everywhere you look, you can sense the first stirrings of spring. It's a time of new beginnings, creativity and purity—it's a time when everything feels young.

Goddess and God

Imbolc is a feast of the Maiden Goddess. At the moment we can picture Her as a teenager. She is really enjoying Her growing sexual maturity and Her independence. She feels excited at all the possibilities that lie before Her, but a little tremulous—like you might feel on a first date. This is reflected in the earth, when the tender shoots are finding their way carefully into the air. Can you identify with this?

The young God grows as the vegetation grows, slowly and secretly, within the ground and the woodland. We can picture Him at rather a wild stage. He's not very concerned with relationships (although He thinks about sex!)—He's more into experiencing life and the capabilities of His own body. In a modern setting He'd be racing around on bikes or in cars, playing around and generally being a guy.

Boys are rarely as rooted in the physical world as are girls. This is partly because girls have their periods to remind them of their bodies and the need to be aware of time and cycles. We might curse our periods (more about this in the chapter on the Moon!) but actually they are part of a truly feminine rhythm that connects us to the earth. During Imbolc the young Goddess might be imagined as having the first of Her periods.

So, in their different ways, our Goddess and God can be seen as feeling their young adulthood and their independence. Each of them is also aware of the beginnings of their creative capabilities, finding out what their bodies and their minds can accomplish.

In times of yore

In the olden days, this was a very important time. The fearsome part of winter was (hopefully) behind them while the first signs that the earth was coming back to life were looked for. It was still a difficult time, being very cold. For people who had been sickly during the dark days of winter, the coming of spring was often a matter of life and death.

Imbolc means "in the belly." In the belly of the land unseen things are happening. From this comes the special connection with

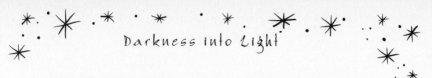
the earliest stages of creativity, which is inspiration. A week before Imbolc comes Burns' *Night in Scotland*, when the work of that famous poet is celebrated. Imbolc is the feast of poets in general.

Imbolc is also called *Oimelc*, which means "ewe's milk." You will see that sheep feature a lot at Imbolc! This is the time the ewe's milk first flows after they have given birth to tiny lambs. Also if you have real free-range hens this may be the time when they start laying their eggs again. It's all happening—but you can miss it if you don't look.

We still celebrate St. Valentine's Day on February 14, two weeks after Imbolc. The original Valentine was a condemned man who wrote a message to his true love on the walls of his cell. This romantic tradition is now celebrated by sending Valentine cards to our partners. However, the fun aspect of Valentine's Day is when cards come from someone unknown. So there may be a romance in the air, but you aren't sure. That's the spirit of the Imbolc season. Birds are choosing their partners to build nests together at this time

Before *in vitro* fertilization and genetic engineering, the ancients celebrated fertility because it was important. On February 15, the Romans celebrated Lupercalia. This was quite a wild time when the priests of the crazy God Pan ran through the streets striking women who wished to conceive with a goatskin whip. The name comes from the Latin *lupus*, which means "wolf."

Perhaps the most notable custom is that of the Bride doll. This doll is a fertility symbol. She could be dressed as a peasant or a queen; her meaning was still the same. She could also be the Corn Dolly from last year. At Imbolc she was put in bed with a piece of wood shaped like a penis, and a candle was left burning beside her all night. Later the doll was placed in the earth. Customs like this are practiced and updated in places where there is an active pagan community such as Glastonbury in Somerset, Britain. Here the Bride—or Bridie—doll is kept and placed with the dolls of former years in a special ceremony. This helps awareness of the Goddess to grow.

The Bride doll is named after the Celtic Goddess Bride (usually pronounced "breed"); her sacred animals were the snake, wolf (remember Lupercalia?), cow and birds of prey. She represents the creative power at all levels. She was also called Brigid or Brigantia, and she became St. Bridget to the Christians, who made her into a Christian saint. She is linked with the sacred flame that was kept burning in temples in honor of the Gods and the process of life.

As with most of the festivals, the Christian Church substituted one of its own—Candlemas, where the Virgin Mary was "purified" after giving birth to Christ. The idea that a woman has to be cleansed after performing such a creative act is not very appealing to the witch mentality! However, the connection with lightness and with cleansing is certainly part of the season. Rituals may be a feast of candles to encourage the growing light.

Things to do

Creativity

In what way are you most creative? Think about this. Now, you may not think that you're artsy, but creativity means many things. Really it is anything you do well. If you are a math whiz, then that is your creative talent. Besides, all knowledge and abilities generate results and move things forward.

If you are good at art, writing, sculpture, sewing, cooking, hairdressing, make-up, gardening, music, drama or any of the obviously creative activities then now is the time to plan to do something as well as you can. Write a poem, paint a picture, make up a story or bake a cake. As you do any or several of these activities, think about how what you are doing connects with the season and the start of things growing.

If you are good at something that isn't usually considered creative, such as sports, socializing or a subject such as history or science, then why not plan a special project connected to what you enjoy? For instance, if you like history then you could investigate some of the history attached to the place you live (and you might find out that there were witches there!). If you like sports, what about a new challenge? If you are Miss Popularity Plus, then get something going with parties. You could even take someone shy under your wing to see if you can bring them out—if that is what they want.

If what you do isn't obviously creative, why not have a clean white folder in which you keep notes of your creative ventures. It can make life more fun—you never know what doors it could open for you. It certainly beats vegetating at home while the nights are still dark!

White and bright

Bring the lightness of Imbolc into your room with some fragrant white hyacinths or snowdrops in a pot. Sort through your old stuff, your papers from school and the piles in your bedroom and chuck everything you don't need. If you received some presents at Christmas that you don't want, pass them on to a charity. You can do all this now in preparation for some spring cleaning at the Equinox. Sound boring? It might seem tedious at first, but as you develop as a witch you will see that many things are a kind of ritual. If you sort out your room, you are sorting out yourself, which leaves room for more interesting things to happen in your life.

Imbolc is particularly linked to candles. Of course, each of the festivals is an occasion to light candles, but during this particular one, candles play a special role. A single, large white candle is best for Imbolc. Put it in a secure place in your room and light it after you have done your sorting. Look at the dancing flame celebrating what you have achieved.

Resolutions

We make resolutions at New Year and most of them are broken within a day. Who's going to keep to a diet when all that holiday food is still around or get going on a new exercise regime when it's cold and you feel bloated? Now, however, the holidays are in the past and the move has been made toward getting in the swing of life again. This is a great time to give yourself a make-over. Try some new cosmetics for a brighter look to your skin, a new skin-care regime with proper cleansing and toning, and perhaps a new hairdo for the spring. It's a great time to start exercising, so get all your friends to go to the gym with you or decide that you will get into the habit of walking each day. Even better, half an hour a day spent dancing to your favorite music will really get you revved up for the longer, lighter days. You can do this alone in your room or invite friends to join you—as long as the neighbors and the floorboards can stand it!

Talk-about

Getting together and talking is a very feminine thing to do. Organize a sleep-over with your best friends and have something special to talk about—something you have done, something creative or any kind of female experience. You can talk about your periods or what you think motherhood would be like, whether you want to be a mother or whether it doesn't really matter, what your own mother is like (whisper!). You may also want to talk about abortion—maybe you or a friend has had to go through that. You could have a shiny white scarf to pass around and the one that is wearing it talks while the others listen—that way everyone gets a chance. It's amazing what you can learn from the experiences of others. Imbolc is about treasuring experiences that are particularly womanly.

Guys tend to prefer active or practical things to do together, though there are men's groups available. Seek them out.

Out and about

Imbolc is a good time to visit sacred wells and springs. You can think of these as the secret life of the earth coming to the surface. The cleansing, purifying quality of water is very special right now. In some places wells are "dressed" at this time. Many wells in Ireland are sacred to St. Bridget, the Goddess Bride. In some places in Britain and Ireland people

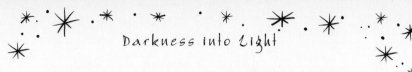

bring pieces of cloth or rags—even bits of their own torn clothing—to hang on trees near sacred wells to bring healing.

If it is frosty, wrap up warm and take a bottle to a well that you know is good and clean. (Make sure the water is safe to drink.) Fill the bottle and take it home with you to drink. Take inside you the sacred, vibrant powers of the awakening earth.

Candle-making

As I mentioned earlier, the festival of Imbolc is especially about candles because the earth is getting brighter, being reborn.

To make your own Imbolc candles you will need molds of your choice—you can use an old margarine tub (that won't melt) or half of an empty eggshell or walnut shell. You will also need an old saucepan, a heat-resistant bowl, some wax of your chosen color (or use old candle stubs), some wick (available from craft stores), an old bobby pin or clothes pin, and a container such as an empty ice cream tub.

First you need to melt your wax by carefully heating it in a bowl over a saucepan of hot water. For scented candles you could add some essential oil such as lavender or ylang-ylang to the melted wax. While the wax is melting, weigh down the mold in a container of cold water so that the water is level with the intended level of the wax. You will also need to suspend the wick in the correct place. You can do this using a bobby pin or a clothes pin balanced on the edges of the mold. If you can weight the other end of the wick with a small metal nut so that it hangs straight, so much the better.

When the wax is melted, pour it slowly and carefully into the mold, leaving some of the wick free. Allow the wax to cool slowly. The wax will shrink slightly as it cools, so add a little more to the mold each hour until it is completely set.

Decorate your Imbolc candle with wax crayons, stick-on stars and anything else you fancy.

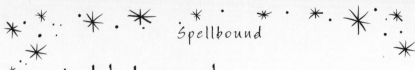

A white banquet

There are many white things you can make for a special Imbolc feast with your friends. The obvious one is to ice a cake with white icing. You could share this to celebrate the newness of the year and the fact that you have everything before you—like a white, clean page you haven't written on.

Spread a green tablecloth and put on it a selection of bowls containing some of the following dishes: hard-boiled eggs, yogurt, bananas, cooked chicken, potato salad, white bread, unsalted butter, cooked leeks, celery, boiled rice, rice pudding, crackers, milk, cheese, pickled onions, apple juice, chopped green-skinned apples, cottage cheese, white marzipan, white chocolate and your iced cake. You can also make a dip with cottage cheese, mayonnaise, pepper and a little garlic and dunk pieces of celery in it. Feta cheese, which is sheep's milk cheese and white in color, is a good food to include. Add any other white foods that appeal to you.

Place a candle in the middle of the table and enjoy your feast. Even if you aren't deliberately thinking about what you are eating, the message will still be getting through to your brain that this is the season of the new and the clean, and that you are part of it. This white banquet would be ideal before your sleep-over.

Do you have a positive attitude?

This time of year is about initiative and new beginnings. You may like to consider how well you use your ability to make new starts and whether you look on life as a series of opportunities or obstacles. This questionnaire will give you a hint as to how you may approach your Imbolc fresh starts.

1) You come across a group of your friends talking about the plans they've made to go out together. After you've been there a minute or two, one of them asks you to come along. You say: a) "No"—after all, they've only asked you as an afterthought; b) "Yes" but feel a bit worried about whether

they really want you or not; c) "Yes" and feel really pleased that you happened to come along at just the right minute.

2) Last week you bought the exact top you needed to wear with some jeans on Saturday. This week someone tells you they've seen the same top reduced in price. You: a) feel really fed up—just your luck—if you'd only waited you could have saved yourself money; b) think, Oh well, at least you got the top; c) couldn't care less—you needed it for Saturday and you feel great in it.

3) Curses, you've just taken your driving test and failed it. You: a) can't stop crying—obviously you're never going to be able to drive; b) feel really low, and you blame the examiner for being unfair; c) are fed up, of course, but you think, At least I know what I did wrong, and you re-apply.

4) Your birthday party coincides with another big event and only ten people turn up. You: a) go off and cry in a corner—what a disaster! b) try to put a brave face on but you feel terrible all night; c) feel really pleased that you have ten such loyal friends and you party on!

5) You spot your latest boy/girlfriend chatting with someone very good-looking of the opposite sex. You: a) think, I knew it, s/he never really liked me anyway!; b) feel really worried that you're going to lose him/her; c) figure that anything done so openly must be innocent—anyway, you're as good as anyone else.

6) You've got a new haircut and your friend says, "You look better with your hair like that." You: a) feel really insulted—so you must have looked awful before? b) find it a doubtful compliment—perhaps by "better" they meant "lovely"; c) feel pleased with the compliment.

7) You go out to dinner with your family but your favorite dish isn't on the menu. How do you react? a) you were really looking forward to smoked salmon and now your evening is ruined; b) you choose something else but the edge is taken off everything; c) it doesn't actually matter—something else will do and it's great to be out.

8) There's a part-time job available that pays well and will look good on your resumé. You: a) try to find ways to get out of it— you don't want to have to get up early; b) feel tired at the thought but know it'll be the best thing; c) feel pleased and excited and are already planning what you'll do with the money.

Your score

Mostly a's. You're so negative it's a wonder you get out of bed in the morning. Haven't you heard that life is what you make it? Perhaps you have had some experiences that have caused you to get depressed and to fear the worst all the time. This doesn't have to continue—you have the power! Use the Imbolc inspiration to get a life.

Mostly b's. Your bottle tends to be half empty rather than half full. You know you should make an effort but sometimes it's difficult. But success breeds success—build on it starting at Imbolc.

Mostly c's. You have positive thinking bursting from every pore! Well done! This is an asset to bring to your spells and seasonal rituals. Make sure you focus your efforts on what really matters to you.

Whatever your score, remember you can only get what you want when you know what that is. Make a list of at least three things you would like to have done or to have set in motion by the time of the Spring Equinox in about six weeks.

Imbolc ritual

For this you will need five white candles, a long white scarf, some lavender oil, white flowers in a pot to place on the altar (together with any seasonal greenery) and a pot of salt. Your incense could contain lavender, lemon peel and frankincense. Have some food items from the white banquet list (see above) for your celebration.

Start your ritual in the usual way, with two of the candles lit on the altar. Consecrate some lavender oil and rub a little into each of the other three candles. Light each one in turn, saying with the first, "I honor the light of the Maiden. May she inspire me"; with the

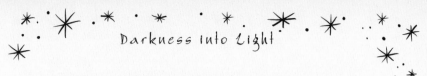

second, "I honor the light of the Mother. May she protect me"; and with the third, "I honor the light of the Crone, may she give me wisdom." If you wish, you can dance to raise power.

Anoint yourself with the lavender oil on your feet, knees, genitals (not too close!), breast, lips and forehead, saying each time, "I pledge myself to the Goddess in truth and freedom." Place now three drops of lavender oil on the white scarf and say, "Goddess bless me and help my creativity." Tie the scarf around your waist, while thinking about the creative things you want to accomplish. Finally, consecrate some salt, then sit and celebrate.

After you have closed your circle, sprinkle the salt around your room, saying, "Be cleansed for spring." Empty the remainder carefully onto the ground outside. Keep the white scarf with you whenever you are studying or doing anything original or creative and sleep with it beneath your pillow for inspiring dreams. If you like the scent of lavender, add a few more drops to your scarf every so often—it encourages peace and sweet dreams.

Spring Equinox

At the Equinoxes light and dark are equal, but in spring, the hours of light are about to increase. Everything is bright and full of promise, and people begin to feel more energetic and hopeful. Everywhere cheerful flowers are breaking through and the earth is coming back to life.

Goddess and God

The Goddess and the God are playful, having fun, exploring possibilities. We can imagine them dating, teasing and laughing. They are enjoying the power of their sexuality and the way it can bring pleasure and love into their lives, but they are not committed. They have no responsibilities. They are carefree and adventurous.

The Equinox is traditionally more a feast of vegetation and the fertility of the land rather than human fertility. The Sacred Marriage of Goddess and God is a Beltane theme generally, although at times this creeps into Spring Equinox themes.

One aspect of the God that seems especially right at this time is the Green Man. The Green Man is a face made up of leaves. You can see this in many churches because the masons who built them were either actual pagans or observed pagan traditions. The Green Man is found in many places in the world—even in India. The idea behind him is that the plant world is alive—alive with the energy of the young God.

The forces of life are "resurrecting" at this time. In the Christian calendar, Easter falls on the first Sunday after the first Full Moon after the Spring Equinox, tying it to pagan nature-observances. Christ died on Good Friday and was resurrected on Easter Sunday. Time and again, at different festivals, the God goes through this painful process! It means we respect the process of change, which means something usually has to give way to enable something new to come about. What is coming now is a time of warmth, hope and promise.

In times of yore

This was a time for the careful sowing of crops and watching with hope that the weather would get warmer. In medieval times New Year's Day was actually March 25. This was because, to people dependent on the land, being able to see the Sun returning meant that the year really was underway. At the Spring Equinox the Sun enters the sign of Aries. This is the first sign of the zodiac and the beginning of the astrological year. The Druids, who also observe eight seasonal festivals, often celebrate the Equinox publicly.

There is a very ancient custom in which the king or queen gives out money to the poor on the Thursday before Easter, which is called Maundy Thursday. The "maund" was originally a type of basket that was filled with goodies. Today the Maundy Money is given out by the queen in red, white and green purses, colors associated with the Faerie Queen or Nature Goddess.

The Easter favorite Hot Cross Buns were eaten long before the Christian festival. The equal-armed cross is not really a Christian symbol at all; a cross within a circle is a symbol for the seasons, the wheel of the year and the magick circle with its four quarters/ Watchtowers. This is also called a Celtic cross and can be seen on many graves. It's a life-affirming symbol and isn't the same as the crucifixion cross. So when you eat your hot cross buns you are being part of a very ancient tradition, just right for a witch!

At Easter there are many lively community events celebrating the resurrection of Christ and the more general Spring holiday, but many of these rites have their roots in pagan worship. One tradition is the wearing of Easter bonnets covered with ribbons and flowers as a way of celebrating and letting it go to your head!

It isn't difficult to work out that Easter eggs are a symbol of fertility. There is a legend that church bells leave Rome during the period of Lent (when, in the Catholic faith, church bells are kept silent) and fly back at Easter, dropping eggs onto the countryside as they go as a symbol of the return of light and life (and we know that the bell relates to the Goddess). Another old tale notes that eggs are brought by the Easter Bunny—biologically impossible but understandable because of the phrase "breeding like rabbits." At Easter it is traditional to have an egg-hunt, which dates back to the worship of the Teutonic Goddess Eostre (who gave her name to Easter), in whose honor the eggs were hidden and found.

So this has long been a time of excitement and new starts.

Things to do

Spring cleaning

At Imbolc you (hopefully!) sorted out some of your stuff, but if not you could do so now. Clear some space so that the energies of spring can come surging into your life. When you have disposed of the junk you could clean your room, perhaps get the curtains washed, the carpet shampooed, and even move the furniture around. This is a signal to your unconscious mind that you are making a new start.

Start something

What have you been thinking about doing all winter yet put off because the weather wasn't very good, you felt too tired or whatever? Kick out all those old excuses and get going. Even if you only start in a small way, at least it's something. The Chinese say, "The journey of a thousand miles starts with the first step." Take it!

Egg-decorating

Hard-boil some eggs with a couple of drops of natural food-coloring added to the water to color the shells. When they are cooled, you can draw on them and give them to your friends. If you aren't artistic, you could just write a message on the shell; but if you're really creative your imagination could run riot! Turn your eggs into faces, animals, birds or anything you like, by adding hats, legs, hands, moustaches or whatever. These will be more welcome gifts than chocolate ones for people who are trying to get trim for summer! Make sure you get free-range eggs to paint. And please don't do what a friend of mine did—fall in love with her egg and keep it on her sunny window-sill for weeks and weeks and then wonder why her bedroom smelled so bad! However pretty the egg is, it needs to be eaten in a day or two—although it will keep longer in the fridge.

Alternatively, you can get rid of the contents of your egg before painting it. Make sure that the egg is at room temperature, then carefully make a hole in the shell at one end of it with a long needle, piercing the yolk. Make another hole at the other end, then blow the contents into a bowl. Wash out the shell and leave it to dry before decorating it.

Planting

Plant seeds in pots in your room or out in the garden. Sow your favorite plants and watch them come up. This is a great example of natural magic as the green shoots push upward to find the light! Sow them when the Moon is waxing (getting bigger). If the weather is clear, you can see the waxing Moon in the early evening. Seeds sprout more quickly when sown by a waxing Moon—you could experiment with this if you like. If your seeds are struggling then bless them by forming a pentagram over them. This is a good opportunity to practice your witch-power.

If you have a group of friends, especially if they are witches, too, then you may want to get together to plant a tree in a suitable place. In doing so you are giving a gift to Nature. Give

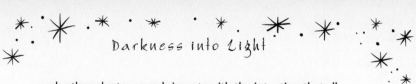
each other plants or seeds in pots with the intention that all
your wishes will come true and your happiness will grow as
the plant grows.

Out and about

With Easter, traditional outdoor events get underway. Many of
these have pagan origins. See if you can spot the Goddess-
links and the cycle-of-the-seasons theme in them. Look out
for primroses in parks and fields—note how they have five
petals and so link to the pentagram. Cowslips also have five
petals shaped into a bell. These wildflowers are exciting proof
that summer is on its way again.

Funky beaded hair clips

Greet the Equinox with bright hair-clips that you have
decorated yourself to make into your own individual celebration—who needs an Easter bonnet? You will need hair-clips,
thin wire (such as fuse wire) and colorful beads of your choice.

First wrap the wire tightly a few times around the loop end of
the hair-clip. Next thread a bead through to the end of the wire
so that it touches the clip. Twist the wire around the clip to
make it secure. Keep doing this with successive beads until
you reach the other end of the clip. You can thread the beads
into the shapes of flowers, stars or even heart shapes just by
twisting the wire. Experiment with the wire and beads to see
what you can form. The clip itself can be brightened up by
painting it with colorful nail polish. Wear it to welcome the Sun!

Wig-wham!

Here is a great way to catch spring fever—if you dare!

Have you ever thought how much your identity is defined by
your hair? Where does the idea "blondes have more fun" come

from? Could it be true that strength lives in your hair, like Samson? What might it be like to have totally different hair, and what could happen to you?

Get some moral support from adventurous friends. Get hold of some wigs and go out on the town with a completely different crowning glory. Some girls have found that going blonde means they get treated totally differently, more wolf-whistles, seats given to them on buses, and so on. Maybe if you have long, black hair people will stare at you but remain at a distance. Do people assume that having red hair means you have a fiery temper? Perhaps having longer hair (even if it isn't really your own!) will make you feel more powerful and sexy.

Or you could just be silly, wear a pink wig and have a giggle. The point is to have fun and the next day go back to being the same old you—if you don't decide that's too boring!

Recipe:

Easter cookies

Ingredients

4 oz butter; 4 oz golden granulated sugar; 8 oz plain organic white flour; 1 teaspoon mixed spice; 4 to 6 oz currants; milk to mix.

Method

Put all the butter, sugar, flour and spices in a food processor. Mix these thoroughly for 30 seconds. Stir and do the same again. Add the currants, mixing in very short bursts (or the processor will mash them). Add milk carefully by hand until you have a dough you can roll out. If you don't have a food processor then cream the butter and sugar together before adding sifted flour and spices and then the milk. Roll the mixture out thinly and cut into rounds with a pastry cutter, or cut around a saucer for large cookies. This should make you about 12 cookies.

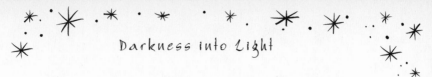

Bake the dough on a lightly greased baking tray, pre-heated to 300°F until golden. Cool on a wire tray. If you like, you can now mark equal-armed crosses on these with icing, chocolate sauce or a whipped cream.

Have you caught spring fever?

If you are in tune with Nature, spring can have a noticeable effect on you. Take this quiz to see if you have spring fever!

1) The lighter nights make you feel like staying up to party. Yes/No

2) Because the Sun's up earlier you find it easier to get out of bed in the morning. Yes/No

3) You can't wait to get into those summer fashions. Yes/No

4) You have plans for all the things you want to do in the brighter weather. Yes/No

5) You feel like clearing out your room. Yes/No

6) You're raring to do sports or anything active. Yes/No

7) Suddenly you're feeling a lot sexier. Yes/No

8) Because it's lighter you find you can't help smiling and laughing more. Yes/No

9) Generally you're in a better mood—you don't get down-in-the-dumps as easily. Yes/No

10) You're enthusiastic about your new skin-care routine to get you glowing for summer. Yes/No

Your score

Mostly Yes: you have spring fever all right, and the more yeses you have the hotter you are. This is great because you're in tune with the season. Make sure that you get on with your plans and make a real difference in your life. You will probably like to try some spells (see Chapter 9) to give you a boost. In all the enthusiasm, don't forget to eat and sleep well so you can hang on to your energy.

Mostly No: you haven't yet made it out of winter, and the more noes you scored, the more you're stuck. Doing your Equinox ritual will help you to get into the spirit of the season. Try burning some orange or sandalwood oil in your burner. If you have been getting lots of colds recently, try taking echinacea tablets. Get out in the fresh air in short bursts that you don't find too daunting. Drink lots of fruit juice and eat as many fresh fruits and vegetables as you can. Remember, try to drink a quart of water a day. Build your energy up slowly so you can take advantage of spring—the gift of the Goddess.

Equinox ritual

For your ritual you will need candles of daffodil yellow or spring green, a round gold or bright yellow dish, some seeds (sunflower seeds are great), paper clips in all the colors of the rainbow and a bell. Have some primroses in a pot for your altar or some daffodils in a vase—or any greenery and early flowers that take your fancy. Orange juice and round cookies, especially cinnamon, would be a good choice for celebration. Incense could contain frankincense, rosemary, dried orange peel and nutmeg.

Start your ritual in the usual way, and then stand before your altar with the candles burning happily. Raise your arms and say, "Welcome to the bright Sun, bringer of joy and life, light and happiness. The sweet Earth holds out her open arms to you."

Pick up your bell and walk deosil around your circle. Ring the bell three times at each of the four quarters, saying, "Earth, awaken, for the great Sun has come." Consecrate some orange juice and drink it in celebration.

Now take up your paper clips one by one and string them together in the order of the colors of the rainbow—red, orange, yellow, green, blue, indigo, violet (dark blue may do for indigo and pink for violet—but don't use black). As you do this, chant, "Power to the Sun returning, Power to the Sun returning…" until you have completed a rainbow circle large enough to place comfortably around one of your candles—you may have to make three or four "rainbows." Link up the last clip with the first. Now place it as a girdle around the candle, letting it rest in a circle on the altar. When you have finished this, say, "Blessed be," and have another drink of juice.

(If you prefer you can wind colored threads together as a rainbow.)

Place the seeds on the golden dish and consecrate them by forming a pentagram over them with your athame or finger. Say, "I bless these seeds in the name of Lady Earth and Lord Sun. And I name three wishes to grow with them." Name your wishes—one for the earth, one for a friend and one for you.

Now you can drink your juice and eat your cookies while thinking of the lovely light days to come, the beautiful flowers, all the fun you'll have, and anything else connected with the coming months. After your ritual pour a little juice onto the earth. Plant your seeds with care and nurture them. Keep the paper clips with your magick bits and pieces, or use them to clip pages in your Book of Shadows or something similar. It's best not to throw anything that you have used magickally out in the trash, and you can't bury paper clips because they won't rot and return to the earth—so use them.

Chapter 7

Light into Darkness: the Celtic Summer

Now we are entering into a different phase of the year, the Celtic summer, when the hours of daylight last longer than the hours of darkness. Like the Celtic winter, this phase of the year has its own special festivals.

Beltane

Beltane is the most glamorous of the festivals. It's delicious, it's vivid and it's very sexy. Beltane is the time to put everything you can into enjoying yourself and into loving yourself. The season tells you it is time for the senses to awaken.

Goddess and God

In terms of our perennial legend of the Goddess and the Horned God, Beltane is the time when they are both in the full bloom of young adulthood, ready to celebrate their union in every way. Despite the fact that girls and women often feel that they give more emotionally in a relationship, it is the man who depletes

himself physically in sex by "giving his seed," as they used to say. Perhaps that's why guys often seem to hold back in other ways. At all events at the time of Beltane there is also one tradition that the young God, in a sense, "dies" in the arms of the Goddess and has to be revived—reborn as the year, the season and the Sun are "reborn." The poor God does a lot of dying in seasonal rituals! This is because the Sun "dies" every day when night falls, and "dies" as well during winter. The point of it all is that He comes back, as all things do. We always honor Nature because we are a part of Her, and by respecting Nature we come to know our own powers.

Lots of stories have undertones of Goddess and God at this time of year. Lady Godiva, who rode naked through the streets of Coventry clad only in her flowing hair, is the Goddess in disguise, flaunting her sex appeal. Maid Marion, lady-love of Robin Hood, is the Goddess, too. She lived in the Greenwood forest with Robin, who represents the Horned God and the Green Man come to life. Robin and his Merry Men were fugitives, and this may have a connection with the fact that the old pagan ways were in a sense "fugitives," too, hiding disguised in surviving customs within the Church calendar.

In times of yore

The Celts had only two seasons, summer and winter, and for them Beltane marked the start of summer. Imagine the delight! Today it doesn't matter too much whether it's cold or hot—we can slip into a slinky silver top and go partying in hot, heated places, with the lights flashing and the rhythms thumping. But not so very long ago winter was a very uncomfortable and unpleasant time, and the long, bright days and the warmth of the Sun were things to get excited about. Back then the drums would pound for the fertility rites and bonfires were lit on the hilltops. Even today something in our blood still stirs at the approach of the summer. In our Beltane rituals and activities, we honor the vibrant season and heighten our awareness of it.

All the festivals have a fertility element within them, but none more so than Beltane. The custom of the May Queen belongs here. In many parts of the world a pretty girl was chosen as Queen of the May, carried around in procession and fêted. Nowadays we may think that isn't really fair because every girl deserves to be regarded as special, and we are right. It may seem a bit sexist to choose a girl by looks alone, as if physical attractiveness was all that mattered and a woman had to get along by pleasing men with her superficial gifts—never mind the person inside. But just stop a minute. Many of these customs may well be far more ancient than we can imagine, dating back to a time in prehistory when women had lots more power and the feminine outlook was greatly respected. So the choosing of a girl as Queen of the May actually meant honoring the Maiden aspect of the Goddess, rejoicing not only in the gifts of the body, but also the vitality and independence of the Maiden. After all, the fact is that "virgin" didn't mean a woman who hadn't had sex (and was therefore okay as far as men and Father God were concerned). Rather, she was her own woman, owned by no one and able to have sex where and when she chose. So the May Queen celebrates feminine power.

A custom that still survives is that of the maypole. Now some feminist writers dislike the old maypole because it's phallic and honors patriarchy. I don't see it that way. After all, what keeps the maypole upright if it isn't the Earth in which it is planted? And the Earth is feminine, of course. And what springs beneath the dancer's feet if not the soft Earth, warming to the Sun? The maypole does indeed honor sexuality—it doesn't take rocket science to work that out! Because of this the Puritans banned it (along with most other things that were fun). Charles II came back to the throne and reinstated the custom. His court was famous for its merrymaking and sexual freedom. The maypole makes the statement that sex is important, and to be enjoyed. The dancers, as they weave the ribbons dangling from the top, are symbolically treading the spiral of life. Some dowsers can use their rods or a pendulum to detect where people danced around maypoles in the past.

Fire in some form is appropriate at all of the festivals, especially at Beltane. ("Beltane" actually means "Bel-fire.") Bel was a Celtic God of the light, and fires sacred to him were lit on hilltops to signal the return of fertility to the countryside. It was considered lucky to jump the Bel-fire (naturally extremely unlucky not to make it all the way over!). Young people did this to get themselves a nice mate. All sorts of goodies were believed to come from the Bel-fire: good health,

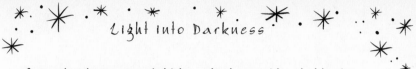

safe travel and pregnancy (which used to be considered a blessing, despite the fact that having a baby was probably the single most dangerous thing to happen to most women). Cows were driven between twin Bel-fires or through the ashes to ensure a good milk yield. This practice might have had a basis in common sense, for certain pests might have been driven off by the heat. Who knows, maybe it prevented the spread of foot-and-mouth, which used to be endemic in Europe. Many old customs have a sound basis in science.

Finally, the symbolism of the Bel-fire is obvious. The Sun has come to Earth. As the electric spring twilight steals over the land one can imagine the Bel-fires twinkling from hilltop to hilltop. There is believed to be a special line of energy in England, running through many sites of importance such as Glastonbury, Avebury, St. Michael's Mount in Cornwall and Lowestoft in the East. Over this line the Sun rises on May Day. Imagine the fiery disc of the Sun rising over the Bel-fire embers, as if they had somehow conjured it into being. Such things can and do emphasize our connection with the cycles of earth and heaven.

Traditionally, Beltane was the time when the Gaels, or the Irish Celts, landed in Ireland. With them we enter the "real time" of history. Before that we are told Ireland had a succession of magical races who invaded by turns, and were driven out by those who followed. The Tuatha de Danaan, the people of the Goddess Dana, still inhabit these isles as the Faerie races who live within barrow mounds and forest depths. You don't believe it? Reality has many layers, which as a witch you will sense. Alone in a shady, wind-whispering place, by a dolmen, in a glen, you may swear you see them, feel them or hear them. They don't fit in to the world as we know it but then we don't know everything about this world, do we? From the point of view of the mythical invasions, Beltane was the time when humans made contact with the land, a time of "earthing" and triumphant celebration.

There are many local customs that still endure, and this is a good time, as the weather improves (we hope!), to get out with some friends and see what may be going on in towns and villages. One well-known tradition is that of the Padstow "Obby" Oss. Padstow is a small town on the coast of North Cornwall, Britain. To celebrate May Day a large round shape of black fabric is carried around by a sturdy dancer, fringed by a black skirt. He wears a mask of red, white and black, and as he dances in and out of pubs to the beat of a drum (getting progressively more unsteady, one might guess!) he is praised and insulted. Then this stops for a sad little song, as the 'Oss dies. But not for long. The rhythm starts up again and he revives, to reel on his way. Everyone gets plastered! It's a great way to start summer, but notice the theme of death and resurrection, which we find year-round because that's what the seasons are all about.

Young people used to go "a-maying," which meant staying up all night to watch the May Day sun rise and gathering hawthorn or blackthorn blossom. I wonder, was the weather more reliable in olden times, or were they just more optimistic? Naturally a lot more interesting things went on than cutting sprigs of blossom, resulting in "greenwood marriages" and lots of babies!

Things to do

You don't need to be surrounded by friends who are all witches to do Beltane things. Look in your local newspaper and see what's going on. Even if the event you choose is very old-fashioned and amateurish you won't find it boring if you go along with your eyes open and look for signs of the old ways of honoring the Goddess and the life-force. Maybe you can even join in and liven things up if you're very extroverted—or very crazy!

This is the time for fêtes and open-air events and you can now go and enjoy them, realizing that there are older, more meaningful traditions that underpin them. If you don't have school the next day, why not stay up to watch the Sun rise, or get up early and climb a local hill for the dawn's rays. It's a brilliant experience because all the birds will be singing and a feeling of vitality vibrates everywhere. Take some sensible friends with you, though, because it's a very bad idea to go to remote places on your own.

Flowers are becoming plentiful and you can start to be lavish with them if you have some cash—or a generous boyfriend! Enjoy the fragrance of roses and lilies. Fill your room with them, if you can. Grow some herbs on your windowsill. Thyme is a Venus-ruled herb and brushing it releases the fragrance. Natural scents can make you

feel really sexy without you really knowing why—it just sort of happens. They make you feel ready to enjoy life, too. Some of the ingredients used in curry powder, such as cumin seed and coriander, are very erotic, smelling like fresh masculine sweat, with a hint of aftershave!

In your room you may like to hang some scarves to give an atmosphere of sensuality and the exotic—like a gypsy's caravan. This is better than those pop-star idols because they leave you free to dream about the ideal guy for you. Some white lace can take the place of hawthorn, and use lots of rose or crimson candles, placed well away from the fabric. Oils to put in your oil burner are ylang-ylang, rose or cardamom, which is spicy and lustful.

If you can afford it, buy something really sexy to wear. If you're short on funds, check out thrift of second-hand stores—it's amazing what other people throw out, and you can have a laugh wearing discount glamour.

Wild woman party

Before the party put all the bright clothes you can find into one room—just pool everything you have: scarves, dresses, nighties, things from the attic—as long as it's interesting, fun and maybe sexy. Include masks, make-up and glitter-paint. You also need to have everyone's favorite food there—just one choice each, plus sensible filling things like bread. Drinks need to be a special choice as well.

Give everyone their favorite drink when they come in, then go into the room where the clothes are and dress up. Just let your imagination or your sense of humor have free rein. Help each other dress up, choose colors, and so on. When you're all changed you can dance and fool around, and then take turns telling everyone your favorite fantasy—preferably sexual or romantic. Describe your fantasy guy—down to the way he smells, the muscles on his arms, the way he touches you and makes you feel. You can have as many go-arounds as you like.

Then choose a name other than the one you usually use and be called that for a while—and then change it again if you like. Act out how you imagine someone with that name might act. If you choose a Goddess-name then you can play-act her personality and mythology.

Dance wildly and sexily; if one of your friends can belly-dance ask her to teach the others. Or someone who feels brave enough could do a strip-tease (but make sure the curtains are drawn!).

Have another drink—by now you'll be all warmed up and the evening is yours!

Guys can do this, too. The point about this party is so that you can talk about your fantasies and dress up.

Making your own massage oil and perfume

If you have been sniffing and using essential oils in your burner or as incense, remember you can use them on your skin, too. Lavender oil is very gentle and can be used straight, but remember don't swallow any of the oils. Many of them can produce an allergic reaction, so test a drop of it on the inside of your wrist and wait twenty-four hours to see if there is an adverse reaction.

In addition to your favorite oil, you will need what is called a "carrier oil," which is a bland and long-lasting oil that dilutes the essential oil. Use pure, cold-pressed oils such as grapeseed or sweet almond. (Don't use mineral oils such as baby lotion.) For a massage, dilute your essential oil using two drops per teaspoon of oil.

You can massage your own feet, legs, arms and neck, or preferably take turns with a friend to massage each other. For perfumes, you ideally need to dilute the oil in alcohol otherwise the fragrance will not keep. Use 2 teaspoons of vodka (or a similar liquor) and add to it about 18 drops of essential oil. Experiment with strengths, making it weaker at first until you find the best concentration for you, and always

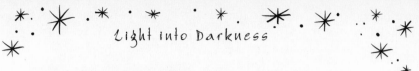

use small amounts to avoid waste. Keep your blends in screw-top bottles somewhere dark.

Samantha's Beltane beauty-spell

Sometimes when you are a teenager you feel insecure about your body. A teenage friend of mine, Samantha, who helped me write this book, devised this spell to help boost your confidence in your looks.

Take a bath with some rose petals floating in it, or use a few drops of rose essential oil. Let your troubles and self-doubt dissolve into the water. Dry yourself on a rose-colored towel, if you have one. Fill your bedroom with candles and/or rose incense (or rose oil in your burner). Stand in front of the mirror in your favorite dress or clothes, or stand naked. Look in the mirror, close your eyes and see before you a beautiful young girl (or handsome fella): this is you! Repeat three times, "My body is glowing. I am beautiful because the Goddess made me." Now open your eyes. Clap your hands together to ground yourself and have something good to eat and drink. You can repeat this spell as often as you like, focusing on all your good points. And remember, everyone is beautiful in her own way.

Recipe:

a simple curry

At Beltane you want a festival for the senses or something really spicy. This curry is best if you make your own spice mixture (called garam masala). You can get all the spices in any large supermarket. First of all, mix together in a small pot two teaspoons of ground cardamom, one teaspoon of ground cinnamon, four teaspoons of ground coriander, four teaspoons of ground cumin seed, two teaspoons of black pepper and two teaspoons of ground ginger.

Stir all these spices carefully together and form a pentagram over them with your athame or your finger. This "witch's blessing" will make the spices all the more special. Use some of the spice mixture now and keep the rest for other times.

Ingredients

About ¹/₂ lb lean minced lamb (preferably organic; chicken will also do—or you can use butter beans if you are vegetarian); 1 onion, finely chopped; 2 cloves garlic, crushed (or use half teaspoon powdered garlic); 1 inch root ginger (this is a gnarled root and can be bought in the vegetable section of most supermarkets); a can of chopped tomatoes; half packet of creamed coconut 4 oz; 1 teaspoon salt; 1 teaspoon chili powder (if you like it hot—if not leave it out or use a smaller amount); 2 teaspoons of your spice mixture; 1 teaspoon turmeric; 1 stock cube; a little sunflower oil.

Method

If you are using meat, set it to simmer on low, with a little oil if it is lean. Stir frequently. Add the finely chopped onion and fry until it is transparent. If you are not using meat, fry the onion first in the oil and then add the drained butter beans. Peel and chop the ginger, then add it to the pot. Now add the mixed spices, turmeric, chili powder and garlic, and stir these into the mixture for a minute or two. Enjoy the lovely, spicy scent. Add the creamed coconut and let it melt over a low heat, stirring often. Then add the tomatoes, salt and stock cube (you may need an extra cube if you aren't using meat, so taste as you go).

Let this simmer for twenty minutes to half an hour. There's enough for two hungry people—you and your boyfriend/girlfriend or best friend. Meanwhile cook some rice. Instructions are usually given on the packet. I find one cup of rice is plenty for two people. Measure it into a pan and add double the amount of water. Basmati rice is best. Bring it to a boil, turn down the heat, cover and simmer until all the liquid is absorbed. This takes about 15 minutes. If you find the rice has gone cakey then rinse it in a sieve, with very hot water, before serving.

Spoon the rice onto warmed plates and ladle the cooked curry over the top. Serve with chutneys—you can make your own by chopping bananas and putting nuts with them in one dish, slicing tomatoes and mild onion in another and in a third try celery, apple and raisins. Eat by candlelight.

Recipe:

chocolate challenge

As Beltane is about self-indulgence, this isn't so much a recipe as an invitation to sling everything yummy you can think of into a very large dish, have two spoons handy (or eat the whole thing if you're on your own) and dig in. Here are my suggestions for ingredients, but you can omit or replace things as you wish.

Ingredients

Chocolate sponge cake; fruit juice; good quality vanilla dairy ice cream—made with real cream if possible; chocolate sauce; a large slab of milk chocolate—Belgian or Swiss is best; several chocolate flakes and/or favorite chocolates; marshmallows; nuts (unsalted); cherries.

Method

First put the sponge cake into the bowl and soak it with the fruit juice. Place the ice cream in layers with the chocolate, which you need to grate, and the chocolate sauce. Chop the marshmallows and put them in here and there. Do likewise with the cherries. Finish off with a layer of ice cream and then stick the flakes and chocolates into the top. A final squeeze of chocolate sauce and a sprinkling of nuts completes the concoction. Now dig in for that first, blissful mouthful! If you can't finish it, stick it in the freezer to enjoy another day.

On your own

Beltane is about spoiling yourself. If you can't afford a massage by a professional, why not give yourself a pedicure? Soak your feet in warm water with a little bath oil dissolved in it. (Don't soak them too long, or the skin will become all wrinkly.) When your toenails are soft, trim them and cut them straight, gently pushing down the cuticles. Rub off any hard skin with a loofah. Dry them thoroughly and rub in some peppermint lotion—available in many shops. Now put on your favorite nail polish, and listen to your favorite music or read a magazine (or both) while it's drying and hardening. If you can give this half an hour, so much the better. Now apply the second coat, leaving that for at least the same amount of time—the second coat takes longer to harden than the first. Once you are sure your toenails are completely dry, rub in more moisturizer—be lavish. Then you can put on some soft socks and sleep through the night with your feet soaking up all that lotion. You'll wake up in the morning with beautiful feet, ready to display in sandals and take you on all those summer walks. Toenail polish usually lasts much longer than fingernail polish and it may be almost a month before it starts to look ratty.

Do you love your body?

Beltane is all about physical joy, reveling in the pleasures of the senses. But all too often we feel guilty about our bodies. Our culture gives us mixed messages about this. We are told it is wrong to be materialistic yet bombarded with all sorts of images about self-indulgence of all kinds. Of course, if something is forbidden we want it all the more! We are also pulled two ways with regard to our bodies. We have all sorts of invitations and suggestions to overeat and overdrink, yet we are told that to be beautiful we have to have a size eight figure with skin that is dew-fresh! So what is a poor girl or boy to do? Take this questionnaire first, to see where you're at. It's mainly for the girls, but with a little imagination it can be adapted for a guy.

1) When you look for clothes your primary feeling is: a) great— I'm going to get something really trendy in a fabulous color

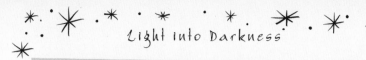

and have lots of fun trying things on; b) I probably won't find anything—not many things suit me; c) hopefully I can at least get something that won't show my bulging stomach!

2) The gang is going swimming—you love the water, but…
a) no *buts* at all, it'll be a great laugh; b) you hope you haven't put on weight since you got that new suit; c) you make excuses not to go so you can keep your cellulite covered.

3) Your favorite dessert is on the menu—how do you react?
a) oooh, yummy, hope there'll be enough for seconds!; b) better try not to eat too much; c) your heart sinks—you know you'll have to starve yourself tomorrow.

4) Someone tells you how nice you look in your new outfit—how do you feel? a) really great—you thought you looked good and it's nice to be told it; b) pleased, but doubtful—probably they're admiring the clothes rather than you; c) embarrassed— they obviously don't mean it and they're just trying to boost your morale.

5) When you go out to a club or dance and the music starts: a) you're first on the floor, shaking your groove thang—you love it! b) you'll have a dance when your friends get up, too; c) you very rarely get out there and shake it up—there are bits of you that don't stop when the music does!

6) It's party night and you know that gorgeous guy you've been fancying for months will be there: a) you dress to kill— something clingy and revealing; b) you wonder what to put on to minimize your fat thighs; c) you think it doesn't matter what you wear because he's never going to look at you anyway.

7) What about your beauty routine? a) you love it—you try on lipsticks and eye shadows for hours; b) your main concern is to try to hide your zits; c) beauty routine?—ugly routine, you mean. You might mess around with your friends' cosmetics but you always look like a disaster.

8) You find you've won a week at a health resort—how do you react? a) ace! All that lying around being massaged and

learning tennis; b) it'll take more than a week to knock this kid into shape; c) you don't want to go—people will look at your body.

9) Your mom has asked you to go shopping to buy chocolate and chips for your little sis: a) it's a drag, so you call up your friends and see if you can work in some talent spotting; b) you hope you'll get home without binging on the junk; c) you feel embarrassed at the thought of openly buying all that— people will think that's why you're so fat.

10) It's happened—he's actually asked you out: a) great—you'll knock his socks off and he'll wonder where you've been all his life; b) you're excited but worried—what are you going to wear? c) you say "No" because it's obviously a joke and his friends are laughing behind your back.

Your score

Mostly a's. You love your body and you've got nothing to learn about enjoying it, pampering it and indulging it. Maybe you do look like Britney Spears, but chances are it has more to do with your internal programming that says you're loveable—and you are! There is much in witchcraft that will naturally appeal to you because it exalts the body and doesn't separate it from the spirit.

Mostly b's. You could feel better about yourself. There's hope, you think, as long as you wear the right thing, do the right thing, don't eat too much . . . . There are lots of things in life that you'd enjoy more if you felt better about yourself. Boost yourself in little ways, such as by smiling at yourself in the mirror, making a note of it when someone pays you a compliment, listing all the good things about yourself, and so on. Remember that your body doesn't have to conform to certain standards in order for you to enjoy yourself. In any case, a fun-loving personality is far more attractive than someone who is beautiful but miserable. What's more, guys tend to prefer girls who are a bit curvy, despite all the propaganda. And most likely, you think you are fatter than you are. So—if you've got it, flaunt it! Witchcraft will encourage you to appreciate yourself.

Mostly c's. It seems that you hate your body and your body responds by being hateful! Chances are you look fine—many beautiful women feel ugly. Whatever size you are, you can look attractive. If the real, inner you (without real or imagined pressure) would really feel happier being thinner, there are ways to lose weight without suffering. To starve yourself is very un-witchy! You might consider some hypnotherapy to boost your self-esteem. Remember, food is a gift of the Goddess and everything we do that is pleasurable and harms no living thing is a ritual in Her worship. Your body itself is a gift of the Goddess—do not punish it and despise it but learn Her message of sensual enjoyment through the ways of the witch.

Body-buddy tips

Your body is the temple of your soul and you need to balance enjoyment with sensible caretaking. When all feelings of guilt, inferiority and inhibition melt away, it is natural for your body to find the right balance in habits and food intake. Here are some Beltane beauty-without-cruelty tips.

✳ Try to drink eight glasses of water a day. This is good for body-tissue and helps with acne. It also reduces your appetite, but don't drink just before meals because it can inhibit the absorption of certain nutrients. Experiment with ways of drinking all this water; tepid water may be best, for instance, or you may find it easier to swallow when drinking from a bottle. Work up to your required intake slowly.

✳ Eat loads and loads of fruit and vegetables. Always have your yummy favorites close at hand. When you feel like snacking, say to yourself, "I'll have something in a minute but I'll just eat an apple and a banana first." Chances are you won't need the snack.

✳ Healthy foods often take longer to prepare—make sure that you have something that you really like ready at hand for when you are hungry.

✳ Don't try to eat food you don't like because it's "healthy"—it isn't! Your mind will send messages to your stomach that make it harder to digest and you won't feel satisfied.

* Exercise speeds up your metabolism but doesn't make you want to eat more. Just ten minutes of exercise each day will up your metabolic rate.

* Never feel guilty about food—if it's what you've chosen, it's good. Eat it slowly, enjoying every mouthful to the max.

Beltane ritual

For this ritual you will need some rose-colored candles, several large scarves in your favorite colors and your favorite perfume—preferably rose oil. Also have a bowl of nuts and as much seasonal greenery and flowers as you can spare. Food and drink to celebrate with should be as delicious as possible. You will also need a cassette player, if possible. Incense could contain rose petals, frankincense, lavender, ylang-ylang, cardamom, vanilla, thyme.

One of the candles may be placed in your cauldron in the center of your circle. After you have cast your circle and summoned the Guardians/Watchtowers, start to play your favorite music and dance around your circle in the sexiest way you can. Make sure it feels good for you. Jump over the cauldron, if this is feasible, because this is your equivalent to the Bel-fire. When you feel you have raised enough energy, stand in front of your altar and say, "Great Mother, I thank you for the beauty and strength of my body. Let me enjoy it, and let me be creative with it. Great Horned One, I thank you for the pulse of life that beats within me. Let me use it well, for the good of all."

If you are wearing a robe, take it off. (If you are working with others you may not wish to do this, so go with your preferences.) Swathe yourself with the scarves (if you are working clad and/or with others and don't wish to be naked you can do this over your clothing), play the music again and slowly take them off, imagining you are doing this for a lover. Anoint yourself with your perfume, close to your genitals (but not on them), and on your belly, breasts and lips, saying: "Blessed be my body, formed in the likeness of the God/dess. Blessed be my sexuality, hot and joyful as the rising Sun. Blessed be my creativity, rich as the greenwood and the fertile fields."

Now celebrate with the food and drink. Consecrate the nuts in the name of the Great Mother and the Horned One. Eat some, give some to friends and family and bury the others. They are the symbol of new life and of fertility. Think of all the things you enjoy doing as you sit in the circle, communing with the Goddess and rejoicing in all She has created. Weave yourself a garland with the greenery and flowers you have, singing along to your music, and place it on your head or around your neck, saying, "I am crowned (or garlanded) by the beauty of Nature." Remember, this really is a celebration, so do what you like to do most and close your circle when you are ready.

Midsummer

Midsummer is the very peak of the year. The lovely thing about this time is that the daylight goes on and on into the evening and the Sun comes up early. It's a high-energy time when almost anything seems possible and everything is vibrant—lots of flowers and everything bright and pretty. We are all making plans for summer holidays, barbecues and outings. But although it may feel strange, the truth is that just when the year is at its very best, it starts to decline. It's the time to grab the moment.

Goddess and God

Here we see our hero and heroine at the height of their fulfillment and creativity. The Goddess is glamorous, strutting her stuff in all the brilliant flowers and sunshine (hopefully!). The God is her strong and handsome champion. However, He is changing as the Sun changes. Reaching His peak, He now begins an inward journey as the Sun starts to go farther away, very gradually. We can picture the God at this time as a man who is conscious of His responsibilities and thinking about things much more. Often when a man has a child he starts to think about things differently. He has been responsible for starting a new life, but, funnily enough, this also makes him think about what will happen when he isn't around anymore, and so he takes out insurance policies and pension plans. The God is joyful, protective, but also aware of the serious business of life and that He has a job to do.

So at this time the Goddess and the God tell us something curious—just when we feel most victorious, on top of the world, flushed with success, we are also vulnerable. Have you ever felt that kind of flat feeling when, say, you have passed with As, won a dance or gymnastics competition or scored the winning goal? You think for a while that things can't get any better and everything about the world is good—and then after the celebrations you're left with a "now what?" sensation. Soon you realize that although you may have done one thing, there are still many things to do, and you have to change gears and get on with it or people may say you are "resting on your laurels." If you have done something really fantastic, like won Wimbledon, you could feel quite depressed for a while, because it may seem as if there is nothing left to prove. The changing seasons and the story of the God and Goddess teach us to make the necessary shifts in life, to go on new quests, to look at things in a different way, and to progress.

As witches we think of everything around us as being part of the Goddess—She is everything and within everything. However, at this time of year, in temperate climates, it is easiest of all to think that we "see" Her, because Nature is so lovely. Life is bursting out all over the place and it is good to enjoy this to the fullest.

In times of yore

Various times of the year were taken to be New Year by different cultures. For the Cretans, Midsummer was New Year. The Cretan civilization was at its height in the Bronze Age and was remarkable for the beauty of its art work, its peace and its worship of the Goddess. The Cretans apparently knew how to live for the moment, aware of the spiritual within the physical world and full of joy.

Midsummer for them was the end of over a month spent collecting honey from bees. Now they stopped to party on for many days, getting drunk on the mead they made from the honey. Bees were considered very sacred because their buzzing was believed to be the voice of the Goddess. Their hives were like great wombs, humming with life, and the bee was a symbol of order and productivity that came directly from nature.

Bulls were also sacred to the Goddess, according to the Cretans. We may believe that all animals are "sacred" because they are a part of creation, but different peoples have spotted qualities in certain animals that have made them special. The Cretans had a myth that bees came from the carcasses of bulls. The interesting thing about a bull is that the head actually looks like the womb of a human

female. Have you ever seen a picture of the cross-section of the womb, with the Fallopian tubes curling up, just like horns? Very much like a bull's head. Links like this are rather interesting because they connect masculine and feminine and show that there are all sorts of threads running through life. This wasn't so good for the poor old bull in Crete, however, because he was sacrificed in honor of the dying and resurrecting God that he represented.

The Cretans also had a story about the Minotaur, which was a half-man half-bull monster who lived in the middle of a labyrinth. He was killed by the hero Theseus, who was helped by the Goddess to find his way in and out of the labyrinth by using her golden thread. The Goddess was represented by Ariadne, who fell in love with Theseus. We have already mentioned that the labyrinth itself is a symbol of the Goddess. So why did She help Theseus in and out, and why did She hide the Minotaur? There are many possible answers, but one explanation is that the Goddess wanted Theseus to understand Her more and to prove his courage by facing all parts of Her and trusting himself to Her. In so doing he was also facing up to things about himself that he may have not liked, such as his fear. This is rather like most women when they want a serious relationship with a man. They want him to understand them, to face up to his own emotions and work through deep things in the relationship rather than going off to hang with the guys all the time. It's about how we all grow through relationships.

Things to do

Great outdoors

Exams are probably finished by now and you'll probably want to get out and about as much as possible. Try camping trips with a crowd of friends. If you can camp near a prehistoric site or standing stone, so much the better. See if you have any special dreams in the place and, if your friends share your beliefs, you can swap stories. In some cultures, such as that of the Native Americans, dreams are taken very seriously. Possibly one of you will have had a dream that is an inspiration and gives you all an idea of what to do, how to spend the day, or just something to talk about. You could have a dream

that relates to the particular site and tells you something about what happened there years ago.

Midsummer night's dream

We all dream, all the time. Anyone watching us while we are asleep can tell when we are dreaming because our eyes move. This is called REM (Rapid Eye Movement) sleep. If you never remember your dreams it's probably because of your sleep rhythms—after all, if you do not wake up during a dream then you aren't going to recall it. During the short summer nights we may sleep less and wake up at different times in our sleep cycle. This may mean dreams are more memorable.

It is a good idea to keep a dream diary, and several things will probably happen. First, you will find you remember your dreams more and more. Secondly, you may start to find that what you dream ties in with your life—as if a part of you *knows* what is going to happen the next day. This doesn't necessarily mean you have major, prophetic dreams but simply little signs that you are in tune with yourself and that your inner wisdom is coming through. Thirdly, you may develop the knack of knowing when you are dreaming—this is called "lucid dreaming." When you know you are dreaming, you have more control over what happens in the dream and you can have wonderful experiences, like flying. These things are all good because they teach us that there is more to life than the everyday. It's called "expanding your consciousness," and that is part of being a witch.

To record your dreams, keep a special notepad and pen near the bed so you can write things down as soon as you wake up. Dreams may be very quickly forgotten if you get up to go to the bathroom or get a cup of cocoa. Always respect what happens. For instance, if you dream of a friend and you tell her and she tells you that she was dreaming about you at the same time, make a note of this. Take this as an indication that the two of you may well have met at that time in the Otherworld, rather than just dismissing it as a coincidence. If you also keep a day-to-day diary of your thoughts and feelings, compare this with your dream diary at a later date. You may find interesting links that you missed at the time.

You can get together with friends and compare your dreams. Sometimes someone else will have an idea about what a dream means when the dreamer just hasn't a clue. There are also lots of books on dream interpretations. However, always take such interpretations with a grain of salt because each dream is individual and there may be many different meanings.

Out and about

This is a time for pilgrimage, and if that sounds dreary remember that witchy pilgrimages are different! They are exciting and expand your inner awareness. Simply head for a special place in nature. Any beautiful tree or grove of trees can serve the purpose, any rock that seems special, or any place where the plants appeal particularly to you. If you're really stuck, even a corner in your garden or local park can be a worthwhile destination!

If you can, walk to the place. Imagine what it was like two or three thousand years ago, to make the same journey on foot. While you walk you will experience so much more of the land than you could ever possibly get in a car. Take a picnic. Take also some dowsing rods or a pendulum. (You will find instructions about dowsing in the Lughnasadh section on page 165. Also take an offering of some herbs, seeds or whatever for the earth at the special site. Always treat the place with respect— please don't fall into the ways of certain present-day pagans (who really should know better!) who leave empty incense jars, bits of string, and so on laying around. Just because you have used something in a ritual doesn't mean that the packaging isn't litter! And just because it's a pentagram that's been scratched on that standing stone, it doesn't mean that the stone hasn't been defaced! So be a friend to the site; clear it of a few nettles if you like, but otherwise leave it unmarked, except by your devotion.

Go to such sites with a group of like-minded friends and see what occurs naturally. Do you all feel like dancing? Going around in a circle? Chanting? Making love? Sitting quietly and meditating? Peeing? (Some say this is a way of making a connection with a place and has pagan meanings.) Perhaps you get a strong sense of something about the place. What do you all think?

Vision quest

The "vision quest" is a Native American tradition where the young brave goes out into the wilds and endures discomfort and even danger in order to get in touch with the Great Spirit. Often spiritual insight would come through being alone with the natural world in some remote place. It can be good for the boys to have a challenge and such traditions are being revived by certain men's groups to initiate young men into adulthood. Because girls don't have the testosterone to contend with, and also because we have our periods as a kind of challenge, it can be easier for girls to understand that life is a serious, deep and mysterious business.

Needless to say, it isn't a good idea to go to remote places by yourself. However, if—and only if—you have friends you can really trust, you can arrange a sort of mini-quest for boys or girls. This could involve merely being on your own on the top of a hill at midnight during Midsummer, when the Moon is full. The arrangement is that you are not truly ever alone, but that your friends are always within earshot. So much the better if you have supportive adults to help. This type of activity must only be done with people who understand what you are doing and take it seriously, not just some friendly jokers who are going to creep up on you—or, far worse, leave you alone.

Only when you are really alone in the natural world can you experience it in a certain way. It is a way that we rarely know about these days. We are used to the urban jungle, but not the power and depth of Nature. If you try it, it could be a memorable experience.

Flower pressing at Midsummer

If you want to preserve some reminders of Midsummer and like flowers, it is very simple to press them. All you need are two sheets of blotting paper and a heavy book or two. Place the blotting paper on a hard surface, put the flower on it, put another piece of blotting paper on top and weight it down with the books. In a few days your flower will be pressed, dried and ready. You can slip it between two sheets of cellophane and use it as a bookmark, if you like. For this you could cut a transparent document wallet down to size, and stick the edges together. Your flower will remind you of summer when the winter darkness is here, and be a promise of sunny days to come in the future. However, please be careful not to pick wildflowers because these may be endangered and it is often illegal to pick them. If you love wildflowers, buy seeds and bulbs from a nursery and grow them in tubs or in your garden.

What is your attitude about Nature?

At Midsummer, Nature may be at its most pleasant and we spend more time in contact with it. But most of us are separated from Nature, lost in a concrete jungle, insulated in our little boxes of bricks and mortar. As witches we know how important it is to connect with the natural world. How easy is this for us? Take this questionnaire to find out how close you are to Nature.

1) Your friends suggest a picnic in the park or nearby woods: a) you think, Great—food tastes better outdoors; b) you can't really be bothered to make sandwiches, and eating is far more comfy sitting at a table; c) you make excuses not to go—you are afraid you'll eat a wasp or sit on an anthill.

2) How do you like your bedroom window? a) you have it open just a teeny bit whatever the weather; b) you open it when the weather is sunny; c) it's locked and you've lost the key, and if it's sunny you draw the curtains so you can see the TV better.

3) What about a lovely walk in the woods? a) great—you just love the feel of the earth under your feet; b) okay if it's not

raining and you can find your boots; c) what's lovely about getting bitten by mosquitoes?

4) It's snowing! What is your impulse? a) get out in it and build a snowman with little sis; b) looks lovely from the window; c) yuck—you hope it melts before you have to go out.

5) It's thundering and lightning and the warm rain is coming down in great big dollops: a) you have a secret desire to throw off your clothes and dance in it; b) you find it quite exciting but you're glad there's a roof over your head; c) you hide in the closet under the stairs.

6) Your next-door neighbors have installed a pond and you find a frog on your patio: a) you pick the poor creature up and put it over the fence before your cat gets it; b) you call the neighbors to come and rescue the frog; c) you poke the horrid thing with a stick.

7) Everyone is sunbathing on a brilliant day: a) you get your sunscreen on and rush out to join them; b) you're worried about looking all blotchy and getting too hot; c) you won't go out because of the flying ants.

8) Do you like helping in the garden? a) if you have time it can be fun because you like the smell of the soil and seeing seeds come up; b) boring, really, but the flowers smell nice; c) never go near it—it's dirty and you hate worms.

9) At the beach you like to: a) swim or paddle and check out the talent; b) sit on a blanket and check out the talent; c) sit in a sports car on the boardwalk and check out the talent.

10) Do you like camping? a) it's great sleeping outdoors and cooking on a campfire; b) it's exciting but you wish it was more comfortable; c) no one will ever catch you in a tent.

Your score

Mostly a's. It's the country life for you! You are really in tune with Nature and never hesitate to get your hands dirty. This may be because you are simply an active, hands-on person, but nonetheless it helps your development as a witch. If you realize this, it should make you love Nature all the more. Enjoy it, especially at Midsummer.

Mostly b's. Understandably for a modern teenager, you aren't keen on some of the discomforts of the outdoors. However, you realize that it has a lot to offer you and you probably feel great making the effort. Make it a little more, especially at Midsummer. It will stand you in good stead—remember, Nature helps develop intuition.

Mostly c's. Lounge lizard, aren't you? You shrink from Nature's unpredictability—and as for insects—they're for the birds (literally, you hope)! Possibly you have phobias about creepy-crawlies, and you're very sensitive. Maybe you lack confidence in your ability to cope, or in your appearance. This doesn't make you less of a witch because your sensitivities may also be psychic ones. However, these can only grow through being with Nature. Take the invitation of Midsummer to open up a bit more. Pick your times—you're in control. See how much you can enjoy it if you try.

Recipe:

summer fruits pudding

The best fruits for this dish are strawberries, raspberries and red currants, but almost any fruit will do. Red fruits are best because they color the bread pink.

Ingredients

About 2 lbs soft fruit (preferably organically grown); a very small amount of water; sugar to taste; 6 slices of organic white bread.

Method

Line a bowl with the bread, saving some for a topping, making sure there are no gaps around the edges. Cook the fruit with the water until just tender. If you are using a microwave, cook for half-minute intervals, checking as you go. Tender fruits like strawberries will soften at high power in a minute or two. When the fruit is soft, stir the sugar into the warm mixture so it dissolves. Taste it to check for sweetness. Then put the fruit mixture into the bread case. Cover the fruit with more bread and put a saucer on top, with something heavy on the saucer so the mixture is pushed down and all the juice soaks into the bread. Leave this in the fridge for 24 hours and turn it out the next day. Serve it with custard, cream or ice cream. Delicious!

Midsummer ritual

For this you will need to put some water in your cauldron or a bowl and float some daisies on top. You will also need a large gold or orange candle, about four yards of red, green or gold thread, some bright flowers for the altar, some honey cake or something similar and fruit juice. Also have a piece of yellow or orange cloth and some dried marjoram. Incense can contain frankincense, lemon peel, rose and rosemary.

Start your ritual in the usual way. Place the cauldron in the South of your circle and light the fat orange candle. Hold this over the water in the cauldron so that you can see the reflection of the flame. Say, "Thank you, Lord Sun, for being with us, for blessing the land and bringing the powers of light to their height." Extinguish the candle in the cauldron and move the cauldron into the West. Re-light the candle and hold it once more above the cauldron (it may take a few goes to light the damp wick). Say, "Now begins a new journey into the mystery. Blessed be." Leave your candle now in the West of your circle and dance, if you wish. Wind the thread thirteen times around your cauldron, widdershins, saying, "What goes around comes around." Now unwind it deosil, saying, "May the blessings of the waning year come to me and mine." Put the thread on your altar for the time being and keep it to burn in a bonfire at some point, perhaps at Samhain. Now consecrate some cake and juice and celebrate the return of the Sun to its zenith. Think about the things you have achieved during the year, and think about how you want to develop them as the year turns inward.

Take up your yellow cloth and place the marjoram in it. Form a pentagram over it and say, "May the light of the Sun stay with me through the dark of the year." Tie it up with some of the thread you used earlier and keep it with you to smell or touch whenever you need cheering up through the autumn and winter. Have some more cake and juice.

After your ritual pour the water from the cauldron, complete with daisies, back onto the earth. Leave some of your cake out for the Faeries; they will take its energy, but probably won't eat the cake itself (but you never know!).

Lughnasadh

At Lughnasadh (Lugh-nasadh means "feast of Lugh") everything is ripe and the weather is often mellow. There are butter-colored fields, buzzing hedges and the harvest waiting to be cut. It's a time when many people are going on vacation or looking forward to vacations. The most joyful time? Maybe. But look closely. Isn't everything looking just a little bit tired? Can you see the Sun slipping away just a little earlier each evening? You may even spot the occasional brown leaf corroding the tops of the laden trees. Truth be told, the year has begun to die. Lughnasadh is a celebration of abundance, it is true, but it is also a "wake," a funeral festival.

Goddess and God

For the Goddess and God this is a time that is both happy and sad. Before them the rich fields and trees are spread out, showing the success of their creation, the continuance of life. Yet the God knows He must go on a long and dangerous journey to experience things He has never seen. The Goddess knows She must let Him go—more than that, She insists that He leave her. She knows that nothing stands still in life, that change must come. She realizes that unless we make changes and take chances everything comes to an end, both inside and outside us. But She is sad—She does not want to be alone.

The God dies—He goes down into the Underworld to experience things that are deep and hidden. This is a symbol for many things that happen to us in life. Because you are young, you may not have experienced this. On the other hand, you may have experienced losses and changes that may seem dreadful at the time, but they make you go within yourself and find something that you didn't know was there. This sort of experience can happen when you come off drugs, change schools, have a fall out with someone you thought was your best friend, or lose a friend or parent. Certainly it can happen if you fall in love with someone and the person doesn't love you back or lets you down. But at the end of it all you may look back and say that in a way it was good it happened to you because it made you stronger—you went down into your own "Underworld" and came up reborn. Nature tells us that the way to grow and to find our "harvest" isn't always smooth—it demands some sacrifice.

"Sacrifice" sounds harsh, unpleasant and tedious, like something people forced on themselves to punish themselves for being human. To a witch, however, the idea of sacrifice isn't about giving up what we hold dear for some stern deity—it's no sin to be glad you're alive. Sacrifice is about realizing that something has to go, to make way for something else and that there is a price to pay for everything in life. It's about progressing, transforming. In order for any creature to go on living, something else must die—even a vegetarian has to kill a lettuce! The death of the God is most dramatically played out in the cutting of the harvest, where all the wealth of vegetation is cut down. However, there is an almost immediate "rebirth" as the grain is made into loaves and produce. This aspect of the God was—and is—known as the Corn King, the spirit of Nature who gives up His life to feed us and yet is twice reincarnated, both as the food on the table and as the new shoots that appear bravely next spring.

There are many stories of Gods who died and were resurrected, such as Greek Adonis and Egyptian Osiris. In particular, the God Lugh, for whom this festival was named, was a shining being who led the Faerie race in their conquest of Ireland. Lugh himself did not die and resurrect, but he killed his grandfather in order to rule. In myths like these, where someone kills his ancestor, it is really a part of himself that is dying.

Lughnasadh, also called "Lammas" or "loaf-mass," is also about a happy time when we should feel great about the generosity of the earth and the warmth of the Sun and enjoy ourselves. The Goddess is preparing to be alone for a while, but Her time on Her own will come to an end. Meanwhile, She holds out her arms to us—full of goodies!

In times of yore

In the olden days, Kings were often sacrificed. People were afraid that the Gods were angry and that if someone didn't die to pay them, everyone would suffer. We met this at Samhain, also. This theme can be linked to most festivals, but Lughnasadh and Samhain are the principle ones.

The king gained his authority from the land herself, which was represented by the High Priestess. He made a "sacred marriage" with the Priestess, and in so doing took the place of the God. When the king's turn came to die he just accepted it. This ancient tradition ran very deep in some peoples. For example, as recently as 1100 CE an English king, King Rufus, or "Rufus the Red," was sacrificed in this manner. We met this openly pagan king briefly in Chapter One. The monks hated him! After calling out to be shot, Rufus was fatally pierced by an arrow near an oak tree. He died in the New Forest, and a plaque marks his passing. (Needless to say, it doesn't tell you about his pagan links!) Rufus was killed on August 2 in the thirteenth year of his reign, which holds significance. A king wasn't sacrificed every year, but only after a certain span, and thirteen is a special number for pagans because the Moon makes thirteen rounds of the zodiac each year.

Natural cycles are things we have to remind ourselves about today, rediscovering them sometimes with a feeling of excitement. However, many years ago people intimately identified with these cycles, even to the point of being prepared to die.

The story of the king mating with the Goddess or High Priestess is found in different themes of many old legends. King Arthur, for instance, drew his power from the land in the shape of Guinevere ("Guinevere" means "white owl," a Goddess-symbol of wisdom), his queen, and when they no longer loved each other the land was laid to waste. Arthur and Lancelot are similar to other pairs of legendary males who were lovers of the Goddess. Guinevere was no weak adulteress as some stories make her out to be, but rather she gave her favors to the man who had most respect for her. Perhaps Arthur had become a little lopsided, losing respect for the feminine and intuitive aspects of life. Arthur's knights went in search of the Grail in order to heal the king and the land. One interpretation is that the Grail is a symbol of the womb, and the knights were searching for something feminine to make things bright and balanced once more.

In the times when harvesting was done by hand, people had an instinctive knowledge of how "sacred" this practice was. They knew they were taking from the generosity of Nature and at the same time "killing" the corn spirit. It was considered to be unlucky to be the person to fell the last stalk. Rather than knowing who had actually done the deed, everyone stood around the tuft and threw their sickles at it. Then the ears would be gathered up together and made into a corn dolly to preserve the Spirit of the Corn. The corn dolly was placed over the hearth until next spring when the seeds were shaken off to be planted with the new harvest. Despite mechanical harvesting, we can still find ways of honoring the Corn Spirit. In what ways can you imagine honoring the Corn Spirit?

Things to do

Your future

You might consider your exams as your "harvest." Are you pleased with them? If so, celebrate; but if you're not, ask yourself why. Was it because the course you took wasn't right for you? Or was it because you didn't work hard enough? Be very honest with yourself. If you have failed, this may seem like the end of the world, as if everything is dead and buried. However, take it from me, your whole life is still before you and you'll have many chances of rebirth. Take time out from the summer fun and sort through your own "wheat from chaff." What have you learned? What has to go in your life and what has to stay? Where can you get help and advice to guide your next step? Let the Underworld journey of the Corn King be an inspiration to you—you are not alone!

If you have achieved the hoped-for results you may soon be planning your next phase of life, either by moving up to a higher grade, leaving for college, or taking a job. Again, plan to get the very best you can from this time by being clear about

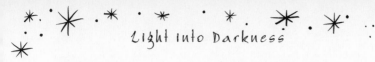

your own needs. For instance, do you really hope for top honors at college or are you really going for the social life? If so, maybe that is what you need—be sure about it. This time next year there will be another "harvest," and as you sow, so you shall reap. Sow only the best!

Visiting the corn spirit

At this time of year going into a field full of ripened wheat is a must. Choose a safe place, not too far off the beaten track, and take some friends with you. Naturally you will make sure that you don't damage anything and upset Farmer MacDonald! Walk into the field quietly and carefully, separating yourself from your friends so you're not conscious of their presence. Listen carefully. Can you hear the breeze in the wheat? What is it whispering? This is a field full of luxuriant, vibrant life, but it will soon be cut down, the field will be bare and the harvest will be rolled up into large stacks and bundles, separated from the good earth. Can you sense anything from all of this doomed plantlife? Take note of all your feelings and compare them with those of your friends or keep them to yourself. Keep a record of them in your Book of Shadows. The feelings you get might inspire a ritual or make you realize that one is necessary.

Crop circles

Strange circles still appear in the ripening wheat fields and, at the time of writing (July 2001), more are being reported in the fields of Wiltshire, Britain. While some circles have been proven to be hoaxes, it seems most unlikely that they all are. These circles can, in fact, appear in any vegetation, in any part of the world, but they seem to be most frequent in a crop that is about to be harvested. What do you think might cause these circles?

Native Americans have said that these circle-based shapes are the mute earth screaming out to be heard because she is being mistreated and exploited—her resources are not being looked after, her soil is being polluted and over-farmed, her creatures and vegetation are not respected and her air is contaminated. Other explanations have included a spiritual, symbolic message being given to us by extraterrestrials or beings from another dimension. There have also been reports of peculiar machines being spotted making the circles.

Crop circles are not a modern phenomenon; in the past they were often attributed to the Faeries. Scientific explanations have included localized whirlwinds or magnetic forces. As far as I am aware, no scientific explanation is consistently forth-coming to explain the majority of crop circles.

Another explanation is that it is human beings who are doing it, or at least involved in it. Not by making the circles mechani-cally, but through "mind-power." Witches know that mind and matter are really part of the same thing—energy. Many people are consciously seeking completeness in themselves and in their personal lives They are also seeking a true connection with the Cosmos. The crop circles could be the land reacting to the vibes that are unconsciously coming out of these people. After all, the circle is a perfect shape, repre-senting infinity. It's all part of the "wholeness" that we live in. (Funny things start to happen when you strongly feel things. You may notice this in your own life; coincidences, happenings that you can't properly explain cluster, making you wonder whether you are actually influencing them. Of course, witches do this consciously with their spells.) My favorite explanation of crop circles is that indeed the minds of people are in some way influencing the land. Of course, I have no proof, and I could be wrong. Maybe you have another, better theory. Is there some way you could test it out?

You can go into a crop circle with the intention of experienc-ing it in the same way you went into the wheat field. If you can get to the circle before it has been trampled down by tourists (and before the farmer has started to sell tickets!), you may sense certain things. Some people have slept out in these circles and had strange dreams. If it's possible, you may like to

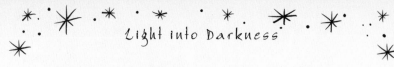

camp out with some friends in one and see what happens. You could also dowse the circle.

Dowsing

Most people know about dowsing as an old way to find water—dowsers are also called "water diviners." The ability to dowse is actually an occult art, but because it has been so tried-and-tested, it has become accepted as a quaint old custom or skill. It is, of course, but it is also more than that. Dowsing implies that we can detect things through senses other than our five "normal" ones.

Traditionally, dowsing was performed with a forked hazel-wood stick, which twitches uncontrollably when the dowser holds it over water. However, you can dowse with such other objects as a rod or pendulum, and you can dowse for almost anything, not just water. And almost anyone can dowse. Like everything else, it is a skill that you can learn and develop, although some people have a greater aptitude for dowsing than others do. Things you can dowse for include water, mineral deposits, lost objects, energy lines, historical remains, and much, much more. You can use a pendulum to dowse food to see if it is good for you. You can dowse a house before you move in to see if it may be a suitable home. You can dowse your garden to discover the best place to plant a new shrub. The list is endless.

Dowsing starts by developing a "relationship" with your dowsing tool. You can buy dowsing rods in many New Age stores but it's fairly easy to make your own with wire from cut coat hangers. You need two rods, each bent at a right angle, one end about 5 inches—long enough to hold in your fist—and the other about 12 inches in length. An easier alternative is a pendulum, which could be an attractive crystal dangling on the end of a chain or a bit of stone on a string—whatever you like.

This is the most important part: you need to "program" your tool. This means you need to decide what means "yes" and what means "no" so that you can ask questions. You can do this either by asking "show me yes" and "show me no," or by saying "counterclockwise is no" or "swinging outward is no" and then testing your tool by holding it over something you know about and asking a question. For instance, you could hold the rods/pendulum over your bed knowing that your purse is in the far corner of the room and say, "Is my purse here?" It may take quite a lot of practice to feel confident about dowsing and you may discover things for yourself that I haven't mentioned. This is because you are developing the skill in your own way.

How you hold the rods and pendulum is important. The rods should be held lightly in your fist so the longer length projects straight ahead of you. Keep your upper arms close to your body and hold the rods at just below shoulder height. Believe me, those rods will move! Many dowsers are very happy to acknowledge that they are moving the rods or pendulum because they say the tool is only a focus and that the "sensing" is coming from their subconscious minds. However, I do not see how a rod can be made to spin like that in a sweaty fist! In the case of the pendulum, it is actually quite hard not to make it move while you are holding it. Many dowsers actually set it swinging backward and forward and then see whether it moves clockwise or counterclockwise. Take plenty of time to practice until you feel familiar with your tool.

When you feel comfortable, you can start visiting ancient sites. It can be pleasant just to wander, rods pointing forward, just to see the places where they move and speculate about them. But that is rather confusing! If you are interested in a site you may want to find out some facts about it and then dowse for more information. In the case of a crop circle, you may want to ask whether there are energy spirals there, which way they are going, whether they are human-originated, whether they are extraterrestrial, whether there is a message to be read there, or anything else you may want to know.

Always remember, there's a learning curve. By no means will everything be clear-cut. Also bear in mind that you may not

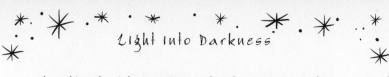

be asking the right questions or that the answers may be something that we cannot quite understand at present. As you continue to dowse you will find that your intuition sharpens as a result. Some dowsers dispense with the tool altogether because their senses become so finely developed that they decide to cut out the middle man. A good thing about dowsing is that you can actually see that something is happening, which increases your faith and your confidence.

What if the rods or pendulum just don't move? This isn't likely, but if so, have patience and relax! They will eventually!

Making a corn dolly

Because we witches are in a distinct minority, there can be no harm in cutting a few spikes (or ears) of wheat to make a corn dolly! The field can spare a small sheaf. Cut some carefully and take them home with you, offering thanks to the land as you take them. If you see the farmer, you should ask him first, of course.

If you are very artistic and creative you can twist your bunch into a real dolly shape. Dress it in dolls' clothes, preferably red, and make a head, arms and legs from the wheat to poke out of the little dress. If you aren't artsy-craftsy (or can't be bothered!) tie up a small bunch in a red ribbon. You will probably be pleased with the look of it, whatever you do, because it will look very traditional and pagan. The corn dolly should now be placed over the hearth. In modern homes, this may well be the stove—put it somewhere where family life is at its warmest and liveliest. Ask your mom where might be best—you may need to explain to her what it represents. If you prefer, put your corn dolly in a special place in your own room. Next spring, take the little dolly and bury her in the good earth, leaving room for you to make another next Lughnasadh.

If you can't get to a field, it is possible to buy wheat spikes at craft stores. Alternatively, you could try picking wild grasses and using them instead.

Moving on, letting go

We all like to hang on to what is familiar. But life is about change, about developing, and we have to let go of the past in order to make way for something better. As a witch your consciousness is likely to be sharper and because of this you may face more transformations than other people. Take this questionnaire to see how easily you adapt and let go.

1) Your dad has been promoted and you are moving to a bigger house in a better area. How do you react? a) with dismay. You can't bear the thought of leaving your familiar house. You run up to your room and lie on the bed crying; b) you feel uneasy—will your friends come the extra distance to see you? How are you going to pack up all your clothes?; c) you feel excited. It will be great to have a bigger house. Perhaps you'll get a bigger allowance, be able to go out more, meet new people.

2) You are very sad because your dog has just died peacefully. So you: a) spend all day crying and looking at photos of old Blackie and you when you were three. How will you ever get over it?; b) you mope around feeling really depressed for a while—perhaps one day you'll get another dog but for now you can't think of it; c) you have a good cry and bury Blackie in the garden. You've chosen some words to say (or made up a little poem). She had a good life and you'll miss her, but you've arranged to see your friends.

3) After all the kissing and the cuddling, the laughter and the promises, s/he doesn't want to go out with you anymore: a) you can't believe s/he really doesn't want to see you. You beg him/her to take you back and keep phoning him/her; b) you go into your shell, hiding under the covers, feeling that your life is over; c) you turn to your friends for support. They come around, do your hair and your nails and drag you out on the town. (Or out to play football, if you're a guy.) It's hard, but you'll get over it.

4) Open your wardrobe—what have you got inside? a) tons of clothes, including an old jacket you had in middle school and

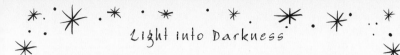

the pants that have been too short in the legs since you were twelve; b) a mess, really, but you push the stuff you don't wear anymore to one side so it doesn't get in the way; c) most of it's cool clothes you bought recently; you can't stand to be out of fashion.

5) What about going out at night? a) you don't go out much— you have a couple of friends who come to your house or you go to theirs; b) you usually just hang out at the corner café, but you do make plans; c) you never know where you'll go from one day to the next.

6) Your school doesn't offer courses in all the subjects you want to study: a) you moan and feel fed up—you just can't be bothered now; b) you think carefully about the options that you do have and where they may lead, and you make your choices accordingly; c) you are determined to do what you want so you talk to your parents about moving to another school.

7) When you go out for a meal, how do you choose from the menu? a) you always have more or less the same thing because you know you'll enjoy it; b) you have several favorites, but there are some things you've never tried; c) you'll try almost anything—calamari, escargots, yak's yogurt—because you might find something really delicious.

8) You feel attracted to witchcraft because: a) it has a really familiar feel and you like to think you're connected to something people did years ago; b) it's traditional but somehow new as well, making you feel both excited and comfortable; c) you love the feeling that anything's possible and that you may discover new powers, new ways of looking at things.

Your score

Mostly a's. You're a sensitive person and you are often rather afraid of life. This could be because you have had some knocks and hurts so you cling all the more to what is familiar. This isn't bad. It could mean that you are an emotional, understanding person who fully realizes all the dangers out there. But you are being negative! Follow the wheel of the year, the turning of the seasons and get in touch with the Goddess. Then you will know that however much things change they are still essentially the same. You are held safe in the undying Cosmos and you will always be home.

Mostly b's. You're a mixture. You rather like the idea of new things but you don't want to let go of the old. You need to learn how to pick and choose, to decide what is best for you and leave the rest. Sometimes you have to let go, and sometimes it is right to hang on. Try to realize the difference and if you hang on do so for the right reasons, not for Auld Lang Syne. As you follow the wheel of the year, let Nature guide your choices and help you to listen to that knowing voice that comes from within.

Mostly c's. You are enthusiastic about new things and don't care about what happened yesterday. What's done is done and if there's half a chance that the next thing will be better, you go for it. This is great because you have a positive attitude, but there are two possible problems. First, be careful you don't throw the potatoes out with the peelings—just because something's old hat doesn't mean it's not worth anything. Secondly, remember that everyone needs to mourn when things pass. Not to do so may mean that you are denying your feelings of loss and so any moving forward is more apparent than real because there is nothing happening inside. Let the wheel of the year put you in tune with gentle nostalgia. Take the time to mourn when summer passes—it will make Yuletide go with an even bigger swing!

Shell pots

Collect shells when you are on vacation and use them to decorate plant pots. All you need are enough shells, some glue and a small pot. Coat the pot with the glue and press the shells onto it. Try to fit them around cleverly so there are no spaces. Buy some compost and plants to go in them to make attractive presents, or keep them on your own windowsill as a reminder of sunny days—for, in a way, the shells are your "harvest."

Recipe:

bread

Bread-making is the obvious recipe for Lughnasadh because the harvested wheat immediately comes back to life in the loaf. Ask mom if you can borrow the kitchen for an afternoon during the holidays. Kneading the dough can also be part of a simple spell. As your fingers press and probe, imagine that you are sending love and healing out into the world. This will grow and rise as the yeast works.

This recipe gives the amounts for a small loaf so you will need a 1 lb loaf pan. Grease this generously inside using a piece of wax paper dabbed with vegetable oil. Cover the grease with a coating of flour so the loaf will come out easily when done.

Ingredients

12 oz flour (preferably organic white flour because it is easier to work with than whole wheat, which can be sticky); 1/2 a level tablespoon of salt; 1/2 oz shortening or butter; 1 teaspoon dried yeast; half teaspoon of sugar; 3/4 cup warm water.

Method

Sift the flour and salt together and rub in the shortening or butter lightly with your fingertips. Dissolve the sugar in the water and sprinkle on the dried yeast. Leave this in a warm place (such as under a slightly warm grill—never use a microwave) until it looks frothy like a half-pint of beer. This will take about ten minutes.

Now, using a wooden spoon, mix the yeast mixture with the flour, then bind it together with your fingers. Knead it gently until it is bound together and the bowl is clean—add just a little flour if you need to. Now put the dough on a floured board and stretch it, fold it and knead it for another ten minutes.

Shape the dough into a ball, replace it in the bowl, cover it with a cloth and put it back in a warm place until it has doubled in size. This should take about an hour. When it has risen nicely punch it down again, kneading, stretching, folding.

(This is what they did in the olden days when there were no such things as supermarkets, sliced loaves or breadmakers, and it has a timeless feeling. In working with the yeast you are actually working with something that is alive. You may like to imagine that you are in a cottage kitchen, 200 years ago, working with flour grown on the land outside your window. In those days, things went at their own pace—the yeast rose, the oven heated slowly, the light began to fade and the candles were lit. There was less rush and struggle and more acceptance because Nature was close at hand. But you might get bored with this and want to listen to music while you're working.)

After ten minutes, place the dough into a greased pan, cover it with a cloth, put it back in the warm place for another 40 minutes or so until the dough rises above the top of the pan.

Bake it in a hot oven for about half an hour. When it's cool, cut it to share with family and friends—it will probably taste so good that all you'll need is some butter. Keep some for your ritual.

Lughnasadh ritual

You will need some ears (spikes) of wheat, red ribbon, gold thread and bread (hopefully that you have made), in addition to your usual ritual requirements. Incense can include frankincense, patchouli and thyme.

Try to get your spikes from a nearby field, but if you can't do this you can get them in craft stores, which make a good substitute to work with. Failing this, you could use grass or any other crop, although some things don't keep as well. If you are using something that is going to decay (wheat spikes keep all year), then bury it outside and be sure you use cotton ribbon so it will decompose.

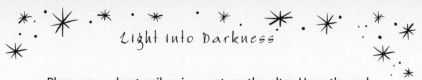

Place your wheat spikes in a pot on the altar. Have the red ribbon and bread close by. You can use red candles (for poppies), green (for the earth) or gold/honey-color (for the wheat) to resemble the earth's bounty. Cast your circle as usual. Consecrate the wheat by forming a pentagram over it with your athame and do the same with the bread. Cut the wheat spikes in groups of three, saying, "I harvest the bounty of the great Mother. Blessed be." Now sit before your altar and bind the wheat into bunches of three with the red ribbon. Make one for yourself, one for your family and as many of your friends as you can, or wish to. Make sure you have at least four spikes left over for the next part of the ritual.

Now harvest four spikes and tie them with lengths of gold thread, long enough to stretch from the center of your circle to the edge. You may like to dance to raise power before the next part. When you are ready, place the wheat at each of the four quarters and sit facing North. Take hold of the end of the gold thread attached to the Northern wheat and start to pull it toward you very slowly, saying, "By the bounty of the Great Mother I call my harvest home." Repeat this over and over again as you slowly pull the wheat toward you. List all the things you would like that are associated with that particular quarter—for instance, in the case of North you may ask for security, material things, blessings for the garden, and so on. Do the same with the East, South and West. When this is complete, bind the gold threads around the spikes, making a bunch, saying, "I bind this spell." Keep this bunch together, placed somewhere safe on your permanent altar or in your cauldron. (Or bury it, if it won't keep.)

Consecrate some fruit juice and drink in honor of the Great Mother and Horned God. Now take up your bread and break off three pieces. Eat one, offer one later to friends or family and keep the other to bury outside. As you are doing this think about the blessings that are on the land and feel joyful. Dance again when you feel refreshed. When you feel you have raised enough power, send it out of your circle as a general blessing for the earth in thanks for your own harvest.

Next year you can dispose of the corn dollies by burying or burning them, then replacing them with new ones during a new ritual. Keep at least one spike of wheat for the Autumn Equinox ritual.

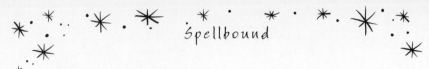

Autumn Equinox

At the Autumn Equinox we enter the most mysterious time of the year. The mist is rising and the days are shrinking, giving way to soft, creeping dusk. The leaves are turning yellow, brown and gold and there are blackberries in the hedges. It may be warm and mellow, but change is in the air. This is the crossover point where day and night are equal all over the world but from now until Yule darkness will be gaining. Not until the Spring Equinox, at the end of March, will light be stronger than darkness once again.

Goddess and God

The Goddess is very much Mother right now; the harvest has been brought in and apples and other fruits are plentiful. At the same time we may feel pleased and thankful that the earth has been so generous; we also know that this is coming to an end and soon the trees and bushes will be bare as winter rides in. Because of this, there is a sadness in the Goddess. She is like a mother saying goodbye to her children, but She is also telling them they must go. She is generous, but She is also the voice saying that everything must change.

The God has departed and gone on His quest to find out more about life in order to show it to us. But of course, Gods and Goddesses are not bound by the usual rules! So just because the God is going down into the Underworld doesn't mean He isn't close by. He is like a shadow near the Goddess, thoughtful and watchful. Both the Goddess and the God are wise and mature, and we can learn from them.

In times of yore

Naturally autumn was an important time, for the storing of the harvest was essential. Grain had to be kept safe and dry while apples and other fruit were preserved so they would not become rotten.

Many years ago in ancient Greece, the Mysteries of Eleusis were celebrated. These rituals centered on the story of Persephone, a maiden Goddess who was abducted by the Lord of the Underworld while she was picking flowers with her friends. Her mother Demeter, the corn Goddess, looked high and low for her beloved child, calling and crying. This went on for many, many months and because Demeter was the Goddess of Nature, the earth was neglected; everything stopped growing and people began to die of famine. The Gods on Olympus decided to take action. It was decided that Persephone should stay in the Underworld as its queen for part of the year, and the other part come back up to be with her mother. This little story was a Greek explanation for the seasons; when Persephone is above ground and re-united with Demeter, the Nature Goddess is delighted—spring comes and summer follows. Then when Persephone has to go down again to the Underworld, Demeter is sad and autumn and winter follow. This story tells us about changes in life, while the "Mysteries" were about accepting these changes and understanding the processes of life and death. They were also about understanding ourselves because the initiates were told "Know thyself."

In England, there are customs, relics of ancient pagan customs, that mark this time of year. One such is the Horn Dance in Abbot's Bromley, held on the first Monday after the Sunday that falls after September 4. Antlers are carried around the streets on poles and imitation stag fights take place. This is the time of year when stags do fight, but the ritual is also about honoring the Horned God, whose power in the world might be waning as the year dies but whose magical power still grows unseen.

The Jewish New Year Rosh Hashanah is also celebrated in September during the New Moon. On the tenth day of the New Moon is Yom Kippur, which is the time when the sins of the community are cast out upon a goat—a "scapegoat"—which is then set free to roam and, thus, cleanse the community. But any time of year can be a time of new beginnings.

Things to do

Serious matters

The new academic year is now underway with its many new demands. You may feel rather overwhelmed, especially if you have just started college, or if you have exams to face. The summer and all the fun and relaxation of vacation is giving way to heavy demands. Try to cope with this by realizing that it's all part of the seasonal cycle and it will pass. Have some early nights and try to prioritize, setting up a homework timetable or such. Remember, Persephone went down into the Underworld—but she came back up. By the time we get to Yule, you'll have a good semester's work under your belt and it'll be time to party again.

Taking stock

Balance is an important theme in your life at present. While it is important to come to grips with the new academic year, it's also important to remember all the other facets of your life. At this inward-turning time take a look at yourself and ask what it is you want to achieve. Are there clubs you want to join, activities you want to be part of, skills you want to learn? Figure out your time commitments and enroll—get involved.

Remember what the priestesses of Eleusis were told—"Know thyself." Do you know yourself? You will naturally change a lot during your life, so getting to know yourself isn't about putting yourself in a box, but rather about finding your direction. You'll naturally be influenced by many things, particularly your parents and your peers. It's quite understandable that they should influence you, but it's also important to be aware of this, not in order to rebel—for it may be right that these people influence you, especially parents, who have your best interests at heart—but to realize exactly what's going on inside you and who you are.

Quickie dough-craft

This is so quick that you don't even need a conventional oven, just a microwave. To make the dough you will need three yogurt cups of plain flour, one yogurt cup of table salt and one yogurt cup of water. Mix the flour and salt thoroughly and slowly add the water. Knead the dough for a few minutes until it is elastic, then roll it into your chosen dough-shape. This can be as imaginative as you like.

For the Equinox, I suggest you make nightlight holders to "cradle" the light as darkness grows. You will need to draw or trace a template in the shape of a star or the Sun, about $3^1/_2$ inches in diameter. Roll out the dough to $^3/_4$ inch thickness. Carefully cut out the shape you have chosen and cut the center to accommodate a nightlight. Make little indentations in the dough for easy baking. Carefully transfer to a microwave plate. Bake the dough at a low temperature for half an hour, then let it rest for two minutes. Bake it another half hour, then again let it rest for two minutes. Bake for 20 minutes on low, let it rest for two minutes, then turn the heat up to medium-low for 15 minutes, let it rest for two, bake again for 15 minutes, let it rest for two again and then bake again for 10 minutes. Now turn the heat up to medium and bake for five minutes, rest it for two and bake it again for five. Let the nightlight holders cool before moving them.

When they have cooled you may decorate them with acrylic paint, and stick gold beads or any other decorations that appeal to you. If making nightlight holders seems too complex, why not just make some dough shapes to paint and hang on a Christmas tree later in the year?

Out and about

These days people are often afraid to eat wild berries, as if the only safe things are cultivated, fertilized, sprayed and generally produced as far from Nature as possible! However, there is nothing like a blackberry picked straight from the bush. If you live near some brambles go out with your friends and pick the berries like people used to do years ago. Avoid bushes that grow along the road, not only because this is a dangerous place to gather berries but because they will have been contaminated by exhaust fumes. As you pick the berries take the time to absorb the gentle and mysterious quality of the season. Even if the sun is quite hot—which it may be—there is still that quality of softness and change in the air. Imagine what it was like hundreds of years ago, gathering food for the cellar, aware of the need to stock up for the coming winter.

Recipe:

blackberry and apple pie

If you like, buy frozen shortcrust pastry for this. Buy enough for an 8 inch pie. Follow the directions on the package regarding defrosting. Grease a suitable dish and cut the pastry in half. Roll it out on a floured board, place it in the dish, gently flatten it and trim it to fit. Place the prepared filling (see below) in the dish, gather the trimmed pastry into a ball with the remaining pastry and roll it out to fit the top. Brush the edges with water and place the pastry lid on top, pressing it down at the sides to seal. Cut a few slits in the top to let the steam escape and brush it with milk. Cook at 400°F for 20 to 25 minutes. Serve with cream or custard.

For the filling you will need enough blackberries to form one layer on the bottom of the dish and two or three apples, peeled, cored and sliced. You will also need between one and three teaspoons of sugar, depending on how sweet you like things and how sweet the fruit is. To prepare the apples stand them so the stem is on top and slice them into four, through the core. Then cut out the core from each segment, peel and chop them. Microwave the apples in a bowl for about two minutes until they go soft. Place the blackberries in the pastry case, then place the softened apples on top, sprinkle with the sugar and put the pastry lid on. As you are filling the pie, fill it also with love for the earth and a special wish for yourself so your pie also becomes a spell. Form a pentagram over it (or cut it into the pastry top) before baking.

You and your friends can enjoy eating this pie knowing that you have been out onto the land to find the fruit and have made your own close contact with Nature. Yummy!

Through the veil

Tradition holds that in autumn the veil between this world and the other is especially thin. Now, as at Samhain, is a time for ghosts, spirits and the people of Faerie. Take some friends with you and go to a grove of ancient trees. Preferably go when it's misty. You are

going in a slightly different spirit than your Midsummer wander, for now the year is turning toward the more eerie and somber season.

Where oak, ash and thorn are found together, the Faeries are traditionally supposed to meet. Don't wear anything made of iron, including jewelry, watches or zippers, and wear a sprig of thyme in a buttonhole. St. John's wort is also good, as are roses and rose petals. However, fresh thyme is easy to buy in supermarkets.

Don't search for Faeries, just look about you in a relaxed way, have a laugh and play around. Remember your pentagram for protection. And if you come back home to find your parents are in an old folks' home and your little brother is old enough to be your dad—we'll just call you Rip Van Winkle!

How happy are you with yourself?

Answer this questionnaire to find out how content you are with yourself and your life.

1) Do you like the course you have chosen? Yes/No/Maybe

2) Are you happy with your friends? Yes/No/Maybe

3) Does your social life satisfy you? Yes/No/Maybe

4) Are you happy with your habits (the time you get up/go to bed, time you spend on grooming, etc.)? Yes/No/Maybe

5) Are you happy with your appearance? Yes/No/Maybe

6) Are you happy with your eating habits? Yes/No/Maybe

7) Do you have the hobbies you would like? Yes/No/Maybe

8) Are you happy with the image you feel you portray? Yes/No/Maybe

9) Do you feel you are on the right route for a career of your choice? Yes/No/Maybe

10) Do you feel you are able to express the real *you* most of the time? Yes/No/Maybe

11) Are you content with the way you spend your spare time? Yes/No/Maybe

12) Do you regularly have a really good laugh? Yes/No/Maybe

13) Are you basically happy with your sexuality (aside from the usual ups and downs)? Yes/No/Maybe

14) Are you generally happy at home? Yes/No/Maybe

Your score

If your answers were mostly "yes," then lucky you—you are a content person and now you know it! If you answered the majority of the questions with "no," then perhaps you need to do something about certain areas of your life to make them work better for you. At least you are aware of this. If you answered mostly with "maybe,"

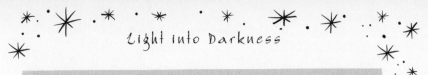

you need to think more about things. It's fine to be uncertain and there is no rush to make up your mind—but keep asking yourself the questions. Knowledge is power to witches, and knowing yourself is some of the greatest power there is. As we said at Imbolc, you can't get what you want unless you know what it is!

Autumn Equinox ritual

Choose candles of blackberry purple, if you can. Decorate your altar with blackberries and any other seasonal produce. Place the spike of wheat you saved from Lughnasadh on a dish and cover it with a dark cloth. Obtain juice and cakes made with berries, if possible. Incense may include frankincense, cypress, bay and patchouli. If you have mixed your own incense, keep some powdered bay leaf separate from the rest to add during your ritual.

Cast your circle as usual. This is a rather sober ritual so sit for a while and meditate as the incense fumes rise. When you are ready, unveil the wheat and, as you look at it, say, "In silence is the seed of wisdom gained." (This is from an ancient rite that came from Eleusis in Greece.) Place your censer in the West and sprinkle upon it some powdered bay and watch as the smoke rises. (Bay was considered an herb that encouraged one to see visions, but you shouldn't find it too strong.) If you feel that you see something in the incense, take note of it. Say, "May my wisdom deepen as the year darkens." Imagine yourself being successful at some mental or insightful task and make another offering of incense. Consecrate your juice and cakes and eat some, saying, "Lady and Lord, I thank you for the bounty of the earth."

When you are ready, blow out all your candles but one, saying, "The year grows dark, the earth grows barren, the Sun retreats, the trees are bare. Let all sleep peacefully until Spring awakens us. Blessed be." Eat and drink some more, move your censer deosil to the East and say, "While the earth rests, let me also feel peace, but let my mind be clear and true and my body strong." Again eat and drink a little. If possible, leave the remaining candle to burn itself out, somewhere safe. Close your ritual when ready. Now you are ready for winter.

Chapter 8

Witch's Moon

We all know that the light of the Moon is witchy and eerie, and that all manner of strange things are supposed to happen during a full Moon. As a witch, moonlight is sure to "do" something to you. However, you may wonder why, or tell yourself this isn't logical. Well, there are some good reasons for thinking the Moon is important. Moonlight is the essence of magick.

Lunar phases

The Moon goes from new to full, then wanes and disappears, only to reappear again a few days later, all sharp, shiny and new. Is there anything else you can think of in Nature that does this over and over again, unfailingly, changing all the time yet always the same? There is nothing quite like the Moon. Her phases taught primitive people that because something went away, it didn't mean it was gone for good. So it could well have been the Moon that taught us to think in the abstract and to hold an idea in our minds even when the thing that had given rise to this idea was gone. Deep in our unconscious we remember this teacher and love her.

When the Moon is full, she looks like a luminous opal on a purple velvet cushion, or a great glistening egg, or a silver ball for a fairy princess or any of the other poetical things we can say. But when we look up and see her, we actually know that she's just a lump of barren rock, reflecting the light of the Sun. So doesn't that kill the magic? It shouldn't. Because the phases of the Moon reflect (literally) the ever-changing relationship between the Sun, Moon and Earth, these fluctuating energies have a profound effect on our lives. Ancient structures like Stonehenge and Avebury were built to mark this cycle. Many present-day thinkers and scientists have observed connections between the cycle of the Moon and events on Earth. But actually we don't need anything or anyone to tell us about the Moon because she tells her own story, straight to our instincts.

The Moon takes about twenty-nine-and-a half days to make her journey from one new Moon to the next. She only takes about twenty-eight days to get back to the same point in the zodiac—so it only takes her twenty-eight days to move from the beginning of the sign Aries all the way around and back to the beginning again. However, in that time the Sun has moved also—or rather, the Sun appears to have moved because the Earth is moving through space. That means that the Sun has moved on one sign of the zodiac and it takes longer for the Moon to catch up—so the cycle from new Moon to new Moon is longer than the cycle from Aries back to Aries. We shall be looking at the phases of the Moon in this chapter, but it is interesting to note that the Moon makes thirteen journeys around the zodiac while the Sun makes one—13 x 28 = 364, and there are 365 days in the year. This is one of the reasons why thirteen is taken to be a witchy number.

You can see the new Moon in the sky in the early evening. If you look up, hold up your right hand and curve your palm you'll see that the new Moon fits into your right hand. (If you live in the Southern Hemisphere it will be your left hand that cups her.) As the Moon waxes she gets up later and later and grows fatter and fatter until she's at the top of the sky at midnight, when she is full—that is when the Sun and Moon are opposite each other and the Earth is in the middle. Then she starts to wane and is only seen in the early hours of the morning, when you can cup her in your left hand (or in your right if you live in the Southern Hemisphere). Gradually she gets closer and closer to the Sun, and thinner and thinner, until she disappears, when she's in what is called the dark of the Moon. This lasts for about three days and isn't a time recommended for most magick. Soon she is seen again in the evening sky. Lunar phases are the same all over the Earth—if it is a full Moon in the U.S., it's also full in Australia.

Eclipses occur during new and full Moons. When the Moon is full, the Sun, Earth and Moon are in line, with the Earth in the middle. Because of the enormous distances involved, the Earth is usually off-center. An eclipse of the Moon occurs when the Earth is exactly in the middle because it gets in the way of the sunlight. During a lunar eclipse, the Moon turns the color of dark blood. Eclipses used to frighten ancient people, and even today astrologers are wary of eclipses because the energies then are sometimes difficult to handle.

An eclipse of the Sun was even scarier in ancient times. An eclipse of the Sun occurs when the Sun, Moon and Earth are in line, with the Moon in the middle during a new Moon. Because the Moon is smaller, solar eclipses are rarely complete. (There was one in the year 2000.) They are quite spectacular. Many years ago it was thought that a solar eclipse would mean the king was going to die because of his direct link to the Sun. Nowadays we have abandoned this particular belief, but astrologers observe that eclipses do have an effect. This may become evident in places where the eclipse was total, and where the point of the eclipse in the zodiac makes a contact in the chart of the country concerned. For instance, if the Sun and the Moon are in 20 degrees of the sign Libra at the time of the eclipse, and Saturn was in 20 degrees of Libra when the constitution of the country came into being, then there could be upheavals in the government, earthquakes or other natural disasters.

Aside from eclipses, the phases of the Moon have been shown to have an effect at other phases. During the full Moon there are more births, accidents and hemorrhages on the operating table. This is confirmed by some surveys and by policemen and midwives who are in the front line. Other surveys and scientists disagree. Do you think the Moon has an effect? It is one of those things about which you can make up your own mind and perhaps do a little research. At full Moon things tend to come to a head, fraught situations explode, energies are high—or you may feel suddenly completely exhausted if you have been overdoing it.

There are other points about moonlight. For instance, the pale light of the Moon reveals certain things while hiding others. You could see a candle flame in moonlight but on a sunlit beach you

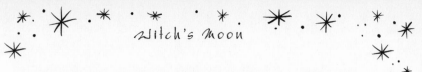

could burn your arm and not realize immediately why. Also, when the light of the Moon is at its brightest, the chemicals in the brain are in the best condition for psychic experiences.

Moon meanings

Witches know that what we see in the world around us has meaning because everything is part of the Goddess and carries Her wisdom. In the Stone Age, people took the phases of the Moon to mean that they too would come back after death, to be reborn either in this life or the next. The Moon also tells us that other things are important besides what we think about and reason with in our conscious minds—because the light of consciousness is symbolized by the Sun. The phases of the Moon have been important for many thousands of years, and notches to mark these have been found on artifacts made 20,000 years ago. In the development of human thought, the Moon has been very important, and she has given her name to many words, such as measurement, dimension, month and many others. These words are often about marking the passage of time, or the extent of something.

Not surprisingly, the Moon has given rise to many myths and stories, and Gods and Goddesses have been linked to her. Witches these days link the Moon especially to the Goddess, as the Sun is linked to the God. The cycle of the Moon ties in with the menstrual cycle, and to some the Moon just looks more feminine! The fact that the Moon reflects light rather than having any light of her own, and that she just isn't as bright as the Sun, echoes the position women have held throughout recent history as rather inferior beings. Of course, we now know that this isn't the case and many feminist witches are a bit unhappy about the Moon being feminine and the Sun being masculine. However, many ancient cultures believed the reverse was the case and thus had lots of Moon Gods.

In reality, you can think of things every which way—or every witch way! For instance, just because the Moon reflects the light of the Sun doesn't mean she isn't as necessary—she is just gentler. The Sun gives life, it is true, but the Moon is in a way the counterpart of the Earth—her sister in the sky, and we all know there would be no life without Mother Earth. The moonlight teaches us things about our inner selves that are as necessary for our spiritual growth as sunlight is for our physical growth. You can see both or either in each, if you wish, and neither is better than the other.

But for now let us think of the beautiful, shining jewel-like Moon as being feminine, and being a sign of the Goddess. You have probably heard of the three phases of womanhood—Maiden, Mother and Crone—and these are reflected in the lunar phases, waxing, full and waning. Many ancient Goddesses had three different aspects to them or came in collections of three, or three-times-three (such as the nine muses). The concept of Maiden, Mother and Crone is a nice one because it gives dignity, loveliness and power to womanliness during every time of life. It is sad in our culture that we don't really respect the elderly and that women feel worthless when they lose their youthful looks and sex appeal. In fact, it is sad that older women think of themselves as having lost their sex appeal because it shouldn't depend on smooth skin. For a woman to feel she's only desirable when conforming to some stereotype isn't good for morale! The Goddess is lovable in all Her aspects.

The Maiden

The Maiden is the fresh, youthful, energetic and exciting aspect of womanhood. You can readily link her with that zingy crescent you see in the sky when it is still tinged pink with the sunset. Today the Maiden dresses in hip clothes, probably has a ring in her navel, tattoos in important places and likes riding motorcycles! She is the breath of young womanhood and she is living proof of the old meaning of the word "virgin." As we've already seen, despite what many of us have been led to believe, the word "virgin" originally didn't mean a woman who had never had sex, but rather a woman who wasn't owned by a man, although she might have chosen to be sexually active. Sex is a gift of the Goddess and to Her there is nothing "purer" or "more spiritual" about a woman who hasn't ever had it, unless that's what she has chosen for herself. The Maiden respects herself, and her body is her temple. If she has sex, it is safe sex, and she makes sure she doesn't get pregnant. She is fit and powerful and knows how to take care of herself. She is an inspiration to young women. Maiden Goddesses include Diana, Artemis, Athena, Eostre and Persephone.

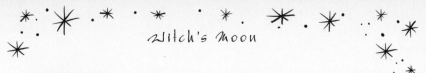

The Mother

The Mother is the most loved aspect of the Goddess, and it's easy to link the glowing sphere of full Moon to the rounded pregnant belly of a mother! (However, the full Moon is a time when all aspects of the Goddess are powerfully present, the three-in-one.) The Mother is actually the most acceptable aspect of womanhood in our culture—not that she has any status, however, especially if she is single! But it is generally felt to be "good" and "worthwhile" to be a mother, while fatherhood makes less difference to the status and respectability of men. There are still these sexist attitudes about!

The Mother is the gentle, nurturing aspect of the Goddess. We can picture her with a baby in her arms. These days she is present in many guises. She is in the young, single mom, struggling to bring up her children on her own; in the woman with a partner, fortunate enough to be able to be at home with her young children most of the time; in the mother who is also a professional, trying hard to be creative and effectual in several areas at once; and even in the woman who has no children and devotes her creativity to other pursuits. (It would be a sadder world without childless women bringing their feminine energies to bear in other spheres.) The Mother is conscious of her creativity and what she has to give. Goddesses who are considered mothers include Demeter, Freya and Hera.

The Crone

The Crone aspect of the Goddess is often regarded with dislike and even fear. The tired, waning crescent that gets lost in the dawn sky is not unlike an old woman. The Crone has had very bad press in fairy tales as the wicked witch who devours children, and who has long, bony fingers and a nose to match! The Crone isn't really the cuddly Nanny that looks after the grandchildren. Although they have some things in common, she is really an older version of the Mother. The true Crone knows a thing or two about life and can be a bit scary because she always seems to sense what is going on and what will happen in the future. This aspect of womanhood was deeply feared in days of yore and is one of the reasons that witches were persecuted. She was a threat to masculine power because she didn't try to please, seduce or nurture—she just knew what was what! The

Crone is a wise-woman and a healer. She has seen so much of life and she knows there are things beyond. Goddesses who are especially Crones were Hecate, Hsi Wang Mu (the Queen Mother of the West in Chinese myth, who gave out wisdom and rewards to heroes), Nokomis and Sheila-na-Gig, the hag with the open vulva whom you occasionally see in stonework on old churches (the masons knew a thing or two not found in the Bible!).

The fourth aspect (and more)

Actually there is a fourth and deeply mysterious aspect of the Goddess that corresponds to the Dark Moon. She is the Goddess Present and Unseen. She is a shadowy figure and it is hard to describe her except to say that while the Crone stands close to the Mystery, this Goddess is the Mystery itself. She is the point of change where death becomes rebirth and she is the very pulse of life. Many Goddesses are linked to her in their stories. Certain Goddesses are also complete—that is, they incorporate all Goddess aspects within their persona and mythology. A good example is the Egyptian Goddess Isis, who appears as a joyful maiden, a Queen, a sorrowing widow and a guardian of the mysteries! This last aspect is how the phases of the Moon link with the Goddess.

As for Gods, today witches usually link their changing aspects to the Sun. Gods linked to the Moon do not seem as welded to the Moon's cyclical aspect. Egyptian Thoth was a Moon God, and very wise. Also it was believed that the Moon was the "other husband" of women, responsible for making them pregnant. We all know about the man in the Moon, do we not?

Menstruation

A woman's periods follow the same cycle as the Moon. Studies have shown that some women's periods tie in with the waxing and waning phases of the Moon. Many girls ovulate at full Moon. (Ovulation is when your ovaries release the eggs that would need to be fertilized for you to become pregnant.) At this time you probably feel very sexy and want to wear more revealing clothes, go partying and dance the night away, attract boys and possibly have sex. Actually you are sending out chemical messages called "pheromones" that heighten your sex appeal. It's Nature's way of ensuring that the species carries on.

When you have your period you may feel moody and prefer to be on your own, especially if you have cramps. You feel irritable and none of the things in life that you enjoy or do well seem quite as appealing or go as smoothly. You feel out of tune with life and you may call your period "the curse."

Throughout the month your hormones are rising and falling, rather like the tides. The tides, of course, are also ruled by the Moon. It is worth studying how your periods correspond with the Moon. Even if you don't have a 28- or 29-day cycle (and many girls don't), it may be possible to see how the Moon affects you. For instance, a girl who has a 40-day cycle may find that her period comes early or late if it is due close to the new or full Moon, "pulled" toward the peak or end of the cycle. Many girls do ovulate at the full Moon (this is called the "mother cycle"), while others menstruate at the new Moon (this is called the "wise-woman cycle"). If your periods are variable you can take note of any differences between a period at new Moon and one at full Moon.

It is a good idea to keep a menstrual diary, charting your periods, linking them with the Moon, noting your dreams, how well you remember them, how they vary, what they are about. Note also your moods and feelings, your sex drive, your powers of concentration, and so on. Draw pictures if you like, write poems, and jot down what music, colors and pictures express your feelings. This all helps you to get to know yourself better.

What does all this have to do with being a witch? Well, menstruation may have a considerable effect on you because during different times of the month you are likely to be more instinctual and magickal, or magickal in different ways. When you are having your period and feeling out of sorts with the world you could be at your most powerful as a witch, the most in tune with unseen forces. In tribal societies women were kept away from everyone when they had their periods. This was assumed to be because they were unclean, but farther back in time it was more likely that they were feared then because they were extra-powerful. During those days women were more likely to be powerful shamans, able to travel into the spirit world for the good of the tribe.

The good thing about being a woman is that we have the opportunity throughout the month to experience the many different sides of ourselves. When we have a period we may feel bad because we are expected to participate in normal activities that don't feel right to us at the time. Maybe it would be better to wander off into the woods and make magick, dance, dream, curl up in peace and quiet, talk to other women and not conform to anything rigid or disciplined. Part of the reason we often find our periods so difficult and such a pain—in more ways than one—is that our society doesn't have a place for this sort of thing. Everyone has to keep to schedules and times and do the same thing day after day, like going to school, taking exams or even doing housework. Perhaps that is a "man thing" and women are better off working harder at certain times of the month, while winding down at others.

So don't call your periods by any nasty names. They are an opportunity to discover the instinctual side of your nature, and the flow of rich blood shows you are truly a fertile, creative woman. Start to chart your periods, flow with your inner tides and you will grow in wisdom, self-knowledge and witch-womanliness.

So what about the guys? From feeling only too pleased that you never have to be "inconvenienced," you may now feel there is something in it! Well, you too can experience the wonders of cycles by studying the Moon. Your cycles will not be as obvious as a girl's, and because of your masculine mind-set it is unlikely that you will be very aware of your body. However, your vitality and energy do ebb and flow and you may indeed discover that they are affected by the Moon. By watching for this, you also may find there are times in the month when you feel more aware of the Otherworld and magickal reality. You may hate to realize this, but you will also be affected by your mother's cycle if you live at home, and your sister's (which will probably tie in with your mom's because women who live together often have their periods at the same time). If you live with your partner, her cycle will certainly affect you and not just because you have to cope with her moods! Learn to flow with the cycle, adjust your responses to hers, try to tune in and you could discover lots about your magickal self. You will also be a lot wiser than the other guys, more like the tribal leaders of yore who were guided by their wise-women and priestesses.

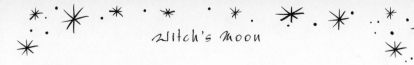

Magick and the Moon

Besides initiating us to the wonders of cycles and mirroring our own bodies, the Moon governs the times for magick. When the Moon is waxing it's the best time for most kinds of magick, as well as anything that is about positive growth, achievement and making things better. The Full Moon is also a good time because it is a psychic "peak." When the Moon is waning it's a good time for spells that are about banishing or decreasing something.

The Moon can turn the way you live into a "spell" if you observe her because activities flow better when timed by the Moon. As a witch, it is very important that you become aware of the Moon and her effects. You should certainly work through several months with the Moon as part of your growing awareness. Phases of the Moon are found in many newspapers, or you can use planetary tables. Some useful books are suggested at the back of the book. Here are some hints.

* When the first sickle of the Moon appears in the sky, just observe her. This time is too fresh, too unstable for anything but plans and ideas—write these down and play with any idea as much as you like.

* When the Moon is about three days old, it's a very good time to start almost anything. Sow seeds, repot houseplants, start rearranging or decorating your room, make contact with all your friends and arrange activities. It's also a good time to get down to work.

* As the Moon gets to her first quarter (she looks like half a sphere now) things may reach a mini-crisis and you realize that some things aren't working so drop them. At this dynamic time, why not get your hair cut or do your nails? This is also a good time to tackle tough jobs. So you could, for example, start your course work in earnest.

* As the full Moon approaches, you can finalize plans for whatever you are doing, and buy new clothes and things for your room. If you love your plants, pay special attention to them now. Pets may be approaching a high-energy time— your dog may want more walks and playtime and your cat

may want to stay out all night. Now is a great time for spells and rites.

* At full Moon you can party on! It's a really good time to go out, but remember that everyone else feels the same and there are more accidents and crime during the full Moon so take extra care. If you feel the urge, work on into the night studying or whatever. You may also try forms of divination now, such as tarot and scrying, as well as spells.

* Just after the full Moon, put the finishing touches on anything you have been doing. This is a good time to plant trees, according to certain lore. Listen to music, do creative things if they appeal to you, and if you've had a fight over something trivial, make up now.

* Now we are coming up to the waning quarter, about 21 days after the new Moon, which is a good time to sort through your things and throw away anything you don't need or give it to charity. Generally think about what you've been doing. Do you want to leave anything behind, or change anything?

* The Moon is getting older and you may feel more tired, less like going out, more like thinking. Don't feel discouraged— this is all part of the cycle. If you want to dry flowers and herbs, now is a good time.

* It's the dark of the Moon again, and a good time to dream and be alone for a bit, even if you are very extroverted. Make endings and clear spaces, emotionally or physically. What do you really want? Make time to discover this and your wish may come to fruition as the Moon waxes again.

Moon spells

As you will see in Chapter 9, all spells are best carried out within a magick circle. However, there are many folk spells associated with the Moon. The Moon is alive and vibrant, she is a tease—she may suddenly appear throwing off her robes of cloud, and just as suddenly disappear again. You may not have time to cast a circle—

if you wait she'll be gone. Everything written in this chapter applies, whether you can see the Moon or not, because her phases are sensed deep inside us. But for some spells it's really great to see her.

It is better to see the new Moon for the first time without glass between you, and it's better to see her over your right shoulder. These are both considered lucky, and as a witch you can take the opportunity to do a quick visualization and make a strong wish for something you need.

A word here about left and right. There was a feeling that the left side was "bad"; the Latin word for left is "sinister"—and we all know what that means! This was probably because most people write and do other precision tasks with the right hand. The conscious mind, which obeys the rules and thinks logically, was considered far superior to the more instinctual part that perceives patterns, follows the laws of nature and is more psychic. However, because the nerve pathways cross over, the right side of the brain rules the left side of the body. So, when you look over your right shoulder you are actually saluting your more instinctual right brain. Everything has the seeds of its opposite within it!

When you see the new Moon, a good spell to make your money increase is to turn over the money in your wallet, purse or pocket, especially the silver coins—silver is linked to the Moon.

When you first see the new Moon, stand on soft ground (not on a tarmac or concrete) and bow three times, or turn around three times, and make a wish.

At the first sight of the new Moon, before saying anything, kiss the first person of the opposite sex that you see—this will bring you a gift within the month.

If you want to know about finding a boyfriend or girlfriend, look at the new Moon over that right shoulder (again) and say:

New Moon, New Moon, tell me true,
When, where, what and who,
New Moon, New Moon, shining clear,
Show my new love, drawing near.

Then take a note of your dreams the following night—they should have a message for you about a relationship that is coming.

If you feel things or people are getting you down and you feel emotionally and mentally "dirty," then the full Moon is a good time to cleanse yourself and your surroundings. If you have a cauldron, fill it with clean water. If not, fill an ordinary bowl. Wash your hands with water containing a little salt or lavender oil, and cast your circle around your room. Now take three lemons, peel them over the water (with your white-handled knife, if you have one) and drop the peel into the water. Now wring out the juice from the lemons into the water and rinse your hands in the water. Stir your cauldron with your wand, if you have one, and if you can get the moonlight to fall onto the water that would be wonderful. Scoop up a little of the water into your chalice, hold it up to the Moon if you can see her, or to your altar if you can't, and say, "Bright Moon, lend me your power." Drink just a little of the mixture (it will be sour!) and say, "May I be cleansed within and without." Take a clean white cloth and carefully wipe over the window and doors of your room and anywhere else you might like to cleanse, such as your headboard, mirror or armoire. You don't need to use the water to cleanse visibly—the acid in the lemons will mark some surfaces so just dab a tiny bit where it won't be noticed—it will have the same effect. Sprinkle some water around your room and wash your feet in it also, if you like. When you have finished, empty your cauldron or bowl in the garden.

Full Moon ritual

Lunar rituals are called "esbats" and may be carried out at any lunar phase. However, the full Moon is traditionally the best time.

The idea of this ritual is to honor the Goddess in all Her forms, but especially as Mother, and to spread Her blessing—for as a witch you are Her priest/ess. It is also the time to bring blessings into your own life.

In addition to the usual magickal tools, you will need a silver dish (or use a white plate if you can't find one), some seeds and/or grated lemon peel for this ritual. The seeds can be some you really intend to plant or they can just be used for the symbolism. Lemon is ruled by the Moon (this means it has long been thought to be connected to it). Other herbs ruled by the Moon are coconut, lemon

balm, myrrh, calamus and willow. You can use any of these if you wish, but you may find lemons easier to come by. Organic lemons from a local or known supplier are by far the best. Poppy seeds are a good choice for the seeds. Also have a piece of white crystal, pearl or moonstone small enough to hold in your hand, or you could use a silver coin or ring that you have cleansed and use only for ritual. A white pebble would also do. For your celebration you could use white grapes, white bread, cheese, white cookies and white grape juice or milk—or even a banana milkshake! You will also need some water for your cauldron or bowl.

Cast your circle in the usual way. If you can, play music in your room. Choose it with special care—it should be gentle but wild, with a low, insistent rhythm. Stravinsky's *Rite of Spring*, some New Age music such as that by Tim Wheater or Carolyn Hillyer or some of Enya's songs are my suggestions, but anything that makes you feel right is fine. Use white or silver candles. Let the moonlight stream in the room if you can (but watch for people being able to see in through your window), and dance to raise power, flowing deosil around your circle.

Place the seeds or herbs on the dish and hold it up to the Moon or over your altar. Say, "Great Mother, Shining One, Lady of the wide sky, Lady of the Secret Heart, bless these seeds with your power. Let them bring fertility and richness to the land and peace and joy to all living things."

Form a pentagram over the seeds with your wand or finger. Keep them now to one side and after your ritual scatter them out on the garden or in the park.

Now take up your piece of crystal and drop it into your cauldron. As the ripples fade, form a pentagram with your wand over the water. Let moonlight fall upon the water if you can. Sit and look into the water and dream. Imagine yourself in a moonlit woodland. Who, or what, comes to share your ritual? Do they have a message for you? For the Maiden make a wish for yourself, for the Mother choose a wish for a friend or family member, for the Crone choose a wish for the world. Dance around the cauldron, and as you name each wish out loud give the water three stirs, deosil, with your wand. Wrap

your crystal, pebble, ring or coin in a soft black cloth and only use it when you need to call upon the power of the full Moon. Pour the water outside afterward.

Consecrate your food and drink with your athame, forming a pentagram over them. Imagine the Great Mother and the Horned God standing over you, smiling at you, their witch and priest/ess. Say, "I eat and drink in honor of the Old Ones. May my heart be filled with love and magick." Eat and drink until you're full, but keep a little to scatter outside with the water and the seeds. Close your ritual when ready.

Chapter 9

Spells

It is easy to find books filled with loads and loads of spells—gypsy spells, folk spells, simple spells using only a few props and complex spells that require things that are not very easy to come by, such as mandrake root. What most of these books fail to tell you is that for spells to be effective they need preparation and thought. Also, no spell should be done lightly—as opposed to lightheartedly, which is a different matter. As you get used to doing spells you will develop the knack of knowing how to approach them. Here are the rules for approaching your spells.

✳ Be careful what you wish for—you'll get it! Getting rid of it again could be another matter.

✳ As a precaution, it's best to include the words "may it harm none" in all of your spells. And never, ever—no matter how bad, angry, desperate or outraged you feel—do any spell that is intended to affect another person directly. Everything you do comes back to you. The only exceptions to this are healing spells, but even then, if the person hasn't specifically asked to be healed you should send "well-being" rather than asking to heal a specific ailment. Why? Because that bout of flu could be just what someone needs to step back from all the stress they're under, which is better than having a heart attack! If you have been abused, attacked or raped then you are a special case, but any magic for this should be carried out by an experienced coven, not by you alone when you are understandably distraught. Do your magick to shield and

calm yourself and to give power to the proper authorities to bring the person to justice.

✳ Spells are best undertaken in a fully prepared magick circle. Occasionally this isn't possible, and occasionally something impromptu harnesses your first, fresh impulse and is great. But mostly the entire process is better.

✳ Don't talk about your spells. "Know, will, dare and be silent" is the motto.

✳ Don't forget, if you don't get out there and make it happen, your magick will be like driving with the brakes on. Do you want to get accepted into that course? Then work for your exams, and spruce yourself up for the interview. Want a wonderful lover? Get out and meet people.

✳ Magick isn't a band-aid for a sore life. Remember, when you are doing magick it is your will and word that mean everything. What does this mean in the everyday world? If you rarely do what you mean to do, if you're always lying, evading and not bothering, then your subconscious mind is thoroughly programmed for failure. If this is you, your magic needs to work on fixing your determination and effectiveness. Being effective doesn't necessarily mean being totally successful, but it does means applying yourself. And if you choose to withhold the truth from others, never lie to yourself.

✳ In case you have any doubts, it's fine to ask for things for yourself. Nature is always balanced, however. Give and be generous and work magick for those you love and for the earth in general.

✳ Never seek to influence the will or life path of another. For example, it is fine to do a spell to bring love into your life, but not to try to cause a specific person to fall in love with you.

Setting about it

There are four essential but unseen components to your spells.

* Belief: you've heard the expression "faith can move mountains"? Even "belief" is too mild—if you *know* deep inside that your magick will work you are 90 percent of the way there. It can work even if you don't believe, but never use it to prove or disprove something. If you have many doubts, don't try to reason them away as you work—just do your best to banish them, blowing them away like grey clouds. In the end, skeptics often make better witches.

* Concentration is important, but you don't have to sit with your face screwed up! Often concentrating in short bursts will do very well. For as long as possible drive everything from your mind but your goal.

* Power needs to be raised, as we explored in Chapter 4. You can do this with dancing and chanting, or just by building it internally, if you can feel it. Your willpower is also important. Be determined.

* Visualization makes things real, first on the astral planes. If you aren't able to visualize I must admit you are starting with a disadvantage, but all is by no means lost. Use pictures and objects that bring to mind what you want, then tell yourself it is there. Not being able to visualize doesn't mean you aren't "magickal"—it could just be that you aren't a very visual person. Try imagining you hear, smell, taste or touch the thing or purpose.

Step-by-step

Here is your checklist for spells and rituals.

* Think about what you are doing—sleep on it for at least one night if it's important. Is it right for you?

* Your unconscious is literal, like a small child, so be exact. What exactly do you mean by "do well in your exam"? If you want money, be clear—asking for "gold" may get you a bunch of daffodils!

* If you're making up your spell, plan with care. Make a list of what you'll need.

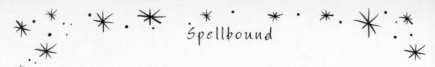

* Choose a time when you won't be interrupted. Check the phase of the Moon, too (see Chapter 8).

* Gather all your bits together—all the usual implements for rituals plus the extras you need for the spell.

* Have a bath or shower, go to the bathroom, then sit peacefully for a minute and relax.

* Cast your circle and invoke the elements.

* If there is a special God or Goddess you would like help from, ask them now for their presence and support.

* Do your spell. State what you intend. Remember—Belief, Concentration, Power and Visualization—but enjoy this part. It's fun.

* Now let go—feel the spell go on its way, like a balloon taking off.

* Say thanks to the Goddess then have a drink of fruit juice in celebration.

* Banish your circle in the usual way and ground yourself.

Making up your own spells

This is easy and by far the best thing, because often the spells given in books or written by other people don't exactly match what you want or are difficult to do for some reason. All you need to remember is that in magick "like attracts like." The Universe is a great big web of connections and many things are on the same strand, like notes that harmonize. There are many notes that harmonize with each other, even ones that are too high or too low for you to hear. So the connection might not be obvious—although you'll probably *feel* it anyway. For example, what sort of spell might involve a red rose, a pink heart and jasmine perfume? I'm sure you guessed right away—a love spell.

This system of links is called "correspondences," and there are several systems. One that is simple but also covers most things is linked to the planets. Here we are only using planets that were known to ancient peoples, for their associations are time-honored.

You should be able to find any goal you want under one heading, or possibly two, in which case you will have to combine.

Here are your correspondences. They will gradually come to be familiar to you. Give yourself time to get acquainted with them. Memorize some of them.

(A word about crystals and precious stones—they all come from the Earth, of course, but so does everything. Thus they are linked to different elements or planets according to color and other properties.)

Sun

Linked to the South of your circle (North, in the Southern Hemisphere), also sometimes with East, and with Fire. Colors (for candles, flowers, cloths, robes, etc.): orange and gold. Animals: cats and lions. Stones: amber, carnelian, tiger's eye, sunstone, diamonds. Plants and herbs: sunflower, bay, cinnamon, frankincense, juniper, orange, rosemary. Use the power of the Sun for spells related to success, creativity, willpower, vitality, feeling fulfilled, succeeding and winning, feeling really healthy, coming out of your shell, being noticed. Gods and Goddesses: Lugh, Apollo, Mithras, Sekhmet, Bast, Bride.

Moon

Linked to the West of your circle, principally, although each of the phases has a link with a different quarter: New Moon with North/Earth, Waxing with East/Air, Full Moon with South/Fire and Waning with West/Water. Colors: white, silver, ivory, sometimes black for the dark Moon and red for the full Moon. Animals: snake, dog, bear, fish, dolphin, wolf. Stones: quartz, moonstone, pearl, aquamarine. Plants and herbs: lemon, lemon balm, myrrh, eucalyptus, coconut, jasmine, willow, poppy seed. Use the power of the Moon for anything to do with home and family, fertility and growing things, gardening, love and sympathy, looking after, caring for, dreams, sound instincts and healing (in the sense of gentle nurture—the Sun is invigorating). Gods and Goddesses: Diana, Artemis, Hecate, Chang-O, Isis, Thoth, possibly Neptune.

A word about lunar phases—it may be confusing that the Moon is linked to the entire circle. The Sun is also, for the eight sabbats celebrate the journey of the Sun and are associated with different points of the circle. You need to be a bit adaptable, use common sense and remember that there are no strict divisions in magick—one thing leads to another. So, although the Moon links with the West/Water quarter for spells involving growth, while the Moon is waxing, you might choose to light a candle in the East, South or Southeast, especially if you can see the Moon. Dreams and intuition, on the other hand, link more with the West. Healing, in the sense of rest or comfort, is West, but increasing vitality would be more South. Don't be afraid to go with your feelings.

Mercury

Linked mostly to East and Air in your circle. Colors: yellow, possibly electric blue. Animals: small swift-flying birds, monkeys. Stones: aventurine, mottled jasper, agate. Plants and herbs: parsley, mace, fennel, lavender, almond, caraway, dill, peppermint. Use Mercury for anything to do with study, the Internet, e-mail, letters, telephone, books, exams, courses, newspapers and magazines, traveling (especially short journeys), communicating, intelligence, lateral thinking, making connections. Gods and Goddesses: Mercury, Hermes, Odin, Bride, Athena, Minerva.

Venus

Venus may be linked to almost any quarter. Use Venus for love in every sense, friendship, pleasure, happiness, compassion and kindness, harmony and unity, creative connections, beauty, youth, joy, parties, outings, making up with someone, clothes, jewelry, make-up. (Friendship could have links with East/Air, passionate love with South/Fire, practical things with North/Earth and compassion with West/Water.) Colors: rose, blue, sometimes green. Animals: doves, swans. Stones: lapis lazuli, turquoise, emerald, coral. Plants and herbs: rose, thyme, ylang-ylang, cardamom, hyacinth, lilac, sweet pea, vanilla, violet. Gods and Goddesses: Venus, Aphrodite, Freya, Oshun, Adonis.

Mars

Linked mostly to South/Fire. Colors: all shades of red. Animals: rams, horses. Stones: bloodstone, garnet, ruby. Plants and herbs: ginger,

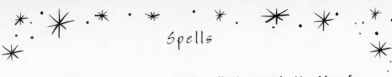

basil, peppermint, cumin, coriander, allspice, nettle. Use Mars for anything that needs courage, assertion and fighting spirit, sport, surgery, passionate love (here it links with Venus), sex, defending yourself, martial arts, protection, banishing. Gods and Goddesses: Mars, Aries, Tyr, Pluto (possibly), Amazons, Valkyries, Morrigan.

Jupiter

Linked mostly to South/Fire but sometimes to other quarters. Colors: purple, wine, magenta and possibly a deep royal blue. Animals: horses, eagles. Stones: amethyst, lepidolite. Plants and herbs: sage, cloves, maple, honeysuckle, nutmeg. Use Jupiter for sheer luck, prosperity, growth, good fortune, philosophy, long-distance travel (especially to study or broaden your outlook), meditation and inspiration, spirituality, being positive, getting fair treatment. Gods and Goddesses: Jupiter, Zeus, Thor, Juno, Kuan-Yin, Hera.

Saturn

Linked mostly to North/Earth. Colors: black, dark brown, very dark green and leaden grey. Animals: goats and animals with horns. Stones: jet, onyx, obsidian, lead, apache tear, coal, salt. Plants and herbs: cypress, comfrey, patchouli, ivy, yew, beetroot. Saturn is very grounding and solid. Use it to bring endings where you have decided they must come, but also to make something last. Grounding, protecting, binding, purifying, fertilizing, making real, solidity, boundaries, preserving, restricting, harvest earned and gathered. Gods and Goddesses: Saturn, Herne/Cernunnos, Maat, Nokomis.

Quick quiz

Now, using your correspondences, devise these two simple spells.

* An herbal sachet to help someone running a marathon.
* A quick spell with a candle and herb/oil to help you with tomorrow's driving test.

Suggested answers are at the end of the chapter.

Some spells to try

A love charm

This is a simple charm to bring love into your life, specifically romantic love.

You will need

A square or circle of rose pink or crimson cloth (choose cloth that doesn't fray), about 4 inches across; about 8 inches of matching ribbon; two or three teaspoonfuls of dried thyme.

What to do

Place the cloth on your altar, or simply face North (if you live in the Northern Hemisphere, South if in the Southern Hemisphere) and place the cloth on the ground before you. Place the thyme in the center of the cloth. Sit quietly for a moment, imagining that you have the love you need in your life. Imagine clearly the sort of person you would like. Take the time to describe him (her) to yourself, his (her) appearance, character, lifestyle, tastes—anything that's important to you. Visualize this for a moment, but be careful not to think about a specific person. Hold your hands, palms downward, over the cloth and send your witch-power into the herbs. Feel it streaming from your palms—they will get warm. Take up your athame and form a pentagram over the herbs, or do this with your index finger if you do not have an athame. Say three times:

Aphrodite, now I pray,
Send my special love my way.

Gather the cloth up carefully so that it makes a small pouch with the herbs inside. Now tie it up with the ribbon. Know that you are tying up your wish and that it's now yours. Give thanks to the Goddess. Keep the little sachet in your purse or pocket and charge it up when you celebrate a festival or full Moon until you get your wish.

To pass an exam

You will need

A yellow candle; some lavender oil; an oil burner; a small piece of mottled jasper or agate.

What to do

Burn the lavender oil in the burner. Cut a small pentagram in the base of the candle with your athame, or use a pin or your fingernail. You may also anoint the candle with the oil. Wait until the scent of the lavender is noticeable. Visualize yourself having passed the exam, and imagine how you will feel and the sense of achievement. Hold up the piece of stone, facing East, the direction of the rising sun. Say three times:

> *Sharp and strong and clear my mind*
> *Success in my......... I find.*
> *(Insert the name of the subject/exam/study)*

Ask for the help of the air spirits, as well as their swiftness and clarity. Imagine the bright rays of the morning sun going into your stone. When you have finished, give thanks. Keep the stone with you when you are studying and during the exam. Light the candle each time you revise or study. If it burns down, consecrate another one until you have taken the exam. Remember, you will need to revise in order to back up your spell.

To keep to a healthier diet

Obviously you should avoid crash or extreme diets because these are unhealthy and in the long run actually make you gain weight because your body immediately goes into a "famine mode" and your metabolism slows down. Besides this, witchcraft is about enjoying life and food is one of its pleasures. However, if you are eating lots of candy bars and chocolates you may want to cut down. It is best to do this spell when the Moon is waning.

You will need

A piece of the food you want to stop eating (there can be several if you wish, and they can be very small); a plant pot; some soil, sand or compost; seven cloves of garlic.

What to do

First lie down and relax. Take your time with this. You may like to listen to some soothing music, or record instructions onto a tape. If you don't like the sound of your own voice, get the help of sweetly spoken friend. Make sure you are deeply relaxed and comfy. Now imagine there is a table laid out with all the foods you know are harmful to you: chocolate bars, candies, cakes, sodas. Really see all the foods. Now imagine all these things being bundled up in the cloth and thrown out. The cloth is spread back on the table and now you imagine all sorts of good food: vegetables, wholegrain bread, fruit, yogurt—make sure that you like the foods that you are putting on the table. Nothing should go there that you don't find delicious. Tell yourself you eat to satisfy your body. You may leave food on your plate, if you wish. You eat slowly, whatever you are doing. You take a small portion of foods that are not healthy and you have had enough. You sensibly eat the good foods and you feel good. Repeat to yourself that you eat sensibly and you feel good.

When you are ready, get up. Put a little of the soil in the pot. Now put the pieces of food in the pot and cover them with the rest of the soil. Place the seven garlic cloves into the top of the soil. Whether the garlic grows or not, it will cleanse you of the wish to eat these foods because they have been returned to the Earth to be neutralized, and the garlic is the seal. Put the pot in the corner of the garden and enjoy your healthy meals.

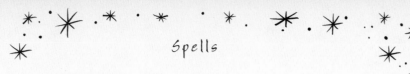

To get rid of anger

Sometimes it is good to be angry. It helps you to speak up for yourself and to insist on fair treatment. Anger should never be suppressed. However, there are times when you may express your anger, have it recognized and even get an apology—but you're still angry! And there are those times when there really is no point being angry because it isn't going to get you anywhere. It's important to be very clear about your anger. Maybe it's a good idea to talk to someone you trust before doing this spell. This spell is to get rid of anger that's only harming you, is pointless and is poisoning your life. Do this spell when the Moon is waning.

You will need

A stone that you can hold in your hand, smooth and dark in color (you may find it lying around, but so much the better if you find it in a stream or dig it up in the garden); a bowl of salt water; washable ink pen; water; lavender oil; rose or ylang-ylang oil; pink rose petals.

What to do

Leave your stone in salt water for 24 hours and allow it to dry naturally. Then hold it in your palm and imagine all your anger running into it. Say:

> *Anger, begone, into the Earth*
> *Blessings to follow, happiness and mirth.*

If you can, write these words upon it with washable ink (it doesn't matter if the writing is all cramped and smeared), then wash them off with the water, to which you added a little lavender oil. Anoint the stone with a little rose or ylang-ylang oil, or wrap it in pink rose petals. Keep it under your pillow until two days after the new Moon—or until you see the new Moon in the sky. Then bury it carefully in a garden, park or wasteland.

To get rid of the blues

This little spell is a good one to do in spring to cheer yourself up.

You will need

A packet of cress seeds; a suitable container for growing the seeds in; water; honey; gold-colored thread; a small pot (such as an empty spice or mustard jar); a picture of the Sun; glue.

What to do

Follow the instructions on the seed packet to sow them. Just sow a few, so you can grow them on your windowsill—you can keep the remainder for another time. Let the little green shoots absorb the Sun. Water them carefully as necessary, saying, "Seeds sprout, seeds grow, away my sorrow, happiness grow." Form a pentagram over them after you have watered them. When the little plants are ready, harvest some and eat them with a little honey, imagining the sunshine entering you. Harvest the rest, tie them in a piece of golden thread, and hang them up to dry. When they are dried, keep them in a little pot. (So much the better if you consecrate the pot first.) Stick a picture of the Sun on the pot. Keep the pot and pick it up and give it a shake if ever you think the blues are coming back.

For protection

This little ritual is a good one to do every so often to keep you safe in all ways. It will help with physical, emotional and psychic protection, but it's not a substitute for common sense.

You will need

An incense made of frankincense/rosemary, cumin/basil and a little patchouli or cypress oil; a thin brown thread (sewing cotton will do).

What to do

When you have cast your circle, started burning the incense and invoked the elements, hold the thread in the incense smoke. Say:

> *By all the powers of sky, land, sea*
> *And all the unseen powers that be,*
> *Safe and sound always keep me.*

Moving deosil, place the thread around you on the floor so that it completely encircles you and overlaps. Starting in the North (or South if you live in the Southern Hemisphere), ask that element for protection, then move around deosil, asking for protection from each element in turn, naming their specific qualities if you like. If you feel you need a specific type of protection, concentrate on the appropriate element (for instance, emotional protection from a lover who is hurting you would be West, physical would be North, gossip East, and another's anger South). Sit in your circle facing your altar and imagine a sphere of golden light around you. Ask the Goddess to bless you and keep your sphere intact when you need it. When you are ready, pick up the thread deosil and keep it in your purse or pocket for added protection.

To stop gossip

Sometimes we feel upset when we think people are talking about us, saying bad things behind our backs. Of course, it's quite possible we imagine things that aren't there or maybe aren't as bad as we think they are.

What you need

Black ink; paper; black thread; rosemary; dried rose petals; dried lavender or lavender oil.

What to do

Write in black ink on a piece of paper: "Lies about me, bad talk about me, all harmful gossip." Roll this up, bind it with black thread and place it in the back of the freezer (or bury it in the garden). Please be very clear that it is the harmful gossip that you want to stop, not any specific person. Follow this by consecrating a mixture of rosemary, dried rose petals and dried lavender (or use lavender oil). Burn this as incense and/or scatter later on the ground outside, saying, "Love peace and healing to me and all concerned."

To find a lost pet

If your dog, cat or other pet has gone missing you may be very upset. This simple spell will either bring your pet home or bring word of him or her, so at least you know what's happened. Take up your pet's favorite toy, or if they don't have one, write their name on a piece of paper. Sit in your circle and repeat, "Monty, (or whatever your pet's name is) come home," three times while holding the toy or paper. Now attach it securely to a long piece of string. After you have banished your circle, dangle the paper or toy out of the window and slowly draw it back inside. Keep it in your pet's favorite sleeping place until you find him or find out what happened to him.

To get rid of an unwanted habit

You will need

Grated rind of two organic lemons; dried sage; rosemary; lavender oil; two cups; boiling water; a drinking straw.

What to do

Mix the lemon rind with two teaspoons of dried sage, two teaspoons of rosemary and a few drops of lavender oil. Put this in two cups, pour a little boiling water over it, and allow it to cool. Cast your circle. Visualize your habit, then blow down the drinking straw into the water in one of the cups, imagining that you are blowing the habit out with the air.

Keep blowing until you feel you have done all you can. Put the contaminated water in the West of your circle. Anoint yourself with the mixture from the other cup on every orifice, especially the one most connected with your habit. Don't swallow the mixture and remember that it will sting sensitive tissues. (Thus if you are ridding yourself of a sexual involvement, anoint yourself close to your genitals, not on them! Ouch!) After your ritual, empty both cups out onto the earth.

For a night to remember

This spell will help you to be really attractive and irresistible to the opposite sex.

You will need

A clean white hanky or a piece of white muslin; cinnamon; ginger; patchouli oil; natural vanilla essence; marjoram; ylang-ylang oil; thread; deep rose-colored candles; a pen; paper.

What to do

Place the herbs, spices and oils in the hanky and tie this up into a secure sachet. Tie it under the hot tap while you run your bath so that the essences run out into the water. (Please note, it is the subtle energies of the herbs that you want, not a lot of dissolved herbs because some can irritate the skin. If you are prone to skin irritation, merely dip the sachet briefly into the bath water, then hang it in the steam.) Light the candles in the bathroom and mentally cast a quick circle around yourself and the bath. Write the symbol for Venus on the paper and place it where you can see it while you bathe. Visualize yourself being charming, attractive, lovable and sexy, having a really good time, laughing, dancing and all the things you like. Imagine all the lovely, warm, gorgeous herbal essences soaking into your skin. Step out of your bath, re-absorb the energies of your circle, place your palms on the ground for a few moments and then put on your most flattering clothes. Knock 'em dead!

Another love spell

You will need

Scissors; rose-colored paper; a pen; 39½ inches of string; oil of rose or ylang-ylang or dried thyme; a cauldron.

What to do

Cut out a heart shape from the paper and write on it everything you want from a lover. Please remember, do not name or visualize a specific person! Attach this securely to the string, then sit in your circle and place the heart in the quarter most appropriate—West for deep, empathic love; North for someone supportive and practical; East for a lover who will also be your best friend; South for sheer passion. Repeating "Come to me, love, come to me, love," over and over again, slowly draw the heart toward you. Anoint it with the oil or sprinkle it with dried thyme and burn it in your cauldron.

To protect your room

To feel safe in your room and to bless and protect it and you, you need first of all to find an oak or mountain ash tree. Preferably find two short twigs of even length but if these cannot be found then ask the tree if you may cut some of it and listen with your intuition for the answer. When you have your twigs, give the tree a generous offering of fruit juice poured on its roots. Bind your twigs together in the form of an equal-armed cross when you are in circle and ask for the special blessing of the Goddess and God. Hang or place your rowan cross in your room.

Ginger spells

Root ginger is delightfully magickal because it comes in so many shapes and many of these look quite human! You can get it in most supermarkets. Take your time to choose your little ginger figures—you could pick some for animals, too, only don't finger too many or the grocer might wonder what's going on! You can use these to make little charms for healing, safety and love. If you have a sick pet, for instance, choose a piece that is as similar to your pet as you can make it, and using a small knife carve it to make it more lifelike. When you are in your circle, place your figure on your pentagram and call it the name of your pet. Then you can anoint the little figure with eucalyptus oil and tie a green ribbon around it, saying, "[Name of pet], be healed." Keep the figure safe until the spell has worked, then take off the ribbon to sever the connection and bury the ginger in the garden.

Calling a suitable figure of ginger by your own name, anointing it with your favorite perfume and tying a red or deep pink ribbon around the neck can be a love spell. Use lavender oil and yellow ribbon to help you study; orange oil and a gold or orange ribbon for sheer good luck and success; a purple ribbon and sage oil to help your intuition; a blue ribbon with lavender oil for pleasure and friendship. Wrap a comfrey leaf around your figure for safety while traveling. You can carve a name or words on your little piece of ginger and be as inventive as you like. Check the correspondences on pages 201–203 for meanings and make up your own spells. Keep your figures *completely* secret and always bury them afterward.

To get fair treatment

Teachers, lecturers, policemen and metermaids—they are all human! If you feel you are not being treated fairly by someone or in some matter—or if you simply want to prevent that from happening—do this spell. Do the spell on a Thursday. Remember what you are asking for must be genuinely fair treatment—not license to park in the red!

You will need

A purple scarf or cloth; two small dishes of equal size; two purple candles; something to represent the organization from which you need fair treatment; chestnuts or figs. If you can obtain a piece of carnelian also, that would be great.

What to do

Spread the cloth, light the candles and place the dishes in front of them. On the left-hand one place your representation of the organization that you want fair treatment from (school report, official document or whatever), with the figs or chestnuts in a pile between the dishes. State what you intend and name what it is to which you have a right. For instance, you might say, "I have a right to be listened to." As you do so, place one fig or nut on the right-hand plate. Then name something you will do in return, such as "I will listen with respect." Repeat as necessary. For example, "I have a right to have my exam marked fairly," combined with, "I will work to the best of my ability." For each thing you ask for, name something you will do in return. Remember, you are not seeking to influence the life path or thoughts of another individual, merely to get what is legitimately yours from the system so don't be personal, and do make sure that you really are entitled to what you ask for.

When you have finished naming the figs or nuts, eat them slowly, chewing deliberately. Bury the rest in the earth.

Place your piece of carnelian in front of you and form a pentagram over it, saying, "Stone of the Sun, bring me justice, courage, protection and peace, in the name of the Goddess." Keep your carnelian with you, especially in situations where you fear you will be victimized in some way.

This spell enables you to get fairness from the Cosmos. It may come in unexpected ways. You aren't trying to change that crabby teacher, who will still look like a Rottweiler sucking a lemon; it's just that you will no longer care!

A healing spell

If you have a friend or relative who is sick, this simple spell will send them soothing love and gentleness.

You will need

A green candle; eucalyptus oil.

What to do

Rub the candle with the oil, and light it. Sit in front of the candle (which you should place in the West of your circle) and visualize the person whom you are healing. Say three times:

> *Peace and love I send to you,*
> *Comfort and true healing too.*

Imagine your loving thoughts gathering in a golden globe above your head and when you feel it is as big or as concentrated as you can make it, send it off as if you were letting go of a balloon in a strong breeze. Send it in the general direction of the person to be healed. You can do this daily, relighting the candle until it has burned away.

Money spell

Do this when the Moon is waxing.

You will need

A green candle; oils of patchouli, orange and vanilla; paper and pen.

What to do

Anoint the candle with the oils. Write the sum you need on a piece of paper. This works best if it is a modest and reasonable amount that you specifically need for something. Say,

As the Moon grows fat, so shall my purse
I call [name the sum] to me by this verse.

Repeat this three times, then say, "May this harm none," three
times. Anoint the slip of paper with the oils and place it in
your purse or wallet. When you get the money burn the
paper. Note, the money will come to you in an ordinary way.
For instance, you may get the chance to earn something extra
over the weekend. Keep a tally—it may come piecemeal.

Success in interviews spell

You will need

A gold candle; a bracelet; things to attach to it, such as charms
or just little pieces of threads.

What to do

Light your candle when you are in your circle and consecrate
your bracelet by forming a pentagram over it with your
athame. (It is better to cleanse the bracelet first if it is not new,
and especially if it has been worn by someone else. You can
do this by leaving it in salt water for 24 hours.) Name several
qualities you know will be essential to successfully get
through the interview, such as calmness, confidence, clear-
thinking. Hold up a thread or charm and say, "I name this for
confidence," and attach it to the bracelet. When you have
completed this, hold the bracelet up to each of the quarters
and ask for their specific blessings. If you are skilled, you could
weave cords together to form a bracelet, naming a quality for
each cord.

Wear the bracelet during the interview, and before you go
into the room, touch each of the charms or threads to bring
that quality to you.

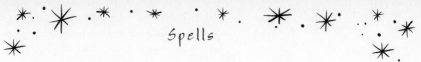

Success in creativity spell

You will need

A strand of ivy; some ribbons in a color appropriate for your type of creativity, chosen from the list of correspondences on pages 201–203 (so if your skill is in computers, that is Mercury and therefore yellow); a symbol of your work (such as a pen, if you are a writer); a small coin; some orange juice.

What to do

Weave a garland with the ivy and ribbons. Place your symbol of your work and the coin in the middle. Toast your creativity with the orange juice, saying, "May my creative fires burn bright." Hang the garland somewhere suitable, and put the coin in a charity box or keep it with your magical things.

Spell for good luck

You will need

A red and a green candle; some nuts or seeds that you like; orange, pineapple or strawberry juice; your pentacle.

What to do

Light your candles, keep your left hand on your pentacle and with your right hand dip a seed or nut into the juice and make a wish. Then eat the nut. You can name several wishes, or several aspects of the same wish or just repeat the same one several times. When you feel you have done enough, drink the rest of the juice and scatter the remaining nuts and seeds outside.

Vitality spell

You will need

A sachet of peppermint tea; honey (optional); some peppermint oil; a large basin of warm water; some yellow candles; a bright yellow shawl or scarf.

What to do

Make yourself the peppermint tea, adding honey if you like. Stir five drops of peppermint oil into the bowl of water, deosil. Drape yourself in the yellow scarf, light the candles and sit sipping the tea with your feet in the water. Feel the vitality and energy rising through your feet while it travels down your throat and meets in the middle, spreading out through your entire body, energizing and vitalizing.

To preserve and increase beauty

You will need

A piece of green tissue paper; oils of rose and patchouli; a lock of your hair; some green ribbon; your pentacle.

What to do

Place the green tissue paper on your pentacle. Take up the lock of hair and anoint it slowly with the oils, stroking it, and say:

> *Beauty stay and beauty grow*
> *Tomorrow and tomorrow*
> *Beauty blossom and beauty be*
> *Ever the Goddess' gift to me.*

Say this six times and wrap the hair in the paper, binding it with the green ribbon. Place it as close as you can to the mirror where you first see yourself each morning.

Candle spells

You can make a simple spell just out of a candle. Choose a candle of the appropriate color from the correspondences list on pages 201–203. For instance, if your spell is about protection you would choose brown candles or even black. Very dark navy could also do. If your spell is about courage and asserting yourself, a red candle would be the choice. Just light the candle and state what you want at least three times. Keep lighting the candle until your spell has worked. White candles will always do as a substitute.

Supply of herbs and essential oils

Suggested suppliers are listed at the back of the book, but apart from frankincense, all herbs and spices can be found at any large supermarket. It is also nice to have myrrh and copal, but you will need to get these from a supplier. Essential oils may be purchased at a natural therapy center, body shop or wholefood shop, and are all selected below for their affordability.

This selection should take you through the rituals and spells given in this book. Store them with care and enjoy their fragrance.

Herbs and spices

Bay, basil, cardamom, cinnamon, clove, coriander, cumin, ginger, nutmeg, patchouli, rosemary, sage, thyme, vanilla food essence (make sure this is natural vanilla extract, not the imitation kind).

Oils

Cypress, eucalyptus, lavender, patchouli, rose, lemon, orange (you can also use fresh lemon or orange peel), myrrh (this may be a little more expensive), ylang-ylang.

Answers to quick quiz (page 203)

✳ Make your sachet with red cloth and fill it with ginger, basil, cumin and/or coriander, all of which you can get in the super-market. Burn a red candle in the South (North, if you live in the Southern Hemisphere) and call on the salamanders, or the god Mars or the brave and warlike Amazon women, to help.

✳ Use a yellow or electric blue candle and rub lavender oil on it. This is inexpensive and can be found in most New Age stores and natural therapy centers. Light your candle in the East, asking for the help of the sylphs and for wing-footed Mercury to keep your mind clear, your reactions quick and smooth and the roads clear, too. For good measure you could light a gold candle in the South and visualize your success.

Well done if you thought of some of these things—and if you thought of all of them, what a witch you are! But if your answers were different, that doesn't mean they were wrong. Why did you choose them? Do you still feel they hold good? The choice is yours.

Chapter 10

Into the Realms of the Gods

Let's start this chapter with a poem to the Goddess, written by my friend Samantha Hudson, who helped me with this book. Sam is 16. Here are her words.

Goddess of Many Faces

The first face I saw was like my own
Curious, bright eyes
Skin radiant and fresh
Body of mid-forming curves
She spoke words of hunger for knowledge
This woman only could be Maidenhood
The second face was wiser, face fully-shaped
Her eyes full of emotion
Her hair the darkest red, defining her face
She gave me knowledge of my purpose in the world
I knew straight away she was Motherhood
The third, a final face, showed limitless lines
Her eyes were tired but true
They warned me of what all emotions—
Love, happiness, sadness can do to you
Her wispy hair of silver crowning her small, shrivelled body

She was the Crone
Remember, my dear friend, the Goddess has many faces
All beautiful in their own way
They all represent her
As One.

The poem beautifully describes one young woman's experience of the Triple Goddess. But during the previous chapters you will have come across the names of many different Goddesses and Gods. Some of these will be familiar to you and some may be new. Some of these have been explained in connection with the eight festivals.

Why are there so many Goddesses and Gods and how does this connect with the idea of one Goddess and one God? The answer is that they are aspects of the one. But they are more than just images—they are real and potent energies. It is important to treat them with respect.

You may like to call upon a God or Goddess for their special help when doing a spell. The obvious example is Venus for love spells. Always do this with respect. For a really important spell, it would be good to back up your request with an offering—for instance, for Venus you could water a rose bush.

For the sake of simplicity, I've put the Greek and Roman Gods together in the list below. However, the pantheons of these two civilizations aren't really one and the same. The Romans were very different from the Greeks, and so their Gods are also different, often being developments of a deity or a mixture of deities. This isn't the place to explore their differences, but it's something to keep in mind if you decide to call upon their help in a spell.

A list of deities

Adonis

Here we have a gorgeous guy—the Leonardo DiCaprio of the Gods. Aphrodite, the Goddess of love and beauty, loved him. He was about everything scrumptiously, erotically male. He was rather passive, actually, and symbolizes a man giving himself, rather than asserting himself. (Greek)

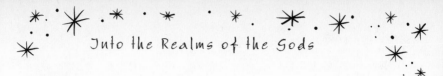

Amazons

The Amazons may have been real warrior women, but they are still Goddesses because they represent an aspect of female nature. Legend tells how they lived in peace in a land entirely peopled by women. They had intercourse with other tribes and sent boy-children to their fathers. They symbolize independent, self-sufficient and sometimes warlike women. (Greek)

Aphrodite

She was the Greek Goddess of sheer, sensual beauty with loads of sex appeal. She was actually a dangerous Goddess, worshiped in shrines out in the wild because people understood her savage power, and that love can hurt. (**Venus** is the Roman counterpart to Aphrodite).

Apollo

He was the God of the Sun and rational thought, fertility, light, life, medicine, beauty and fine arts. He represents all that is noble, cultured and civilized (Greek).

Aries

Aries was the Greek God of war, son of Zeus and Hera, and not very popular with the Greeks because he was overly fond of strife, anger and bloodletting. **Mars** was his Roman counterpart and lover of Venus. He was very warlike and disciplined, whereas Aries was a little more thoughtless. Mars really was the Roman war machine. Aries and Mars represent assertion, desire, conquest, physical prowess and mental determination. They are inspiring for their guts and fighting spirit.

Artemis

She was the Greek virgin Moon Goddess who was also a huntress. Artemis guarded her privacy and her maidenhood fiercely. She was the lady of the beasts and Goddess of the greenwood, a free spirit. Artemis represents freedom and maidenhood. **Diana** is the Roman counterpart of Artemis. She was also a Maiden and Moon Goddess.

Athena
She was a wise and skillful Goddess but also very warlike when the need arose. She was also very just, fair and clear-thinking. Legend tells that she was born from the head of her father Zeus, so she is a "head-stuff"-Goddess, very clever. Athena represents wisdom. **Minerva** is the Roman counterpart of Athena, Goddess of crafts, war, music, math and the arts.

Bast
She was an Egyptian cat-headed Goddess who brought joy and music and whose gifts were mental and physical health. To Ancient Egyptians, the cat was sacred.

Bel
A Celtic God of lightness and brightness (linked to the Middle Eastern God Baal), and also of fire. He represents energy and love of life. He gives his name to Beltane.

Bride
She was the Celtic Goddess (pronounced "breed"), also known as **Brigid**, **Brigit** and **Brigantia**. She was a triple Goddess: Maiden, Mother and Crone in one. And she was a Goddess of fire, inspiration and crafts. She was "converted" to St. Bridget, and her sacred flame was tended by virgins at Kildare in Ireland.

Cernunnos
He was the Celtic horned God, keeper of the animals, hunter and hunted (the hunter must always understand his prey). He was also a God of the natural order, deep in the woods, out in the fields.

Chang-O
She was the Chinese Moon Goddess who greedily took the pill of immortality the Queen Mother of the West had given to Chang-O's husband Hou Yi. She became lighter and lighter and floated into the sky, landing on the Moon. A bit of a cheat, an opportunist, a moody lady.

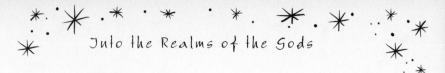

Chronos and Saturn

Chronos was the father of Zeus and son of Uranus (Heaven) and Gaia (Earth). **Saturn**, his Roman counterpart, was God of the land and a generous king; he was harvest lord in the Golden Age and God of time, earth, stone, bone, structures and limits. Legend says that Saturn killed his father in order to take his power and then feared the same fate at the hands of his children so he ate them! But Jupiter escaped and deposed him in turn. However, good old Saturn is still with us, giving us our boundaries and our ambitions because he is very much a God who embodies the real and the tangible.

Demeter

The Greek story of Demeter and her daughter Persephone is found under the Autumn Equinox section of this book. **Ceres** was her Roman counterpart, a Goddess of fertility, the corn and the harvest. Ceres represents life and abundance, but also the realization that all must be returned to the earth for life to go on.

Eostre

This is the Anglo-Saxon Goddess of spring, rebirth, fertility and lots of energy. All things bright and beautiful. She gave her name to Easter.

Father Christmas or Santa Claus

Yes, he is a type of god! Some witches honor two aspects of Father Christmas, one as the Holly King and the other as the Oak King. Holly is king of the Waning Year, from Midsummer to Yule, while the Oak King rules the Waxing Year, from Yule to Midsummer. Like many pairs of Gods in mythology, they battle for the hand of the Goddess at Midsummer (Holly always wins, while at Yule, Oak always wins). They represent both a dark and light side of life, or growth and decline. The dark side isn't evil; it's about the hidden things, and the things that have to go in order for other things to take their place. The fact that the dark aspect has hidden blessings is shown by the fact that Father Christmas has a sleigh-full of presents! (This is one interpretation.)

Freya
She was a very powerful Scandinavian Goddess who was, like Aphrodite, a very beautiful Goddess of lust and sexual love. But Freya also kept hold of the powers that Aphrodite used to have before the Greeks brought her from the Middle East and restricted her to the bedroom. She was a creator Goddess, mistress of life and death—girl power plus!

Green Man
He was really the heart of Nature and he represents the intelligent power within Nature. He is shown as a face made of leaves and you can find him in many churches because masons weren't always as Christian as they made out to be! Legendary figures that live within the Greenwood, such as Robin Hood, are really the good old Green Man.

Hades
He was the mysterious lord of the Underworld and the generous God of wealth. **Pluto** was his Roman equivalent, a mighty God who ruled the process of regeneration, evolvement and deep-rooted transformation. He wore a helmet that made him invisible. He was God of all things that are hidden that can later erupt, changing everything. He was persistent, secret, resourceful and determined. He was also God of gold because he represents the life that waits underground.

Hecate
Scary, witchy, black-gowned Greek Goddess Hecate ruled the Dark of the Moon and haunted crossroads with her great black dog by her side. She was mistress of sorcery and ruled the spirits of the dead. Actually she represents an aspect of female power that society isn't too keen about! But really she's about hidden wisdom, and she's fascinating. Because she rules the dead she also gives the supreme gift of rebirth.

Hera
She was the sky-queen of the Greek Gods and wife of Zeus. She nagged him about his affairs with other Goddesses and mortal

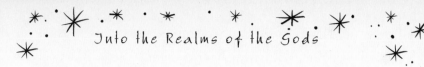

women, and he bullied her. In earlier times, before patriarchy took over, she was supreme, a Goddess of female dignity and very queenly. Hera was a female version of "hero." She was Goddess of feminine sexuality. **Juno** was the Roman counterpart to Hera and she ruled marriage and the process of time.

Hermes

He was the messenger of the Greek Gods, very quick in mind and body. He was clever and tricky, and the patron of commerce. He was a traveler and he could even be a bit of a thief. He was also the only God who could go down into the Underworld and come back in one piece so he guided the souls of the dead. **Mercury** is the Roman counterpart of Hermes.

Herne

He was more or less the same God as Cernunnos, a horned God who lived with the animals. He ruled fertility and represented the wild heart of nature.

Isis

Egyptian Isis was the most "complete" form of the Goddess because she represented every Goddess aspect. She guided humans in developing crafts and farming in addition to looking after them. She loved Osiris, and when he was killed and chopped into pieces she gathered the pieces together and magically made herself pregnant by him. Osiris became king of the Underworld. Isis was the Lady of Ten Thousand Names, magical Goddess, Goddess in mourning, mother, wife, daughter, sister, Goddess of the Moon, mother of the Sun, Goddess of the sea and cornfield. Protective, nurturing, powerful and wise, Isis was the "throne" that Egyptian kings wore on their heads to show that they ruled by the grace of the Goddess.

Kali

She was the Hindu Goddess of destruction who had hidden gifts and helped us deal with our fears.

Kuan Yin

She was a Buddhist Goddess, the most powerful being in the pantheon of China. She was a great lover of humanity; a compassionate, gentle and caring Goddess. Courier of all the feminine virtues, she was peaceful, loving and wise, and her name is called repeatedly in meditation. She keeps people safe if they call upon her and her message is of nonviolence, harmony and generosity.

Lakshmi

This is the Hindu Goddess of light. Homes are cleaned and lamps are lit to honor her, and in return she brings blessings.

Lugh

Lugh Longhand was one of Ireland's Faerie races, the Tuatha de Danaan. He was a God of the light and the bright, but also linked to Gods that die and are reborn in another form. He was a young and brilliant God, skilled in many arts and crafts.

Maat

The Egyptian Goddess of justice and truth, Maat weighed the souls of the dead against a feather and if the soul was light with truth then the dead person passed into the afterlife to mingle with the Gods. She was a Goddess of deep wisdom and represents the inescapable idea, "as you sow, so shall you reap."

Mithras

He was originally a Persian Sun God, but Mithras' cult spread among the Romans and their emperors. He was a great and shining being; his gifts were victory in war and purity of intent and action.

Morrigan

She was a sinister war Goddess in Ireland, the gaunt and terrifying Washer-at-the-Ford, washing the clothing of those doomed to die in battle. Crows were sacred to her and she took on their shape to fly over the battlefield. She sang magical chants before battle to help her favorites—presumably those who had real respect for the power of the Goddess and who didn't expect women to be soft and compliant! The Morrigan is savage and deathly and isn't an "easy"

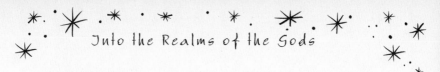

form of the Goddess. She represents the most raw and ruthless side of feminine power.

Nokomis
An Algonquin Goddess whose name means "grandmother," Nokomis created food for the people and for all the animals on the land. In a way, she was the land itself. The Indians also thought of her as feeding herself to the people and animals because of their belief that life depends on life, and life only exists through the devouring of other life. Nokomis was Goddess of natural process. Some say Nokomis had a daughter who was abducted and taken to the Underworld, later to be rescued by the Sun, a tale similar to the Greek's Persephone and her mother Demeter.

Odin
He was the chief Scandinavian God, the All-father, who ruled magic, war, poetry, cleverness and cunning, and the shades of the departed. Odin was a God of shamanic revelation, who hung on the World Tree Yggdrasil until he learned the secret of the runes in a mystical vision. So he is God representative of wisdom, the "sight" and all forms of mental inspiration and lateral thinking.

Oshun
She was a Brazilian Macumba Goddess who ruled beauty, love and flirting. She was also a Goddess of the waters.

Persephone
Daughter of Demeter, the earth Goddess, Persephone was abducted by Hades and became queen of the Underworld. Persephone was a gracious and gentle Goddess of death and rebirth. The myth goes that because her mother mourned her passing and the land withered, the Gods agreed that Persephone could return to the earth for part of the year. This formed a story of the seasons—spring and summer came when Persephone returned and winter came again when she rejoined her dark lord. Forming a trinity, Persephone is the Maiden Goddess, Demeter the Mother Goddess and Hecate the Crone.

Poseidon

Great God of the sea who ruled the waves with his awesome trident, he also ruled earthquakes. He even ruled the earth and heavens at one point until he was supplanted by Zeus. **Neptune** was his Roman counterpart, a God of dreams and psychic powers, who dissolves and changes. Neptune was God of illusion and mysticism. He enables us to seek our ideals and have a sense of things we can't see, but we need to be careful of self-deception.

Sekhmet

She was the lion-headed Goddess of the Sun in ancient Egypt. She was fierce and strong. She became disgusted with humans and enjoyed destroying them until Ra managed to get her drunk! Symbolizing the destructive power of the Sun, Sekhmet may be the other side of Bast, who represents the Sun's life-giving qualities. But Sekhmet isn't all bad; she represents power of females to be warlike and fierce. So, if your rage is righteous and you have to fight, Sekhmet is your gal!

Thor

He was a Scandinavian God of sky and thunder and broke the ice every spring with his magic hammer Mjolnir. He was beloved by ordinary people and was the patron of sailors, farmers and emigrants. He had a red beard and his strength was unsurpassed. He was protective and forceful and offered the common touch. He was also a law-giver and dispenser of justice.

Thoth

Egyptian God of wisdom, he measured time and was associated with the Moon. His sphere was science and precise observation. He was God of knowledge, wisdom, mathematics, architecture, writing, archives and arbitration. He was also concerned with justice. He is pictured as having the head of an ibis, or the form of a baboon (possibly because baboons "talk" at the Sun as it rises). Thoth had a very subtle power because early stories tell how he created Gods and Goddesses from the sound of his voice. Because all existence is composed of vibration and sound is a vibration, Thoth was potently

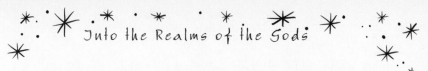

creative and magical. He was a healer and the magical partner of the Goddess Isis.

Tyr

This Scandinavian God was a great athlete and warrior, rather like Mars, but with the additional quality of caring for the social order.

Valkyries

These Scandinavian Goddesses were a bit like the Morrigan, but a little more pro-active. These maidens flew over battlefields on their spirit-horses, choosing the unfortunates who would be slain. But more than this, they were the Goddesses who wove the web of war with spears and human heads. They represent fate and vengeance, and are not to be trifled with. They had their favorites among the brave and were a law unto themselves, blood-thirsty, merciless. In a similar way to the Hindu Goddess Kali, they teach us that facing our worst fears makes us strong.

Zeus

Zeus was the king of the Greek Gods, the greatest and the best. He was commanding, jovial and wise. A law-giver, he wielded thunder-bolts and had lots of testosterone! Generous and larger-than-life, he gives a feeling that all is possible and that everything is getting better and better. **Jupiter**, the Roman counterpart to Zeus, was fatherly, regal and rather liked his own way!

Who is your Goddess?

This questionnaire is for girls only! There's one for the guys on page 233. Which Goddess comes closest to expressing the real you? Answer the following questions to find out.

1) A distressed friend comes to you for help when she has trouble in her relationship. You: a) suggest things you can do together to jolt her out of it; b) find something beautiful to give her to cheer her up; c) put your arms around her and make her a cup of tea; d) try to get her to analyze why these things keep happening to her.

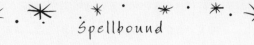

2) How do you prefer to travel? a) biking, horseback riding or motorcycling; b) a plush sporty number; c) a nice comfy car or the bus with your friends; d) a limo with tinted windows.

3) What sort of hobbies do you prefer? a) sports, mostly—you like to get out and work up a sweat; b) retail therapy—trying on clothes, buying make-up; c) cooking and gardening; d) your tarot cards.

4) Choose your favorite night out: a) going bowling or something similar; b) partying; c) a nice meal with your friends; d) a masked ball.

5) When you buy clothes what do you look for? a) something sporty that allows you to move freely; b) the latest hot fashions that show off your figure; c) something that's going to last and go with everything; d) something unique and unusual.

6) What kind of guy turns you on? a) he needs to be independent and active; b) just gorgeous will do; c) you like the boy-next-door type; d) you can't help it—the forbidden and dangerous attracts you.

7) What effect do you want to create with your make-up? a) you rarely bother with make-up; b) you spend ages making up so you look really seductive; c) you like to look fresh and clean; d) you like to create a slightly Gothic look.

8) What are your favorite colors? a) bright red, white, clean colors; b) blues, pinks and pastels; c) greens, golds and browns; d) purple, mauve, black.

9) What's your favorite vacation? a) walking, camping, backpacking; b) lazy days in the sun with a fantastic guy to rub in the sunscreen; c) the cozy B&B you went to last year; d) India, Bali—anywhere exotic.

10) Which is the greatest compliment? a) you've really got guts! b) you're so beautiful! c) how creative and caring you are! d) you're so fascinating and mysterious.

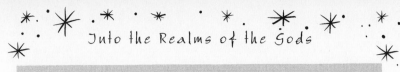

Your score

Mostly a's. Your Goddess is Artemis/Diana, the Maiden Goddess. You're independent, outgoing, energetic and active. You want to feel inspired to challenge life and to feel that spirit flare inside you. You don't mind people knowing you're a witch—if they don't like it it's their problem! You're going to set the world on fire and the Goddess is on your side

Mostly b's. Your Goddess is Aphrodite/Venus. You're a girly-girl and you love all things feminine and glamorous—and you love the boys! It's important to you to look your best at all times and you value your sex appeal. You enjoy the sensuous things in life and you feel it's here to be enjoyed. You love the way witchcraft reveals the joy in life—and the Goddess is with you as you grab your share.

Mostly c's. Your Goddess is Demeter/Ceres. You're a creative, caring person. You like to feel you've done something productive and you like the thought that your friends come to you to be mothered. The Nature-worship aspect of witchcraft is especially attractive to you and the Goddess walks close by as you send out your love to all of her creation.

Mostly d's. Your Goddess is Hecate. You are a private and intense person and you have a deep understanding of life. Sometimes it is hard for you to convey all that is in your heart and mind. You always look below the surface and you can be quite analytical. You like the mysterious aspect of witchcraft and the exploration of subtle power. The Goddess is with you as you delve and explore.

Who is your God?

This one is just for the boys! Which God expresses the energies that you exhibit most strongly? Answer the following questionnaire to find out.

1) What is your attitude toward team games? a) winning's the thing—get in there and give them hell; b) you rely on your quick thinking and dexterity; c) you aren't that keen on games

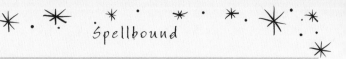

but if you have to play you plan your strategy; d) you have a trick or two up your sleeve—silent but deadly.

2) Everyone wants to make a move on the Jennifer Lopez look-alike that has just walked into the party: a) you go for it—she can only say no; b) you play it by ear—if there's an opportunity you'll grab it; c) you aren't confident but you start thinking of things to say; d) what would you do?—that's for you to know and the rest of us to wonder!

3) Your career needs to be: a) physically demanding or fast-track up the ladder; b) varied and mentally stimulating; c) reliable and well-paid; d) challenging, exciting and unpredictable.

4) Your favorite films are: a) you don't go to the movies much because you're usually out playing sports, but when you do it's all-action movies; b) something with a clever plot that you have to work out like a mystery or whodunnit; c) informative movies and stories about big business; d) horror movies and spine-chillers.

5) What about your clothes? a) you can't be bothered with clothes—as long as they cover you, they're okay; b) you like plenty of fashionable clothes for all your different activities; c) good quality gear—you like to make an impression; d) serviceable and usually dark in color.

6) Your friends are generally: a) guys who like the same sports, teammates, comrades-in-arms; b) guys who'll give you a laugh and who are up for anything; c) You don't make friends easily—you hang around with a few old-faithfuls from school; d) a friend is someone who'd die with you—all the rest are just wallpaper.

7) Choose your favorite car: a) something very fast; b) something trendy, with a great stereo that you can trade in next year for the latest model; c) something reliable; d) something that can't be broken into.

8) What are your favorite colors? a) reds and oranges; b) yellows and bright blues; c) sober colors like navy, green and brown; d) paint it black.

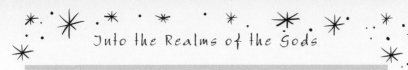

9) Your heroes are: a) sports figures; b) clever ones or inventors;
c) high achievers in business and industry; d) people who
have been very brave.

10) How do you manage your money? a) generally it manages
itself—you buy what you need and when it's gone it's gone; b)
you plan and work out your finances—you like a good deal; c)
you save and invest—you worry about the future; d) you're
well-insured but you keep quiet about your finances and you
have more money than people realize.

Your score

Mostly a's. Your God is the warlike Aries or Mars. You're a man of
action, gung-ho at times and very assertive. A man's man with lots
of energy, you tend to see life as uncomplicated, which works for
you. People have to accept you for what you are. If you choose to
be a witch you'll tell it like it is and your fiery energy will be a great
asset in circle.

Mostly b's. Your God is the clever and resourceful Hermes or
Mercury. You're a happening sort of guy with lots of friends who
always has an answer for everything and a ready line. If you choose
to be a witch, your inventiveness will stand you in good stead when
you compose rituals. You probably understand magic as energy and
vibration.

Mostly c's. Your God is the sensible and controlled Saturn. You plan
your life and are practical, realistic and reliable. Your hands-on
attitude and organizational abilities will be a great help in collecting the necessities for rituals and you have a common-sense,
down-to-earth approach, although you are skeptical and like to
have proof. Your witchcraft is for a purpose.

Mostly d's. Your God is the mysterious and powerful Hades or Pluto.
You feel that knowledge is power and that the less people know
about you the better. You have a trick or two up your sleeve and few
people know the real you. You possess great depth, concentration

and intuition, and your awareness of subtle power will stand you in good stead in circle. If you decide to use magic be very careful that you use it well.

Your God/dess connection

Do you feel the answer to the questionnaire is really *you*? If not, which God or Goddess do you feel most in tune with? Make a space for her or him on your altar. Collect objects that you feel are connected—there are clues in this book. All the deities mentioned are either listed in the correspondences list in Chapter 9 or described in the section on the Eight Festivals. Light a candle to your God or Goddess at the Moon phase you feel is most appropriate. Read up about the mythology of the God/dess. Talk to him or her—ask for advice. Make up poetry, little prayers, etc. Your God/dess will help you increase your magickal awareness and deepen your identity.

Magickal you

By now you have some idea of your magickal identity. Your magickal identity is the subtle part of you that is your strongest expression in the realms of the Otherworld. You will know which is your strongest element. You've taken an inward journey to experience it and others. You've built your inner temple and have embarked on spells and rituals that are opening your inner eyes. You also have some idea which Gods and Goddesses feel closest to you. You can wear jewelry and collect items that help you express this more. But always remember, this is a starting point, not the final goal. Explore and develop from your familiar territory and feel yourself expand. Good journey!

Initiation ritual

You may decide you definitely want to be a witch and you may want to affirm this by ritual. Such a ritual is called an initiation ritual, or dedication ritual. It's a statement of a commitment and the beginning of an inner change. It isn't to be taken lightly because, like all properly conducted rituals, it has a deep effect, which may not be obvious at first. If you decide to initiate yourself, this can be

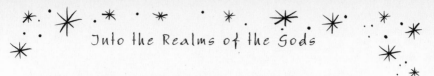
just as powerful and meaningful as being initiated by another person or a group of people. It can make you feel special and renewed.

At any time in our lives we may change our minds, but when you are young this is even more likely to happen. Please remember that any commitment you make to the Craft can be left behind if you so wish. Nothing and no one can ever bind you against your will or past the time that is right for you—always remember this.

So if you feel the path of the witch is for you there is no harm in initiating yourself. This is a statement of your choice of the path and your love of the Goddess. However, please be very wary of any adult or group of adults who offers to initiate you before you are 18 because, it's sad to say, they may have mixed motives.

Having said that your initiation is not binding, do still think very carefully before committing yourself. You should meditate daily over at least the space of a lunar month (and a year is much better), recording your dreams and also your waking thoughts before taking the step. Don't do it in a rush. You can do simple magick before you are initiated, although you should always make your circle and protect yourself. If you take things slowly and work through this book thoroughly, believe me, by the time you reach your 20s you will be a person of depth and knowledge. You may feel raring to go and very impatient, but if you do something and learn something each day you will be getting somewhere steadily and you may well know considerably more than many people who are neophytes (beginners) in a coven.

So if you wish to initiate or dedicate yourself to the Craft, here is what you do.

A self-dedication rite

First contemplate and meditate as described above. Certainly you should do the guided visualizations suggested earlier in this book and/or others first because these will begin to open your inner sight. Remember, being a witch comes from inside, not outside.

Secondly, it is usual to choose a witch-name. This is a name for your magical self that you call yourself when in your circle. Witches in a coven are always addressed by their witch-name. This name can be that of a Goddess or God, a name from mythology, an animal, a precious stone, mineral, plant or tree. Some examples are Diana, Morgan, Gawain, Fox, Amber, Silver and Rowan. When choosing your name, try not to be pretentious. For instance, calling yourself Aphrodite won't make you special in itself or get you tons of admirers. Your name needs to mean something to you, something deep. Take care if you choose a name from mythology or the name of a Goddess or God because sometimes the stories and character-istics associated with the deity come along with the name as symbolic baggage. "Big" names like Jupiter and Hecate are best avoided.

Choose the third day or so of the new Moon to initiate yourself. Make sure you have some time alone to take a short walk and to take a leisurely bath containing lavender oil or salt for purification. It's good to have an old shirt or other garment you no longer need with you as well as a new robe. You will also need some lavender oil, white candles and a yard or so of black thread. For incense you could use frankincense, lemon and rosemary. Juice and some cake or cookies will be needed, plus a pair of scissors.

Cast your circle wearing your old shirt, nothing more. Place the black thread about a foot and a half in front of your altar so that you can reach over it to pick up what you need from the altar, but do not step over it as yet. Sit and meditate for a while as the incense smoke rises.

Take off the old garment and stand naked in front of your altar. Raise your arms and say, "Great Mother, Mighty Horned God, I stand before you as you made me, and ask that you accept me as witch and priest/ess." Take up your pentacle and place it to your forehead, saying, "May I be cleansed and blessed by the powers of Earth." Now take up your censer, wafting the smoke over your body (if you are burning your incense in a pot that you can't move then stand close to it and direct the incense smoke toward you with your hand). Say, "May I be cleansed and blessed by the powers of Air." Carefully take up one of your candles and move it around your body, saying, "May I be cleansed and blessed by the powers of Fire," and then take water from your chalice and sprinkle your body, saying, "May I be cleansed and blessed by the powers of Water."

Facing your altar, say, "I, [insert your witch-name], dedicate myself to the Old Ones, as witch and priest/ess. Lady of the soul's

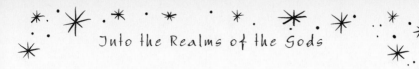

inner fire, Lord of the life that surges within me, my life is now yours in joy, love and creativity." (You may call on the Goddess and God by any names that have special meaning for you—for instance, Isis or Lugh—to add power and poetry to your dedication.)

Take up your lavender oil and anoint yourself on the feet, saying, "May my feet lead me by the sacred paths"; knees, saying, "My knees shall kneel at the holy altars"; close to your genitals, saying, "My sexuality is a celebration of the Goddess"; breast, saying, "My heart is true, loving and free"; and your brow, saying, "May wisdom grow in me and light my way."

Starting in the North and with Earth, offer yourself to the elemental powers in turn and ask for their help and protection in words of your own choosing. Take your time. For instance, you could say, "Powers of Elemental Earth, I ask for your protection, grounding and good sense on my path as a witch, and I pledge to care for the Earth and the life upon her." When you have completed the circuit of the four, deosil, sit before your altar and meditate for a while again.

Now stand up and slowly and solemnly step over your black thread. Say, "I enter the magickal realms in truth and faith. Blessed be." Stand quietly for a few moments. You have crossed the threshold and are now a witch. Gather up your black thread and place it on your altar.

Celebrate with the juice and cake that you have consecrated. Drink a toast to the Great Mother and Horned God in whose presence you now find yourself. Consecrate your new robe and put it on if you wish. Ceremoniously shred your old shirt. Think about your future path. Dance or celebrate in any form you like. Close down when you are ready and keep your black thread as a reminder of your dedication.

Note your dreams that night. Your initiation will not turn you into some powerful being—it is the beginning of your inner journey as a witch and priest/ess.

And from here?

Now that you are well-informed and have made your choice, you can now feel that you are truly a witch. What do you do? This is just a beginning. You will grow in wisdom with everything you practice.

Here is a list of suggestions.

* Observe the cycles of the Moon, how they affect you, and every so often conduct an esbat at full Moon.

* Observe the cycle of the seasons, celebrating each of the festivals inwardly and outwardly.

* Practice regular meditation using the visualizations given in this book.

* Keep a note of your dreams and other meaningful experiences.

* Practice forms of divination such as those given under the section on Samhain.

* Open yourself to the joy in life and let the Goddess be your guide.

Visualization

Here is a final visualization to meet your inner guide. It is best to record it on a tape and take it very slowly so that you can explore your inner landscapes and see with your inner sight—that's why I don't offer too much detail about the scenery.

Relax and turn your consciousness inward. Enter the subtle realms and go into your temple. Ask for the help and guidance from the Goddess. State that your quest is for greater wisdom and a companion to guide you.

When you are ready, leave your temple with your athame in your hand. Find yourself on a winding path, leading through a wheat field and into a forest. Enter the forest. It is dark, secret and sweet-smelling, and the path meanders through the trees. What plants and flowers do you see? What are the scents that you are conscious of? What creatures do you meet? If you feel threatened by anything, hold your athame out toward it and challenge it, saying, "Do you come with pure intent in the name of the Goddess?" Anything that isn't okay will disappear. Remember your pentagram for added protection.

Follow the path, going deeper and deeper into the forest. Here there is no sunlight—it is dark, fragrant and mysterious. The plants are different here. How do they look? What do you see and hear?

In front of you now you see a large shelter made of wood and straw. Animal skins hang over the doorway and through them you can see the flicker of candlelight. You smell the scent of incense and it seems to you that someone is singing a soft, wild chant.

Go up to the shelter, part the skins and stand respectfully at the doorway until you are invited in. What happens now is up to you. Do not be disappointed if you do not go in this time, or if you choose not to go in, the choice is entirely yours.

When your encounter is over, tread the path back through the forest—do not rush. If you are given a gift, take it with you. Walk until you come out into the sunshine through the wheat field and back into your temple, where you should put down your spirit athame and store the gift you have.

Come back to everyday awareness, pat yourself all over and eat and drink something to ground yourself. Make a note of what has happened while it is fresh in your mind.

You are on the path of the witch. Travel wisely, sisters and brothers.

Merry meet, merry part, and merry meet again!

Further Reading and Resources

There are many books on witchcraft that you can buy. Here are some that I recommend that will take you farther.

Books by me

Faeries and Nature Spirits: A Beginner's Guide (Hodder & Stoughton, 1999) Faeries are companions to the witch—learn about them.

Herbs for Magic and Ritual (Hodder & Stoughton, 1999) You will find this useful for incense recipes, magickal use of herbs, etc.

The Magic and Mystery of Trees: A Beginner's Guide (Hodder & Stoughton, 1999) Tree lore that you might enjoy.

Spells & Rituals: A Beginner's Guide (Hodder & Stoughton, 1999) More spells and rituals for you to try out.

Wheel of the Year: Myth and Magic through the Seasons (Capall Bann) This was co-written by Jane Brideson. It contains lots of ways to celebrate the eight seasonal festivals.

Witchcraft: A Complete Guide (Hodder & Stoughton, 2000) This is a more-adult training manual to take you through all the steps.

Other books

An ABC of Witchcraft, Past and Present by Doreen Valiente (Bookpeople, 1989) Doreen was a much-respected witch and priestess of the twentieth century and she died just before the millennium came in. All her books are worth reading and loving.

The Complete Book of Incense Oils and Brews (Llewellyn, 1991), *Cunningham's Encyclopedia of Magical Herbs* (Llewellyn, 1994),

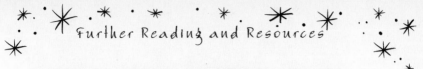

Cunningham's Crystal, Gem and Metal Magic (Llewellyn, 1994)
Good reference works by Scott Cunningham.

Eight Sabbats for Witches by Janet & Stewart Farrar (Phoenix
Publishing, 1988) All the Farrars' books are very informative and if
you want to know more about Wicca as practiced in a coven, they
are an excellent source.

Every Woman a Witch by Cassandra Eason (Quantum, 1996)
Interesting lively and varied.

The Hedge Witch's Way by Rae Beth (Hale, 2002) A lovely spiritual
and also practical book to take your understanding deeper.

A Witch Alone by Marion Green (Aquarian, 1991) An excellent book
for grounding in the Craft. All books by Marion Green are recommended. She runs courses in Natural Magick and produces *Quest*
magazine. BCM-SCL QUEST, London WC1N 3XX.

Supplies

Herbs and oils can be ordered worldwide from the following, but
sometimes you may have to send a small sum for a catalog.

Enchantments, 341 East Ninth Street, New York City, NY 10003. Tel:
212-228-4394. Catalog. Fee.

Eye of the Cat, 3314 East Broadway, Long Beach, CA 90803.
Catalog. Fee, includes refund on first order.

Mystery's, 386, Darling Street, Balmain, NSW 2041, Australia.

The Sorceror's Apprentice, 6–8 Burley Lodge Road, Leeds, LS6 1QP,
UK. Tel: 011-0113-245-1309. Fee.

Starchild, The Courtyard, 2–4 High Street, Glastonbury, Somerset
BA6 9DU, UK. Tel: 011-0145-883-4663. Catalog. Fee.

Resources

There are few resources for young witches because older witches
usually do not want to influence them. However, the Pagan Federation can be contacted at BM Box 7097, London WC1 N 3XX, United
Kingdom. They have a branch called Minor Arcana for young people: PO Box 615, Norwich, Norfolk NR1 4QQ, United Kingdom.

The Internet

The Internet is alive with witchcraft sites and resources. Don't take notice of anyone who offers to cast spells for you or anything similar!

Please, never give your address or telephone number to contacts you make over the net. If you have been in contact with someone for several weeks you might feel that you would like to meet them. If you do this, it should be somewhere public like a café, and you should take along your friends and parents. Never go alone! Obviously this will only be possible if you live fairly close to your contact. You can establish this by giving the name of your home town—no more.

You can e-mail me at undines@freeuk.com. I try to give a brief reply to all correspondence but I cannot answer detailed inquiries, give special spells or help with specific problems—sorry! But anything you say will be kept in mind for future books and is very valuable to me.

Recommended sites

Children of Artemis: **www.witchcraft.org.** This website has a lively online chatroom used by many teens. It's monitored to make sure people with dubious motives are made to leave right away.

www.witchvox.com/wxwotw.html

www.bookofshadows.net

For witch artwork: **www.darkmoondesign.free-online.co.uk**

email: morrigan@mac.com

A Letter to Parents

If you've found this book in your daughter or son's room, you may be worried. Please don't be! You may have heard stories in the media about witches and think that we're devil worshippers—but nothing could be further from the truth. Not only do we not believe in him, but witchcraft, as a spiritual path, is far older than any religion that believes in the devil.

Witches are Nature worshippers, and while we have no dogma, we do have one rule and that is "Harm none." By that we *mean* "none"—not other people, animals, plants, the environment nor, of course, oneself. By teaching self-respect, self-knowledge and personal empowerment, witchcraft not only discourages drug-using and irre-sponsible living—it offers an alternative. This alternative is finding the magick in life and in oneself—and it is fun!

Through following the witchcraft path, your sons or daughters can find a way to feel in control of their life, and to realize that life has meaning. This can help them avoid some of the pitfalls we worry about. In a world where so many things have become mean-ingless and dry, where there is so much exploitation, hypocrisy and cruelty, witchcraft offers an alternative that is as time-honored as it is fresh and inspiring.

This is the way of the ancient Mother Goddess, strengthening for girls while giving boys a greater appreciation of the depth and responsibility of their manhood. This is not through boring "shoulds" and "oughts" or by frightening and threatening them, but rather in an atmosphere of celebration.

Covens of witches are not out to "get" young people, corrupt them and use them, sexually or otherwise. If you hear of anybody who is taking that attitude toward your son or daughter you are right to worry—whatever religion that person purports to follow. In general, witches are very concerned not to be drawing young people into the Craft before they are old enough to make mature judgments, (the minimum age is 18 or even 21). Of course, this means that many young seekers have little guidance and that is what this book is for.

If you want to know more about the Craft, please read through the book. Hopefully it will answer your questions, too.

And what about me, the author? Am I some nutty old bag that lives in a cottage in the woods with 20 cats and a broomstick? No. Do I belong to some sinister coven that holds orgies and lures the innocent into our evil rituals? No, no, no! I am the mother of four children, ages 22, 19, 7 and 4; I'm married, live in an ordinary house, drive an ordinary car and worry about the same things you do— paying the mortgage and the welfare of my children. My eldest isn't interested in the Craft, and that is his choice; my 19-year-old is, but only casually; the little ones are too young to get involved, but we do introduce them to things like Halloween and the pagan meanings of Christmas, in ways they can understand.

Like you, the most important thing for me is to feel that my children are safe, happy and fulfilled. I believe that witchcraft and all it entails is one of the best hopes for them and for the planet. I hope you will read this book and agree with me, at least to some extent.

With Blessings,

Teresa Moorey,

Lughnasadh 2002

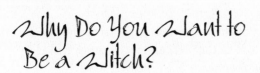

Why Do You Want to Be a Witch?

In Chapter 1 I asked you to think carefully about why you want to become a witch.

✳ If it's because you like the thought of being special and powerful—ten out of ten for honesty! Yes, we all like that because we all have an ego. Witchcraft does have the aura of the "powerful" and mysterious. But it also brings responsibility, and it's hard work. Any "power" is hard won and doesn't mean you will win the lottery or star in the re-make of *Titanic*. Hopefully this wasn't the reason you wanted to be a witch!

✳ If you like the thought of wearing black—be a Goth. It's less troublesome and will fit your image better. Some witches don't like black because it's a cliché.

✳ You want to get back at people who have been nasty to you—forget it. The Craft is not for that. Join the Mafia!

✳ You want to be able to do spells and make things change in your life—fine. But it doesn't happen overnight. Keep your ambitions modest and work hard.

✳ You feel strongly drawn to The Craft, you know it's for you—that's great. Try to learn a few rational ways of explaining yourself so that people will understand you. This book should help.

✳ You would like to develop your psychic senses. Well, you can do that but you don't need to be a witch to do it.

✳ Nature appeals to your heart and you want to be a part of her—you've come to the right place.

* The thought of the Goddess is very magnetic and you want to know more, to get closer to the Goddess—again, you're in the right place.

* You like the thought of a spiritual path that has no dogma and teaches love for the body, love for Nature as well as personal empowerment—you're halfway there!

Whatever your answers and reasons are now, they can and will change. Keep your list to refer to in the future to see how you change and develop.

Index